THE
Innovator's
TOOLKIT

THE Innovator's TOOLKIT

SECOND EDITION

50+ TECHNIQUES

FOR PREDICTABLE

AND SUSTAINABLE

ORGANIC GROWTH

David Silverstein | **Philip Samuel** | **Neil DeCarlo**

WILEY

John Wiley & Sons, Inc.

Dedicated to our co-author, Neil DeCarlo. Your passion and dedication have been an inspiration to us all. We couldn't have done it without you. You will be missed.

CONTENTS

CONTENTS

PART II
Discover the Ideas

PART III
Develop the Designs

PART IV
Demonstrate the Innovation   315

We've updated this book because of you. We've received so many kind words and terrific feedback, and the first edition exceeded most everyone's expectations, that our editor at Wiley asked us to consider writing a second edition. Unlike most books, *The Innovator's Toolkit* sold more copies in its second year than in its first, and more in its third than either the first or second. Clearly the need for help with innovation is growing.

We didn't have any trouble agreeing to write a second edition because we ourselves learned so much about innovation as we worked with clients. We learned about why innovation is so highly touted in the marketplace yet so rarely achieved. We consulted with and advised the leadership of many companies, divisions, and R&D organizations. We got our hands quite dirty as we trained many individuals and shepherded many teams through the innovation process.

Many along the way weren't shy to tell us what they liked about our book—and what they didn't like. When they told us certain explanations didn't help, we changed them. When they said they needed a better example, we developed one and replaced what we had. Of course we didn't heed every complaint, but we sure listened when people or groups had the same problems or suggestions.

Specifically, this second edition provides:

- A new introduction that shows why so many fail at innovation—and how you can succeed.
- Several new techniques, and modifications to existing techniques, that better enable initial problem definition and ideation—leading to the population of a risk-mitigated innovation portfolio.

• Updated exhibits and examples to make the techniques more readily understandable, useable, and current.

This updated and revised edition of *The Innovator's Toolkit* simply helps innovation leaders, managers, and specialists do their jobs better than ever—giving them more confidence, reducing the chance of expensive failures, and packing more practical innovation know-how under one cover than we did before.

Please use what's in this book to become the very best innovator you can possibly be. We wish you amazing success!

DAVID SILVERSTEIN
PHILIP SAMUEL
NEIL DECARLO

Growing an already sizeable company isn't an easy feat, and it's even more difficult to do on a sustainable basis. Two avenues exist: You can grow from the outside through mergers and acquisitions, or you can grow from the inside through organically engineered innovation. The problem is that both approaches tend to fall short of expectations, even when used in combination.

Leaving the problem of M&As to others, we wrote this book to take the mystery out of organic growth. Why is it that only a special few companies seem to have a grip on innovation? We watch a company like Apple in reverence as it releases new product after new product that meets or beats expectations in the marketplace (or at least did for an amazing period of time if this is not true after publication of this book).

Executives in every industry wish they could be more like Apple. Or, they come up with reasons why their companies just aren't and never could be:

"We're not a technology company and don't have the ability to make so many product revisions."

"Our core technology simply isn't as robust as Apple's, so our opportunities are limited."

You name it. Sometimes it's easier to make excuses than to admit your company just doesn't get it.

Under Armour is an apparel company, but it's not an apparel company that considers itself like others. That's why it's been pursuing innovation like a tech company. No, that's why it's become relentless about innovation, putting most tech companies to shame and outdoing them at their own game.

CNBC's Jim Cramer said this in a March 2012 television segment: "Tech stocks don't have a monopoly on using innovation to win new business. A lot of what we now consider tech isn't innovative at all. When was the last time Hewlett-Packard invented something new? Can you even remember? I know I can't . . . The real essence of tech is innovation . . . . I think we need to cast our net wider to hunt for game-changing inventions in places where you'd least expect them."

Under Armour invented moisture-wicking compression fit clothes, a new category of apparel that regulates body temperature. But the company didn't stop there. In 2011, it rolled out *charged cotton*, which dries five times faster than ordinary cotton and is incredibly soft. Under Armour has a cotton, hooded sweatshirt (called Storm) that is *waterproof*. They've built an ultra-light running shoe that, as of this writing, Morgan Stanley says will take share away from Nike.

These and more planned product releases are the reasons for Under Armour's greatly enviable growth rate (at the time of this writing, Q4 2011 revenue growth of 34 percent and EPS growth of 40 percent). The company's innovation and resulting pricing power is also responsible for its long-term growth target of between 20 and 25 percent.

Impressive indeed, but what lies at the core of this success? Under Armour's mission is to make all athletes better through passion, design, and the relentless pursuit of innovation. But how can any company really achieve innovation, much less on any consistent basis?

There is a host of managerial principles and practices that must be adopted by all companies aspiring to organic growth. These include passionate and galvanized leaders who get what it takes to innovate—who not only inspire but also provide the rationale, create the roadmap, set up the systems, establish the processes, deploy the know-how, staff the teams, run the committees, and otherwise actively lead and manage the innovation lifecycle.

This book is obviously a very practical guide focused on the innovation process and the many techniques that enable it. It doesn't cover all the leadership or managerial aspects of successful innovation, namely, what executives need to know (and do) to create the right climate and set the organization up for continual reinvention of its products, processes, and business models. (We address these leadership topics in our seminars and consulting.)

Innovation Is a Two-Faceted Process

Exhibit I.1 shows what the innovation process should look like in any company or organization. But we create a misnomer when we say process, singular—because *the key to successful innovation is that it is really two separate processes*, not one. This is where most companies fall down: They either focus on the left (front-end innovation) or the right (back-end exploitation), but not on both.

Let's define each side, and then look at some scenarios of what happens in real business life. The left side, *front-end innovation*, is a fluid, playful, nonlinear pursuit of new products, processes, and business models—new *solutions* as we call them throughout this book. The right side, *back-end exploitation*, is more of a stage-gated, linear, systematic approach for commercializing new designs that have already been proven viable by the activities on the left.

If you mix the left with the right, confuse one for the other, have a process for innovation but not exploitation, or have the same people dominating both sides—failure will be your friend.

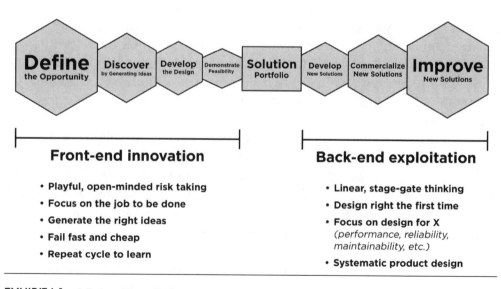

EXHIBIT I.1   A Tale of Two Cultures.

We mentioned Under Armour, but we didn't mention the innovation lab it established in 2011. Adjacent to its headquarters building in Baltimore, the lab exists to "build the world's best product with no restrictions," according to what the company's senior vice president of sports marketing Kevin Haley told the *Baltimore Business Journal* ("Under Armour Debuts 'Innovation Lab' at Tide Point," February 15, 2011).

A YouTube video shows snippets of what goes on at the lab—whether it's testing the body suit used by NFL players to monitor their breathing and heart rates, or to perfect sewing methods, or to analyze just how people run, or to see how stable Under Armour bras are under real usage conditions (www.youtube.com/watch?v=cSc8m46RPPQ). Says a company spokesperson in the video: What happens at the lab "takes the guesswork out of product development and helps us really understand what our product is doing."

This is one of the keys to innovation's front end: If you're going to fail, fail fast and fail cheap (before what you're doing becomes a financial disaster). But you can only do this if you have the proper culture, people, mind-set, and tools. And you'll only do this if you have the right organization in place and a team of innovators who march to a different beat than their operational counterparts.

Nike, for instance, has a separate business unit that lives only in the world of innovation's front end. The unit generates thousands of ideas, makes detailed engineering drawings for those ideas, tests them, prototypes them, and above all, discards them. Nike accepts failure when it needs to be accepted—before the company bets large sums of money by engaging too deeply in the development and commercialization phases on the right side of the process.

If you're in Nike's innovation business unit, you might be playing basketball in the middle of the day to free the mind from its endless concentration, or to get creation-friendly endorphins flowing. Or, you'll find yourself at a nice dinner celebrating the fact that you've bailed on a great idea because it's just not economically feasible, or because it's predicted to simply suck up too many resources in the process of making it into a final, commercialized product.

Contrast this with the standard practice in many Asian companies, which operate in a culture where failure is synonymous with shame. In such organizations, and in more U.S. companies than we'd like to admit, R&D happens inside a black box—not so much to keep the activities secret but to avoid the embarrassment of examining the amount of resources going in versus the new revenue coming out.

So many companies don't have a front-end process because the steps and activities, as we said a moment ago, aren't linear or stage-gated. Since these organizations are used to processes having very defined steps and tollgates and metrics, they either have a front-end process that is too systematic or they don't have a process at all.

Remember Iridium's attempt to bring a satellite phone to market? With a $5 billion budget, the company gathered inputs from 200,000 potential customers in 42 countries, secured about 1,000 patents, and spent more than 10 years perfecting the system and product. About as fast as the product was launched, it failed, and the company went bankrupt.

Anyone interested in this famous case study can find gobs of articles discussing what went wrong. Didn't anticipate the build out of digital cellular networks. Target market of traveling executives was too small. Price way too high ($3,000 for handset and $3 to $8 per minute). Phones didn't work in moving vehicles or inside buildings. And in the end, company executives were highly reluctant to bail on the business since so much was already invested.

We can break it down in terms of our two-faceted innovation model. Iridium focused all of its efforts on the right side of the innovation equation, on the exploitation aspects rather than the front-end aspects. In the words of Iridium's Interim CEO John A. Richardson: "We're a classic MBA case in how not to introduce a product. First we created a marvelous technological achievement. Then we asked how to make money on it."

Iridium should have been asking far to the left, and making sound calculations, about the feasibility of making money on its grand vision.

If you don't worry about how to make money on an innovation until you're into full design and production mode—especially a big, complex, marvelous innovation—it could bankrupt your company (and for Iridium, it did). It's better to spend focused time and effort on innovation's front end where you can fail fast and cheap.

So what about the opposite problem we said other companies have? What about an overemphasis on the creative front end of innovation to the exclusion of the more mechanical actions needed on the back end to exploit and commercialize? This happens, too, although less commonly, and it can also destroy value.

In its past, Microsoft was rightly known for using the market as its testing ground. It developed and launched an operating system in accordance with a good grasp of customer Jobs to be Done (Technique 1) and a focus on *certain* Outcome Expectations (Technique 3), like speed and reliability.

But it didn't perfect its designs before releasing them into the market. As a result, users had to endure frequent crashes of the operating system and several rounds of bug fixes. In this sense, Microsoft did a decent job with the front end but not so well with the back end.

Boeing's Dreamliner 787 is a great example of a highly complex product that managed its innovation risk by relying on already known and proven technologies. Like all companies, Boeing has to innovate, but if it fails to innovate a major release like a new jumbo jet, that easily puts the company at risk of extinction.

The vast majority of the many innovations in the Dreamliner had already been ideated, developed, tested, and proven—either at Boeing or elsewhere. Advances in composite materials. Innovations in air quality, humidity, and cabin pressure systems. Low-noise engines. These are a few innovations that Boeing incorporated into its designs.

So why has the company struggled so badly to meet its obligations to customers? All we have to do is look to the far right of our model. Most of the delays in delivering Dreamliners have been due to manufacturing and assembly problems (due in large part to outsourcing issues)—not problems with the airplane's core technologies.

We can imagine or name several companies that bring the left and right sides of innovation together for competitive advantage. Apple's doing it. Under Armour has achieved great success. Nike's done very well at bringing countless new products to market. (It's innovation production facility is the third largest footwear manufacturer in the world by volume.) You don't have to look so far, like *Fast Company*'s 50 most innovative companies in the world, to find stories and examples of those that have properly managed the different cultures needed for achieving greenfield innovation (the left) and success in the marketplace (the right).

Innovation's Front Edge—the D⁴ Model

Many articles, books, and texts have been written—and many consultants can tell you—about how to engage in design excellence. This is where, for example, Design for Lean Six Sigma fits into overall business excellence—the right side of the model (develop, commercialize, and improve new solutions). Lean Six Sigma also obviously fits into this part of the model, as solutions are brought to market and improved over time.

But this book is about bringing substance to that very vague aspect of business we call innovation; and it's especially about providing much needed knowledge and clarity to the front end of innovation, since very little has been documented about how this can be done with any degree of predictability.

We've established that when a company has the right formula for perennial and pervasive innovation, it creates a special process and organization that functions quite differently from the rest of the organization. This organization plays. It works relentlessly at changing the game and seeking new growth opportunities. It rewards rather than eschews the right kind of failure at the right time. And it does this according to a process that is flexible, agile, and just systematic enough to breed success while keeping painful failure at bay.

So, in more detail, when we look at the front end of innovation, what do we really see? You'll note in Exhibit I.1 that we've chosen to depict both the left and right sides as a series of hexagons—and that the hexagons get smaller over time on the left and larger over time on the right.

Simply stated, when moving through the phases of innovation's front end, people and teams move from divergent thinking and action toward convergent thinking and action; we start by generating all kinds of ideas—sane, crazy, whatever—then use the techniques to hone in on the ideas that really do carry the promise of success. On the other side, we generally move from convergent to divergent thinking and action; we bring our feasible solution to market, and then keep improving it, expanding it, creating more options and customers (think iPod, followed by all the new features upon new releases, and any associated products like iTunes and iPad).

But *within* any phase of any part of the model, innovators both *diverge and converge*, and it's vitally important to keep this discipline. If we're only diverging or converging during any phase, we introduce risk and compromise our chances of achieving any true innovation. Exhibit I.2 characterizes how people and teams progressively diverge and converge as they move through the front end of innovation.

In the **Define the Opportunity** phase (Part I), we want to divergently explore as many opportunities for innovation as possible—using Jobs to be Done (Technique 1) as our overarching guide. Then, such techniques as Ethnography (Technique 5), Nine Windows (Technique 8), and Job Scoping (Technique 9) enable us to reframe the problem in many different ways.

D⁴ Phase	Diverge	Converge
Define the opportunity	Many problems to solve	Choose one or few problems to solve
Discover the ideas	Explore many ideas to solve problem	Choose most attractive ideas
Develop designs	Create many different design concepts based on core ideas	Choose most attractive design concept(s)
Demonstrate feasibility	Explore different ways to convert assumptions to knowledge	Narrow down to final, most feasible concept

EXHIBIT I.2 Diverge and Converge within Each Phase.

After this, when we want to narrow our set of innovation problems down to a finite few, we look to Value Quotient (Technique 4), Project Charter (Technique 12), and others to help with such convergence. Some techniques in this part of the book can be used to either help when in divergence or convergence mode—like Job Mapping (Technique 2), and Outcome Expectations (Technique 3).

In the **Discover the Ideas** phase (Part II), the task is to first divergently explore as many ideas for solving the innovation problem as possible—using HIT Matrix (Technique 18), Concept Tree (Technique 22), and other techniques. Some techniques can push the innovator to new creative heights within the paradigm of the business, industry, and current solution—like Brainwriting 6-3-5 (Technique 20); others, like Forced Association (Technique 25) and Structured Abstraction (Technique 26), force the innovator outside the current paradigm into unknown industries and realms.

Then, after this, the objective is to narrow down the many options/ideas to the one(s) that are the most attractive in terms of their predicted feasibility. Will customers buy? Is the new product cheap enough to make? Does the new solution forcefully fill a large outcome expectation gap? See Value Quotient (Technique 4), KJ method (Technique 30), Six Thinking Modes (Technique 32), and Paired Comparison (Technique 39) to achieve this narrowing job.

During the **Develop the Design** (Part III) phase, we take our core idea and ask ourselves how we can build the solution by focusing on the key functions the design must perform. By this, we don't mean to place emphasis on building it for reliability, usability, maintainability, and other such functional requirements that come into play on the right side of the innovation model—although we do keep these dimensions somewhat in mind as we develop design ideas.

For example, an innovator in the food industry might ask how to conveniently heat a beverage, soup, or a meal. There would be many ways to explore multiple design concepts using Axiomatic Design (Technique 34), Function Structure (Technique 35), TILMAG (Technique 37), and other techniques. But then the task quickly becomes one of converging on the best and most feasible design concept(s) to solve the problem or answer the question—using the Work Cell Design (Technique 38), Pugh Matrix (Technique 40), Robust Design (Technique 42), or other techniques.

In our example, the innovator might converge on a design idea for creating self-heating packages or containers: compress a designated spot on the container to cause an internal exothermic reaction that heats the food.

Last on the front-end frontier is to **Demonstrate the Innovation (Part IV)** of the final planned design, which is also achieved by both diverging and converging. This is the stage at which the innovator's *assumption-to-knowledge ratio* should dramatically improve (meaning more knowledge, fewer assumptions)—enabling the innovator to better predict market success or failure.

To do this, we use Innovation Financial Management (Technique 13), Prototyping (Technique 48), Piloting (Technique 49), Conjoint Analysis (Technique 54), and other techniques used in a way that explores different ways of testing, making, delivering, or otherwise commercializing the new solution design. Then other techniques are used to converge on the final design that is carried forward into the innovation portfolio—such as Process Behavior Charts (Technique 55), Cause & Effect Diagram (Technique 56), and Control Plan (Technique 58).

Having laid out the land in this manner, we, of course, recognize that many of the techniques in the Develop and Demonstrate phases of D^4 are also heavily used when further developing, commercializing, and improving innovative solutions (exploiting solutions on the back end). Lean Six Sigma and operational excellence practitioners even use, at times, various front-end techniques from the Define and Discover phases as they engage in back-end activities.

While our innovation model is presented and generally followed in a progressive manner, well over half of the techniques in this book have many lives; they are robust in nature and can be applied by smart innovators, optimizers, waste reducers, and facilitators at any point in the larger innovation process—from the very left to the extreme right of the model. They are really, in the end, simply problem-solving tools.

In fact, some techniques can and are applied even to the left of the left—meaning there is a managerial domain that surrounds the innovation process. We mentioned above that this domain falls outside the scope of this book, but for context we should mention that it entails creating the proper organizational climate and culture for innovation, and directing the organization toward its well-intentioned vision. This entails harnessing human talent, implementing and managing innovation projects, installing an infrastructure for rapid and successful innovation deployment, and otherwise governing and leading the charge for tomorrow.

All told, we think of the techniques in this book as the innovator's core knowledge; how these techniques are applied and on what scale is a matter of management at the project level and leadership at the organizational level. But for our purpose here, the techniques enable innovators to safely navigate their way through the front end to a risk-mitigated portfolio of projects (when practiced on a larger scale).

A Balanced Innovation Portfolio

A robust portfolio of innovation projects should be balanced along the lines of product, process, and business model innovations—as well as innovations that are incremental, substantial, or radical in nature. (See Exhibit I.3.) We use the term *process innovation* to mean either noncustomer facing processes or customer-facing processes, the former of which many call *internal processes* and latter of which many call *services*.

Examples of product innovation include Sanyo's introduction of washing machines that don't use detergent, Apple's iPhone, and Procter & Gamble's Whitestrips. Customer-facing process (or service) examples are progressive Insurance's on-site claim adjustments, self-service check-ins at hotels and airlines, Skype for phone calling, and Facebook for social networking.

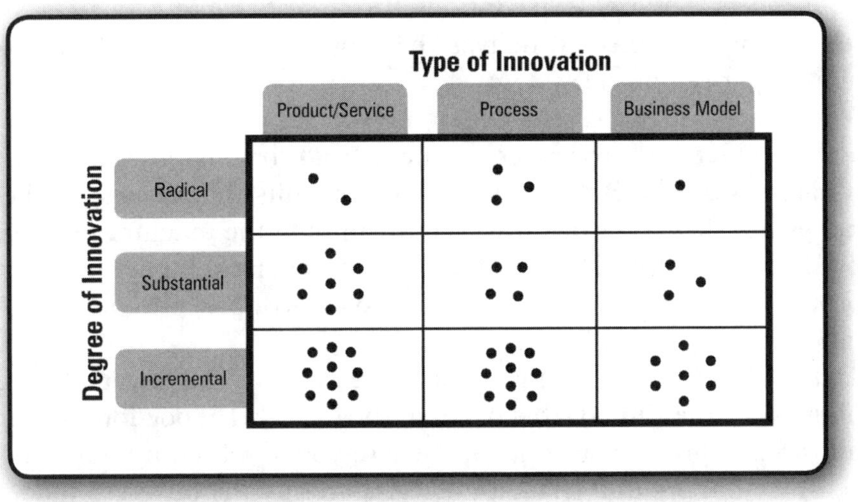

EXHIBIT I.3   Balanced Innovation Portfolio.

Noncustomer-facing process (or even product) innovations provide more value to the customer in the form of expedited service and higher quality. Bottoms Up beer (www.bottomsupbeer.com) is a rogue and beautiful startup based in Montesano, Washington. A look at the company's website can show you that the Bottoms Up beer machine and ancillary products provide a compelling alternative to the traditional beer keg or bartender options for *getting a cold, delicious beer quickly.*

We wonder if, by the time of this book's publication, this beer machine company (Grinon Industries) will still be in its infantile stage. Watch the videos on the website; the commercial machines produce 44 cups of beer a minute (using one person), using special cups that seal themselves with gravity after the beer fills the glass *from the bottom.* Properly trained Bottoms Up beer dispensers (people) make the beers with the exact amount of foam, so no mess—and up to nine times faster than traditional methods.

No wonder the company's slogan is *pushing draft beer to new heights*; this is a case in which the slogan actually fits the facts.

GrinOn has done a great job in meeting several customer and provider Outcome Expectations (see Technique 3)—such as *getting a consistent beer fast* (for the customer) and supplying the beer with *greater efficiency, less waste,* and at a *lower cost* (for the provider). GrinOn goes even further to ensure it meets outcome expectations through its *rapid education system*, whereby labor is trained to deliver the most value possible to customers through proper use of the system.

While this case represents a customer-facing process innovation, it also has both product and process components that the customer doesn't really see or care about (the Bottoms Up dispenser units themselves, the behind-the-scenes training, the skills involved in running the machines to their full potential and capacity). Therefore, we can at least loosely call this a product and process innovation of substantial import (as opposed to incremental or radical).

But don't try to call GrinOn Industries to have a conversation about anything. As of the time of this writing, the *Call Us Up* portion of GrinOn's website simply directs you to a page where you can fill out your name and contact information, and write a note. Apparently the business model part of this solution has been designed to meet the provider outcome expectation of *minimizing the cost of labor*, and *increasing the ability to work whenever, wherever one wants*.

This is not to say that Bottoms Up is a Podunk outfit; it boasts such large customers as Fenway Park in Boston, Invesco Field in Denver, and Wells Fargo Center in Philadelphia. Not bad when you consider the original technology was developed by Native Americans of the Montesano tribe in Washington state.

Other examples of process innovation include Wal-Mart's *everyday low prices*, which is really a conglomeration of behind-the-scenes business process innovations, as is Amazon's *Buy now with 1-click* feature. At the same time, such process innovations provide great value to businesses in the form of higher productivity, lower lead times, improved employee morale, and increased profitability.

An example of a business-model innovation is when Dell began selling computers directly to customers (innovating the distribution channels), avoiding the retail link in the chain. With minimal inventories to manage (core process innovation), cash up-front from customers, and delayed payment terms to suppliers, Dell redefined working capital management (revenue stream and cost structure innovation). In addition, Dell enabled customers to customize their solution and receive the computer within a few days (customer experience innovation).

eBay also changed the business-model landscape when it enabled buyers and sellers to come together outside the inefficient confines of former person-to-person venues. As Dell did, eBay changed the rules of an industry (buying and selling used goods) by implementing a host of innovations from among the list of what constitutes a business model innovation at large.

Companies can rewrite the rules of their industry by innovating around many of these 11 components: customer segment, customer experience, distribution channels, brand strategy, revenue streams, core offering, complementary offering, core processes and resources, enabling processes and resources, value creation partners, and cost structure.

We can take a more recent example of business model innovation from high-end, power-toolmaker Hilti Group, based in the very small country of Liechtenstein in central Europe. According to a *Harvard Business Review* article, Hilti went through a process of rethinking the job its customers wanted to accomplish with its tools. ("Reinventing Your Business Model," December 2008).

Written by Mark W. Johnson, Clayton M. Christensen, and Henning Kagermann, the article points out that contractors make money by completing jobs, and that they just need functioning tools to get this done. In other words, they don't need to own the tools themselves; they just need to hire the tools in the interest of the *job to be done* — in this case, *complete the work according to specification* (our words, not the authors).

Therefore, Hilti investigated the feasibility of helping contractors get their jobs done by offering them the use of tools, shifting the burden of ownership from the customer to the company. The new business model called for Hilti to manage "its customers' tool inventory by providing the best tool at the right time and quickly furnishing tool repairs, replacements, and upgrades, all for a monthly fee."

The authors conclude: "To deliver on that value proposition, the company needed to create a fleet-management program for tools and in the process shift its focus from manufacturing and distribution to service. That meant Hilti had to construct a new profit formula and develop new resources and new processes."

A rounded innovation project portfolio should also be distributed according to degree of import (incremental, substantial, radical). Obviously, the magnitude of investment, risk, and potential impact on profit increases as you move up the chain from incremental to radical innovation.

Some examples of incremental innovation include improving the check-in process at a hotel or airline, or implementing an employee idea-solicitation program. A substantial innovation might be replacing an electric toothbrush with one that adds sound waves, or allowing consumers to purchase their own plane tickets online. You still need to brush your teeth and get a plane ticket, but the means by which you do so materially changes.

Of course, radical innovations generate tremendous value for customers and for the business. The discovery of antibiotics, the printing press, gunpowder, airplanes, portable computers, and the World Wide Web are all examples of radical innovation. Less magnanimous, we could pigeonhole such innovations as handheld mobile television, self-cleaning clothes, and 3D printers as at least substantial if not radical; 3D printing, which enables retail customers to design and manufacture products at home, could for sure become a radical innovation that changes the world.

While it's difficult to firmly establish what constitutes incremental versus substantial versus radical innovation, each company can define these terms for itself. The Chemical division of Royal Dutch Shell, for instance, said at one time it needed to generate $100 million or more in revenue for an innovation to be classified as radical (or breakthrough). Whatever the criteria, every company needs to constantly populate and refresh its innovation project pipeline.

Exhibit I.3 shows the relative proportions of a typical innovation portfolio. Usually you will have more product, process, and service innovations—and fewer business model innovations. As well, most organizations aim for more incremental and substantial innovations—and fewer radical innovations.

Of course, true competitive advantage is usually the result of making coordinated innovations on multiple fronts. According to a study by Kaiser Associates, there was a three-year time period during which Apple combined its iPod, iPhone, and other products with its iTunes business model to create about $70 billion in shareholder value. Today (2012), the company's market capitalization exceeds $500 billion, and Apple holds about $100 billion in cash assets.

Amazon is another high performer in terms of how it pursues and implements business model innovation. Cutting out the brick-and-mortar store is coupled with such service innovations as *1-click, recently viewed items, customer reviews,* and *books you might also like.* Add to this the rate at which Amazon piles new products into its kingdom (unknown by us but observed as "quite healthy")—and keep examining such other customer delights as making faster-than-promised shipments—and you'll see the picture of business model innovation unfolding.

Compare what you know or think about Amazon with the list of 11 business model components above to get an impression of how Amazon has innovated across the board. To name a few, think about *customer segment, customer experience, distribution channels, brand strategy, complimentary offering*—heck, think about the whole list of 11 components.

How People Solve Problems

All the identified growth projects in the world won't result in even one profitable innovation if at the end of the day you don't have the right people solving the right problems. Therefore, to close out this introduction, we'll summarize the way humans solve problems, as well as what types of problems are (and are not) appropriate to solve with the techniques in this book.

Every innovation is the result of solving some important problem, like how to get an army across an ocean (naval ship), or how to put a man on the moon (rocket). Even simpler problems lead to simpler but no less important innovations, like using a net to catch fish and secure a food supply. Still other problems lead to solutions that save lives: vaccines, portable water purifiers, bulletproof vests, and the like.

Each stage of the problem-solving process is associated with two fundamental cognitive operations, namely *divergent thinking* and *convergent thinking*. The divergent thinking operation involves searching for ideas and increasing one's options through elaboration of the problem, redefinition of the problem, and by exploring, connecting, and/or combining potential ideas and solutions. In contrast, the convergent thinking operation involves evaluating ideas and narrowing or reducing one's options through the imposition of value judgments, exploiting the information available about the ideas, and then prioritizing and selecting.

In both cases (divergent and convergent thinking), the resulting ideas and solutions may fall inside, at the edges of, or outside the relevant technical domain or paradigm. We make this statement to ensure that divergent thinking is not considered synonymous with *out of the box* thinking, nor convergent thinking with *in the box* thinking. All problem solvers both diverge and converge, at different cognitive levels and with different preferred styles; these operations lead to solutions throughout the problem-solving space.

Another way to look at the problem-solving approach is in terms of *exploration* versus *exploitation*. Exploration is about searching for new ideas both inside and outside the paradigm, whereas exploitation is about taking advantage of an idea within the paradigm and perfecting it (as reflected in Exhibit I.1). Some business problems require mostly exploitation, while others require mostly exploration, but all problems require some mixture of the two.

Thomas Edison is often called an inventor, but he mostly developed basic discoveries into better solutions for commercialization. Often credited with inventing the lightbulb, Edison really conducted extensive experimentation and analysis to find the optimal conditions under which the tungsten wire in a bulb would glow continuously without interruption. While Edison did his own share of exploration, his basic strength and passion was in taking what was already known and refining it until it could solve some known problem.

Einstein, on the other hand, thought mostly outside the box of his day's prevailing wisdom, or what was known at the time, and such exploration is the essence of solving problems in untried and untested ways. His theory of relativity questioned key assumptions of Newtonian physics. Einstein even characterized himself as a little strange—but strangeness is what it takes to solve ill-defined problems, or to solve fairly well-defined problems in new and unusual ways.

People in your organization, including you, are either more like Edison or more like Einstein. You might tend to solve problems through study, analysis, and working within known domains (exploitation). Or you might tend to explore new domains, question assumptions, and generate many hair-brained ideas until you solve your problem (exploration). See Technique 11, Cognitive Style, for an interesting breakdown of these two approaches and why they are the most important yet most overlooked aspect of how certain innovation teams succeed while others fail.

To reiterate, different types of innovation problems require different degrees of exploitation and exploration to solve, as shown in Exhibit I.4. The solid boxes and lines represent the convergent exploitation, while the dotted boxes and lines represent divergent exploration.

Understanding each of these four problem-solving classes will enable you to characterize any problem in your organization. From there, you can

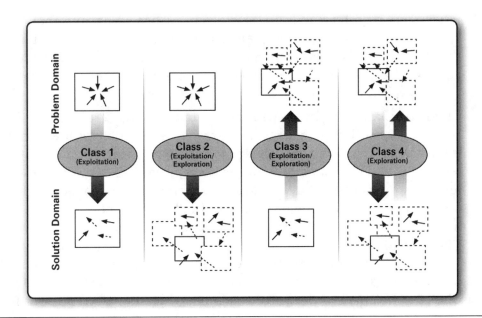

EXHIBIT I.4 Four Classes of Problem Solving.

select the best and most appropriate techniques for solving your particular problem.

Class 1—The problem and the solution space are both well-defined, and this dictates mostly exploitation activities within the current paradigm. Defects on a production line are a good example of Class-1 problems, which are usually solved with such process-improvement methods as PDCA (Plan-Do-Check-Act), Six Sigma, Lean, and the like. See mostly the Develop and Demonstrate techniques to solve Class-1 problems.

Class 2—The problem is well-defined but the solution pathway is not so clear or directly discoverable. Therefore, the task is to explore new ideas and realms, searching for better solutions, while also exploiting known knowledge when necessary. For example, the job of illuminating a room in the dark was once accomplished with a candle, but candles have drawbacks, like dripping wax. Some important customer expectations were not met very well by candles, so this opened the door for better solutions.

When your customers tell you they are largely satisfied with your product or service, you have a Class-1 problem: Just optimize. If, on the other hand, customers tell you they are unsatisfied with your product or service, you have a Class-2 problem: Discover or invent a better solution that closes the dissatisfaction gap. Stated differently, if customers are generally happy with candles, make better candles; if they are unhappy, discover a better way to illuminate the darkness.

Class 3—Class-3 problems are the reverse of Class-2 problems: The solution is clear but the problem is fuzzy. Class-3 problems are intriguing because they force you to consider new applications for existing technologies. For instance, engineer Richard James was working with tension springs in 1943 to develop a meter for monitoring horsepower on naval battleships. One of his springs fell to the ground and offered him a new idea about a different job to be done in a different market. Thus, the Slinky was born.

Sometimes, your existing solutions can be put to a different use, thereby solving a problem and opening a new market. In effect, Class-3 problems require you to turn your ideation efforts upward— beyond where your solutions reside into the realm of higher human needs—asking what jobs your solutions could do that they don't do today?

Class-2 and -3 problems are by far the ripest classes on which to focus organic growth efforts, and all 58 techniques in this book were chosen because they primarily solve these types of organic growth problems.

Class 4—These problems are undefined, and their solutions are undefined, as well. There is no particular mandate to solve any problem, and the objective is to simply explore, as both the problem and the solution reside in unknown territory. Medical researchers, for instance, are always looking for new molecules—just for the sake of finding them. Once they're found, they can always be studied, manipulated, and exploited.

Solving Class-4 problems is what you do when you don't know what you're doing—basic research, where discoveries are made but the path to commercialization is unclear. As such, they fall outside the scope of this book—although Trend Prediction (Technique 16), Provocation and Movement (Technique 24), Biomimicry (Technique 29), and Design of Experiments (Technique 53) can help the Class-4 problem solver.

There you have it. We only hope you can use some of the techniques in this book to write your own innovation story.

PART I

DEFINE THE OPPORTUNITY

Taking thousands of shots at an undefined target (unfocused ideation) won't result in an innovation goal. Yet, the very nature of innovation seems to imply that the target is hazy and disguised—but this is a myth. Those who know how to clear the haze will see that the front edge of innovation isn't as elusive as it may seem; it's only unreachable by those who don't know how to find it and bring it into focus for their own advantage.

This first phase of innovation enables you to bring the aims of organic growth into focus and *create viable innovation opportunities*. Use the Jobs to be Done (JTBD), Job Mapping, Outcome Expectations, and Value Quotient techniques to identify actionable innovation gaps, or high-potential innovation projects based on the identification of unmet customer needs and new market territory. Also, use the Ethnography technique to directly observe how customers struggle with existing solutions so you can understand their unarticulated needs.

Once you've defined your opportunity, you can *scope and focus your innovation projects*. The Scenario Planning technique will facilitate your thoughts about the future, so you put some stakes in the ground about the developments you expect to occur in your environment. The Heuristic Redefinition technique will help you do this by identifying all the elements of your current solution and how they relate to one another. The Nine Windows technique will do this as well, adding the dimensions of time and scale to your innovation problem. Then, Job Scoping is a simple but powerful technique for either narrowing or broadening your project's focus.

Also in Part I, we give you techniques to *manage people, projects, and return on innovation investment.* Specifically, the Stakeholder Management technique helps get all pertinent people lined up to support organic growth projects. The Cognitive Style technique ensures your team is staffed with the right people. The Project Charter technique is a living document used to keep the project on time and on task. And the Innovation Financial Management technique keeps you on the straight-and-narrow fiscal path, even enabling you to discontinue your project if it becomes too risky.

Jobs to be Done

Highlight the human need you're trying to fulfill.

A *job to be done* (JTBD) is a revolutionary concept that guides you toward innovation and helps you move beyond the norm of only improving current solutions. A JTBD is not a product, service, or a specific solution; it's the higher purpose for which customers buy products, services, and solutions.

For instance, most people would say they buy a lawnmower to "cut the grass," and this is true. But if a lawnmower company examines the higher purpose of cutting the grass, say, "keep the grass low and beautiful at all times," then it might forgo some efforts to make better lawnmowers in lieu of developing a genetically engineered grass seed that never needs to be cut.

This is the power of the JTBD concept and technique: It helps the innovator understand that customers don't buy products and services; they hire various solutions at various times to get a wide array of jobs done. You may need light survey design and sampling help from a statistician to apply this technique, but for the most part, it requires no expert assistance.

Background

Harvard Business School professor Clayton Christensen and coauthors articulated the JTBD concept in a *Sloan Management Review* article (Spring 2007) as follows: "Most companies segment their markets by customer demographics or product characteristics and differentiate their offerings by adding features and functions. But the consumer has a different view of the marketplace. He simply has a job to be done and is seeking to 'hire' the best product or service to do it."

Therefore, if you understand the jobs your customers want done, you gain new market insights and create viable growth strategies. Sometimes a good solution for a JTBD, or a family of JTBDs, does not exist; when this is the case, you have a great opportunity to innovate.

Jobs to be Done Breakdown

There are two different types of JTBDs:

1. *Main jobs to be done,* which describe the tasks that customers want to achieve.
2. *Related jobs to be done,* which customers want to accomplish in conjunction with the main jobs to be done.

Then, within each of these two types of JTBDs, there are:

- *Functional job aspects*—the practical and objective customer requirements.
- *Emotional job aspects*—the subjective customer requirements related to feelings and perceptions.

Finally, emotional job aspects are further broken down into:

- *Personal dimension*—how the customer feels about the solution.
- *Social dimension*—how the customer believes he or she is perceived by others while using the solution.
- See Exhibit 1.1 for a visual representation of the different types of jobs to be done and breakdown into aspects and dimensions.

Let's develop an example. Say the main JTBD is to clean one's teeth and gums. Then related jobs might be to create lasting fresh breath, whiten one's teeth, and even achieve such other grooming objectives as a clean face and/or neat eyebrows.

We can break the main and related JTBDs into their functional and emotional aspects. One wants to remove foreign particles from one's teeth, along with any bacteria and associated odor. These are some functional aspects of the JTBD. A customer also wants his or her teeth and gum

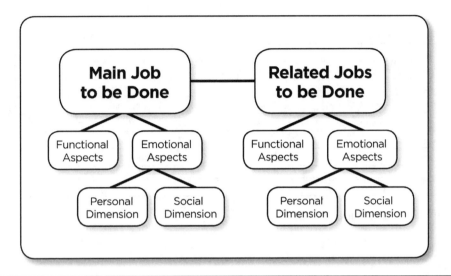

EXHIBIT 1.1   Jobs to be Done Breakdown.

cleaning experience to be pleasant. It should feel good, not painful. It should make the customer feel good about him- or herself (personal dimension), as well as help him or her be perceived as a person who has clean teeth, healthy gums, and fresh breath.

The better a solution can fulfill all of these job levels and layers, the better chance it has in the marketplace. Also, the better the solution either achieves or nicely dovetails with related JTBDs, the better chance of success it has. In short, the JTBD concept is a guide for thinking beyond to make your current solutions, and your competitors' solutions, obsolete.

You can tell when a company thinks in terms of JTBDs because the result not only fulfills a need, but is often quite innovative. Consider the recent developments in self-cleaning glass for cars and high-rise buildings, or in car paint that *heals itself* and, thereby, removes the need to paint over scratches. While you could think of *painting scratches* as a JTBD, it really isn't. Painting scratches is actually a solution for accomplishing the JTBD called *maintain a blemish-free vehicle*.

Consider the examples of new solutions for old JTBDs in Exhibit 1.2. Then, ask not how you can make your current products and services better, but instead, ask how you can fulfill your customers' JTBDs in unexpected and more effective ways.

Jobs to be Done	Old Solution	New Solution
Ingest medicine	Pills and shots	Skin patches
Make many products for mass market	Many craftsman	Production line
Execute rote legal functions	Lawyers	legalzoom.com
Detect enemy at night	Flares	Night vision
Keep windows clean	Clean with squeegee	Self-cleaning glass
Clean teeth	Manual brushing	Automated with sound waves
Search for information	Library	Internet

EXHIBIT 1.2   New Solutions for Old Jobs.

The Triune Brain

Metaphorically speaking, our brains have three parts as per the *triune brain model*: reptilian, emotional, and intellectual. The reptilian part is related to our basic survival and biological needs; we eat when we're hungry, and we either fight or flee when we are threatened. The emotional (or paleomammalian) part of our brain, directed by the limbic system, guides many or most decisions we make in life. The intellectual (or neomammalian) part, guided by the neocortex, is the logical, methodical, and analytical part of the brain.

Psychologists have discovered that when these three parts are in conflict, the reptilian takes precedent over the other two. When there is a conflict between the emotional and intellectual parts, the emotional part wins over. This is why people often make poor, emotionally based decisions, and then find an intellectual alibi to justify themselves.

So what is the implication for companies that want to innovate? One, make solutions that appeal to all three parts of the brain—especially the emotional and intellectual since only a small set of solutions are truly a matter of life or death (reptilian). Apple does a good job of this. Its products are functionally sound (intellectual)—plus, they're cool and stylish (emotional). Although we know one iPod user who returned the product six times due to functional challenges, the customer was willing to tolerate this because the product was so emotionally appealing.

But there's another interesting implication. If your industry is mainly focused on the functional aspects of the JTBD, then differentiate yourself with the emotional aspect. Make the surgical instrument look really cool with an appealing design and shape that fits the hand better. Or, start to emphasize the functional aspects of your products in industries that are typically driven by image and emotion. Many Body Shop products, for example, are organic (noncarcinogenic), and they improve the quality of one's skin (anti-aging properties)—blending function with emotion.

This is the story of innovation in a nutshell: While some companies went about making better pills, or becoming better law firms, or making their flares better and brighter, others went about breaking the mold. No new solution automatically or instantly makes an old solution obsolete, but change does happen as a result of finding new ways to fulfill the jobs customers need to get done.

If you remember anything about jobs to be done, remember this: they are completely neutral of the solutions you create (your products and services). While a customer JTBD remains fairly stable over time, your products and services should change at strategic intervals as you strive to provide ever-increasing value.

Steps

1. Identify a Focus Market

Markets can be identified by considering any one of the following organic growth strategies: core growth, disruptive growth, related job growth, and new job growth.

Core growth is the act of meeting unmet outcome expectations associated with a job that customers want to achieve. For example, customers want to pour juice into a cup with greater ease (desired outcome expectation) and without the risk of spilling (undesired outcome expectation). So the juice bottle is redesigned to have an indentation for easy gripping. This is the easiest way to innovate for most companies because it entails perfecting the current paradigm. (See Technique 3, Outcome Expectations, for more on this).

Related job growth is the next easiest way to innovate and entails bundling solutions that achieve the outcome expectations of more than one main or related JTBD. Starbucks is an example of a solution that addresses many jobs, such as *drink caffeinated beverages*, *drink healthy alternative beverages*, *carry on business conversations*, *surf the Internet*, or *study and read books in a relaxing environment*.

The key is to focus on *adjacency*: I want coffee, but I also want to read a book and get on the Internet, or socialize with my friends. Or, I want a car to rent so I can get from here to there, but I also want easy directions so I also get a GPS in the car.

New job growth is the product of evolving technology and change, and it's more difficult to achieve than core or related job growth. It entails expanding the solution space to accomplish different JTBDs. Candle companies that existed for decades, for instance, had to look for new applications after the advent of the lightbulb. So they made products that were appealing to those who wanted to decorate their homes or to create a romantic environment for dinner. The JTBD was no longer to illuminate.

Some medical companies are migrating their technologies from use by humans to new jobs for animals, especially after patents expire. Another example might be an organization well-versed in emergency response processes expanding itself to get into the ambulance business.

Disruptive growth focuses on what the literature and innovation experts call *nonconsumption*. Certain solutions are available to certain classes of people, but not all or more people. Remember when going to a dentist's office was the only way to get your teeth whitened? But now the job of whitening teeth can be sufficiently accomplished by anyone nearly anywhere due to such disruptive, over-the-counter products as Crest Whitestrips (which became a $300 million product within two years for Procter & Gamble).

There are four drivers of nonconsumption: price, time, skill, and access to the technology or solution. The Whitestrips example fits all four criteria. Prior to Whitestrips, it was too expensive to whiten one's teeth. It took too much time. Individuals didn't have access to the needed technology, and they didn't have the skills to apply that technology at home.

This is the most difficult growth strategy to enact because it entails cannibalizing what you and others in your industry do. Other examples of disruptive growth are home pregnancy tests, online stock trading, and self-administered medical monitoring and treatment devices.

Core and disruptive growth strategies are focused on existing JTBDs, while related and new job growth strategies are focused on new JTBDs. Also, core and related growth strategies are about serving existing customers, while new and disruptive growth strategies are about adding and serving new customers.

2. Identify Jobs Customers Are Trying to Get Done

You want to study customers and find out what they are trying to accomplish—especially under circumstances that leave them with insufficient solutions relative to available processes and technologies. What jobs have ad hoc solutions or no good solutions? When you see customers piecing together solutions themselves, these are great clues for innovation.

Several methods exist to help an innovator study customers and the way they use solutions to get their jobs done. Ethnography (Technique 5) and cultural archetype research are especially useful in this regard. Other techniques include observation, interviews, customer complaints, and focus groups.

Sometimes jobs to be done are not as straightforward as one might think. For instance, a fast-food provider found that its customers were buying flavored milkshakes when faced with a long, boring commute in traffic; they were not only looking for convenient, non-messy nourishment in the morning, but they also wanted to make their commute more interesting by entertaining themselves with a breakfast that took a while to consume.

3. Categorize the Jobs to be Done

Jobs can be main jobs or related jobs. Some jobs are parents of other jobs. If a person wants to self-actualize, for instance, this job could be the parent to any number of lower-order jobs having to do with a person's physical, mental, social, emotional, financial, and spiritual well-being.

There is no one way or standardized, commonly used scheme for categorizing JTBDs—so our best advice is to use a scheme that makes sense for you and your industry. In the retail sales industry, for instance, many main JTBDs are related to how you make people feel (emotional aspects) rather than what a product or service actually does (functional aspects). Many non-customer-facing jobs in the engineering industry are functional rather than emotional in nature. But recall earlier that we discussed the potential value of focusing on either functional or emotional aspects *in contrast with* industry norms.

We also mentioned earlier that jobs have functional and emotional aspects (and personal and social dimensions). One JTBD is to *organize and manage music for personal use.* An important functional aspect of this job is to *listen to the music.* A related emotional/personal job is to *organize and manage music in a way that feels good;* a related emotional/social job is to *share songs with friends.* Related jobs might be to *download songs from the Internet, make playlists, discard unwanted songs,* and *pass the time.*

4. Create Job Statements

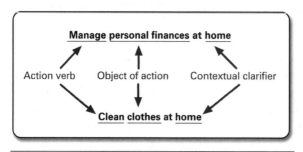

EXHIBIT 1.3 Structure of a Job Statement (Downloadable).

Copyright © 2012, BMGI. A blank version of this customized form is available for download at www.innovatorstoolkit.com.

The *job statement* is used to describe a JTBD. Key components of a job statement are an action verb, the object of the action, and clarification of the context in which the job is performed. *Manage personal finances at home* is a job statement. So is *clean clothes at home,* as shown in Exhibit 1.3. *Listen to music while jogging* is also an example of a job statement.

5. Prioritize the JTBD Opportunities

There are hundreds of jobs that customers are trying to get done in every market. Which one of these offers the best opportunities for you? Which ones provide opportunities to create uncontested market space? In most situations, the jobs that customers want to get done for which no good solutions exist are the ones that provide the greatest opportunity for innovation.

Prioritizing JTBDs is a function of how *important* they are, how *satisfied* customers are with existing solutions, the general potential for developing new (or more ideal) solutions, and the specific potential of the provider for creating new solutions that better meet Outcome Expectations (see Technique 3). As shown in Exhibit 1.4, the importance-satisfaction dimensions establish priority from the customers' perspective. But we also consider new solution potential from the provider's perspective.

You can use different assessment and rating schemes to determine which JTBDs should be a priority for innovation. One way to measure the importance of a job is by asking customers based on a Likert Scale (degree of importance to them), using sound *sampling* techniques. A Likert Scale can also work for assessing the level of satisfaction customers have with current solutions.

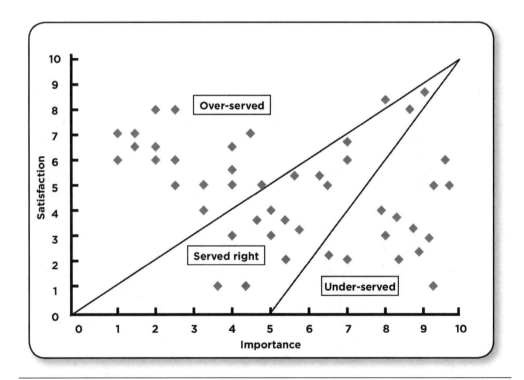

EXHIBIT 1.4   JTBD Prioritization (Downloadable).

In any case, under-served JTBDs are generally ripe for a core growth innovation strategy (make the existing solution better); over-served items are ripe for a disruptive innovation strategy (remake the solution so it becomes available to those who can't afford the existing solution). When your assessment shows opportunities in the middle that are served right, you should focus on related jobs to be done.

Sometimes innovation is as simple as finding a new JTBD that your existing solution meets. Post-it Notes, for example, were developed by a 3M scientist looking for a new and better adhesive compound. The scientist didn't quite reach his goal because his adhesive was weak. Ten years later, another 3M scientist led the way in applying the adhesive for jobs that fit the solution perfectly.

Resources

For more on the Jobs to be Done concept and technique, see:

Christensen, C. M., S. D. Anthony, G. Berstell, and D. Nitterhouse. "Finding the Right Job for Your Product." *MIT Sloan Management Review* (Spring 2007): 2–11.

Christensen, C. M., and M. E. Raynor. *The Innovator's Solution: Using Good Theory to Solve the Dilemmas of Growth*. Watertown, MA: Harvard Business School Press, 2003.

Ulwick, A. *What Customers Want: Using Outcome-Driven Innovation to Create Breakthrough Products and Services*. New York: McGraw-Hill, 2005.

Ulwick, A., and L. A. Bettencourt. "Giving Customers a Fair Hearing." *Sloan Management Review* 49, no. 3 (2008): 62–68.

Job Mapping

Determine how customers are getting jobs done.

Job mapping is a technique that helps break down the customer Jobs to be Done (JTBD, Technique 1) into eight categories of activities (define, locate, prepare, confirm, execute, monitor, modify, and conclude). We do this to extract associated solution-neutral criteria (Outcome Expectations, Technique 3) that the customer will use to hire a solution. We use the phrase, *hire a solution*, to shape the mind toward solution indifference; we want to offer whatever solution that gets the job done today with the most value for the provider and customer.

For example, suppose we want to understand the subtle nuances of getting the following JTBD accomplished: *Withdraw cash from an ATM associated with your current bank.* Imagine that we want to truly understand how customers are getting this job done today and extract their solution-neutral hiring criteria; we would break this JTBD down into its various job steps and then extract the outcome expectations.

The job map is typically used after the JTBD has been scoped to the right level (see Job Scoping, Technique 9). It quickly enables the problem solver to identify opportunities for innovation by extracting the needs associated with each step the customer is trying to get done to achieve the JTBD. This technique is often used in conjunction with Ethnography (Technique 5).

Background

Bettencourt and Ulwick articulated the job mapping concept in a *Harvard Business Review* article (April 2008) as follows:

> By thoroughly mapping the job a customer is trying to get done, a company can discover opportunities for breakthrough products and services.... The goal of creating a job map is not to find out how the customer is executing a job—that only generates maps of existing activities and solutions. Instead the aim is to discover what the customer is trying to get done at different points in executing a job and what must happen at each juncture in order for the job to be carried out successfully.

Therefore, if a solution provider dissects the steps of the job the customer is trying to get done and extracts its customers' expectations for each of the steps, it can uncover innovation opportunities that will fuel its growth agenda. (See Exhibit 2.1.)

A job map differs from a process map in that it identifies the fundamental goal associated with the steps a customer is trying to complete (including the cognitive activities)—as opposed to the actual process steps (solution dependent) a customer may perform.

Steps

Scenario: Let's say we want to innovate around the process of returning a rental car at an airport location before catching a flight. Currently the rental car return process is tedious, time-consuming, and prone to errors even if you hold elite status with the agency. So, our goal is to identify opportunities for innovation around this JTBD.

1. Determine the JTBD

Observe and interact with customers to determine the job they're trying to get done—especially under circumstances that leave them with insufficient solutions relative to available processes and technologies. What jobs have ad

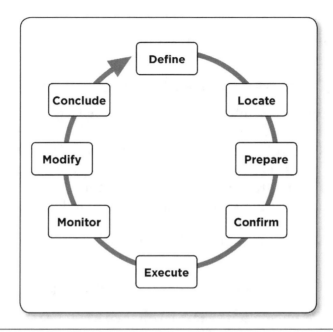

EXHIBIT 2.1 Customer Job Map. *Define* the cognitive steps taken before this job is executed, *locate* all enablers for achieving this job, *prepare* these enablers so the job can be executed, *confirm* that all decisions have been made and enablers have been collated, *execute* the JTBD, *monitor* the experience, *modify* the experience (in real time or in future job cycles), and *conclude* by closing out the transaction to move on to the next JTBD.

hoc solutions or inadequate solutions? In our example, the JTBD is *return the rented vehicle to the agency's airport location.*

2. *Define* the Cognitive Portion of the JTBD

What are essential planning steps the customer must cognitively process when trying to get a job done? Create a list of all different aspects of the JTBD that need to be defined. This includes establishing the objective, planning the approach, and identifying the resources needed.

In our example JTBD, this entails the objective of returning the vehicle at the airport location. The approach entails how long before flight departure time the renter must start the journey towards the airport return location, the shortest route to the return location, fitting the luggage in the trunk of the vehicle, how all the fellow passengers will travel to the return location, and how the vehicle will be refueled before its return.

By simplifying the planning process for the customer, the solution provider can make life easier and worry-free for the customer.

3. *Locate* the Enablers for Achieving the JTBD

List out all the items and information that is needed (needs to be located) to get the job done. This includes both tangible resources as well as intangible information. The job of *performing a kidney transplant*, for instance, requires the surgical team to locate all the instruments necessary to conduct the surgery, ahead of the transplant. Similarly, in our example, the rental car customer must locate the rental return location address, the vehicle and keys, the luggage, people traveling with the renter, personal belongings to be taken, and refueling options.

4. *Prepare* All Located Enablers for Achieving the JTBD

This step lists the activities associated with preparing the inputs (organizing and environment setup) to efficiently execute the JTBD. In our example, the rental car must be loaded with the luggage for travel, co-travelers must be seated and buckled in, and the car must be refueled for return. Solution providers can innovate by enabling customers to minimize the time it takes to prepare the inputs needed to get the job done, thereby simplifying the preparation step.

5. *Confirm* that All Preparations Are Complete

The purpose here is to ensure that all necessary process steps are taken to confirm JTBD readiness for execution. This provides peace of mind to the customer that everything is ready and the chances of making errors are minimized. It is also an essential step to ensure that rework is minimized.

Before starting a surgery, a surgeon must ensure that the patient is ready for the procedure and all the inputs are in their place. For the returning a rental vehicle example, the renter must ensure that the vehicle is ready for return (i.e., fuel gauge shows a full tank, contract ready, no dents/scratches, keys are in the ignition, and so forth), all the luggage is in the vehicle, the route is accurate (ensure that the GPS unit pulled up the right return location), there is sufficient time to reach the return location, and travel time allows drop-off and travel to the airport.

Again, the provider can anticipate these customer needs and design solutions that meet them better, faster, and more cost-effectively than the alternatives.

6. *Execute* the JTBD

The most visible and prevalent aspect of job mapping, this step identifies the key activities involved in executing the JTBD. It's important that customers can perform the job easily, in minimal time, with quality output.

The most obvious execution steps for returning the rental car to the airport location include driving to the rental agency, finding the exact drop-off location when one arrives, enabling the vehicle-return staff to evaluate the vehicle, closing out the contract and handing over the receipt, transporting luggage to the airport shuttle and waiting, then boarding the shuttle with luggage and traveling to the airport.

By gaining insight regarding the detailed aspects of the steps, solution providers can innovate by simplifying and automating many of these steps and aspects.

7. *Monitor* the Experience

This step is carried out to verify the necessity of making adjustments or modification to the execution step, if necessary. If the job was executed correctly, it will provide peace of mind for the customer. If the job wasn't executed correctly, the customer can be alerted on steps (or how) to fix the errors. How can solution providers alert the customer about whether the job was executed correctly?

In the rental return example, some of the mistakes in job execution could include the GPS system not finding the return location or providing erroneous directions, the driver not finding a gas station on the way to the agency, rental return staff giving confusing hand signals, and the driver parking in the wrong return lane. More opportunities for error include damaging luggage when removing it from the vehicle, waiting too long for vehicle-return staff to arrive, vehicle-return staff taking too long to evaluate the vehicle and conducting performance checks, and the amount charged not matching the price shown when the booking was made.

The consequences of these mistakes can be time-consuming or resource demanding on the part of the customer (and the provider). Therefore, the solution provider could proactively think about these issues and come up with innovative strategies to reduce the errors during job execution.

8. *Modify* the Experience

Based on learning in the preceding steps, the activities in this step include all that is performed to modify the experience either in real time or in future executions of the same JTBD. What adjustments should customers make if the job wasn't executed as expected? How can the customer minimize the time and effort required to perform the needed modifications?

In our example of returning a car to the rental location, some of the modifications could include rerouting the car to the actual return location when the GPS or operator fails, providing a detour to locate a gas station, reparking the vehicle in the right return spot, working the dent out of the luggage, calling out to cut vehicle-return staff when waiting too long, and going to the rental desk and sorting out the erroneous charges.

Of course, these are not preferred modifications because they are after the fact. The provider can anticipate so many problems and install measures to prevent them, according to the job map steps above and other techniques like Mistake Proofing (Technique 45) and Robust Design (Technique 42). In other words, what can be done upstream to minimize the need for modifying steps later?

9. *Conclude* the Job

In this step, the customer is focused on performing all the cognitive and physical activities necessary to conclude the job. So how can customers minimize the non-value-added activities during this step while improving the throughput, quality, and time it takes to complete the value-added activities?

Again, in our example, some of the activities associated with this step include receiving a rebate on the incorrect amount charged (if an error was made), collecting the receipt, traveling to the airport, checking the credit card statement to ensure transaction accuracy, and deciding on whether to rent from this agency again. The solution provider can innovate in this step by simplifying any or all such activities.

Identify Opportunities for Innovation

After the job map is complete, identify the outcome expectations associated with each of the job steps. These are the solution-neutral criteria customers will use to determine which solution to hire.

In our rental return example, during **define**, customers would like to *increase the likelihood of remembering to define all relevant cognitive aspects of the JTBD*. During **locate**, customers would like to *increase the ease of locating the address of the rental car return location*. During **prepare**, customers would like *to minimize the time it takes to prepare enablers*. During **execute**, customers would like to *minimize the time it takes to drop off the vehicle at the return location*. Also, during this step, customers would like to *minimize the time it takes to reach the airport from the return location*. During **conclude**, customers would like to *minimize the time it takes to conclude the JTBD*.

Of course, this is not a comprehensive listing of outcome expectations for each job map step. It's not uncommon to identify between 50 and 150 outcome expectations for a given job map that, in turn, become the basis for developing innovative solutions to accomplish the JTBD. One can then subsequently leverage any number of Discover tools to identify innovative solutions for the identified opportunities.

Resource

For more on the Job Mapping technique, see:

Bettencourt, L. A., and A. W. Ulwick. "The Customer-Centered Innovation Map." *Harvard Business Review*, April 2008.

Outcome Expectations

Give customers more of what they desire.

Outcome expectations are a direct outgrowth of innovation jobs to be done (JTBDs), and they lead to eventual new solutions that create more value and customer satisfaction than existing products and services. For example, the job of cleaning your clothes has many associated outcome expectations, such as *minimize the time it takes to clean clothes, increase the likelihood of stain removal,* and *increase the ease with which clothes are cleaned.*

It's important to define any outcome expectations associated with a JTBD when pursuing an innovation based on that JTBD. Understanding these expectations, and knowing how satisfied (or unsatisfied) customers are with current solutions, helps you identify unidentified market space and possibly fill that space with better solutions than what exists today. You may need light survey design and sampling help from a statistician to apply this technique, but for the most part it requires no expert assistance.

Background

There are four types of outcome expectations:

1. Desired outcomes customers want to achieve.
2. Undesired outcomes customers want to avoid.

3. Desired outcomes providers want to achieve.

4. Undesired outcomes providers want to avoid (see Exhibit 3.1).

By segmenting outcome expectations in this manner, you can look at the JTBD through the lens of what the customer wants and doesn't want, as well as what the provider wants and doesn't want. Both parties must benefit from the innovation or it will never reach viable commercialization.

We can view outcome expectations as *hiring criteria*, a notion set forth by Harvard Business School professor Clayton Christensen, the originator of the Jobs to be Done concept. In his own words at the 2009 World Innovation Forum in New York: "What are the experiences in purchase and use which, if all provided, would sum up to nailing the job perfectly?"

Customers typically hire the solution that gives them more of the desired outcomes (benefits) and less of the undesired outcomes (cost and harm). As a provider, you want the solution that maximizes desired outcomes and minimizes undesired outcomes—for your customers and yourself. When you accomplish this, you position yourself to create high-value (innovative) solutions that address your customers' JTBDs better than competitors.

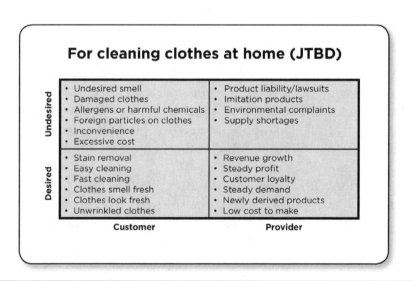

EXHIBIT 3.1 Outcome Expectations.

People don't buy quarter-inch drills; they buy quarter-inch holes. The drill just happens to be the best means available to get that job done.

—Ted Leavitt of Harvard Business School

We know of at least one company that was working on innovating a better detergent while another innovated a washing machine that doesn't need detergent. Whose solution will capture more market share or be more profitable? It depends on which company can better fulfill the outcome expectations for itself and its customers.

Steps

1. Identify the Job to be Done

In Jobs to be Done (Technique 1), we provide instructions for how to develop job statements and how to determine which JTBDs are priorities for innovation. Follow these steps to select the JTBD for which you'll develop related outcome expectations.

2. List the JTBD's Related Outcome Expectations

You can use a simple table like Exhibit 3.1 to brainstorm the four types of outcome expectations that relate to your selected JTBD. Keep asking, "What criteria would the customer use to decide which solution to hire or use?" Think in terms of time, cost, potential errors, quality, dependability, availability, ease of use, maintainability, and any number of other satisfaction and dissatisfaction dimensions.

Do not confuse this exercise with Functional Requirements (see Technique 33), which are solution-specific performance characteristics, such as *candle burn time* (target = 32 hours), or *PC battery life* (target = 6 hours). Outcome expectations are solution-neutral and reside at a higher level; they are JTBD-specific desires, such as *increase the duration of illumination* (using any solution), or *increase operating time* (in whatever way possible).

See the discussion on Job Mapping (Technique 2) for more help in creating your list of outcome expectations. Create a list of outcome expectations for each step in your job map.

3. Create Outcome Statements

Since the job of innovation is to meet expectations to a greater extent than they are met today, they should be stated in imperative terms, using a standard structure. That structure is:

- The direction of action (minimize, increase).
- The unit of measurement (time, cost, probability, defects, errors, etc.).
- The object of control (what it is you're influencing).
- The context (where or under what circumstances).

Consider this customer outcome statement: *Increase the likelihood that clothes appear fresh after home cleaning. Increase* denotes the direction, *likelihood* is the unit of measure, *clothes appear fresh* is the object of control, and *at home* is the context.

Other outcome statements related to the job of cleaning clothes at home might be:

- Minimize the time it takes to clean clothes.
- Minimize the cost of cleaning clothes.
- Increase the likelihood of stain removal.
- Minimize any damage to clothes.
- Minimize the effort needed to clean clothes.
- Increase the likelihood that clothes look fresh.
- Increase the likelihood of an appealing smell from clothes.
- Minimize the likelihood of any wrinkles in clothes.
- Increase the likelihood of removing all foreign particles, germs and bacteria from clothes.
- Increase the ease of cleaning clothes.
- Minimize the use of resources (water, energy, detergent) in cleaning clothes.

Some example outcome statements from the provider's perspective include:

- Increase the revenue growth from innovations.
- Increase the likelihood of maximum profit from innovations.

- Increase customer loyalty from using solutions.
- Increase the likelihood of deriving new products from current innovations.
- Minimize the cost of developing and providing solutions.
- Minimize the likelihood of product liability litigation.
- Minimize the likelihood of imitation products or services.
- Minimize damage to the environment.

Provider-related outcome statements tend to be similar with little variation due to the commonality of why companies exist. All corporations, public or private, exist to provide valuable products and services, to make a profit, and to do so safely and without harm.

The outcome statements improve the consistency and reliability of collecting useful information regarding the job to be done. It is very important to follow the outcome statement structure to enhance repeatability and avoid confusion.

---

4. Determine Priority Outcome Expectations

You can use different assessment and rating schemes to determine which specific outcome statements to pursue right away. One way to measure the importance of an outcome statement is to use a Likert Scale along with sound sampling techniques.

Examine the list of customer and provider outcome statements in light of how important they are and how satisfied each constituent (customer or provider) is with the extent to which current solutions fulfill these statements. Using a Likert approach, both the extent of *importance* and *satisfaction* are derived by averaging all responses (say, on a scale from 0 to 10) into a single score for each outcome expectation. As shown by Exhibit 3.2, these responses can then be plotted and categorized as *over-served*, *served right*, or *under-served*.

Your analysis should also include an examination of how likely it is that competitors will implement new solutions to fulfill priority outcome expectations better, and how likely it is that the provider (you) will fulfill them better with new solutions.

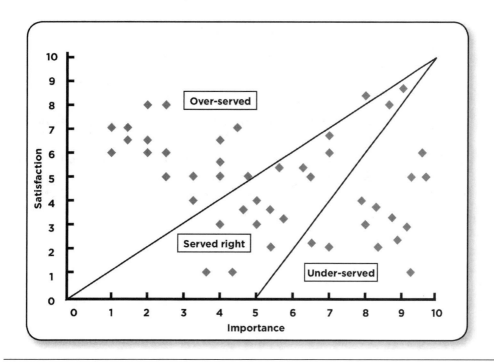

EXHIBIT 3.2 Opportunity Prioritization (Downloadable).

Copyright © 2012, BMGI. A blank version of this customized form is available for download at www
.innovatorstoolkit.com.

In general, under-served outcome expectations are high-priority and
are best addressed with a core-growth strategy of making the solution better
(see Technique 1, Jobs to be Done). Over-served outcome expectations lead
you to make existing solutions simpler, cheaper, and more available to
more people (or nonconsumers)—looking through the lens of a disruptive
growth strategy (again, see Technique 1). If the outcome expectations
are served right, don't do anything; focus instead on the other outcome
expectations.

> You can plot outcome expectations (or JTBDs) on an XY graph, with *importance*
> on the *y*-axis and *satisfaction* on the *x*-axis. Based on the location in the graph,
> you can then determine opportunities for the various categories of organic
> growth: disruption, core growth, new job growth, and related jobs growth.

Resources

Christensen, C. M., and M. E. Raynor. *The Innovator's Solution: Using Good Theory to Solve the Dilemmas of Growth*. Watertown, MA: Harvard Business School Press, 2003.

Ulwick, A. "Turn Customer Input into Innovation." *Harvard Business Review*, January 2002.

Ulwick, A. *What Customers Want: Using Outcome-Driven Innovation to Create Breakthrough Products and Services*. New York: McGraw-Hill, 2005.

Ulwick, A., and L. A. Bettencourt. "Giving Customers a Fair Hearing." *Sloan Management Review* 49, no. 3 (2008): 62–68.

Value Quotient

Identify opportunity gaps in the marketplace.

Value quotient is the ratio of a solution's desired outcomes to its undesired outcomes—relative to some job to be done (JTBD). For example, if one key desired outcome for a driver is to *increase visibility at all times,* then a car window that cleans itself has a higher value quotient than a window you have to clean—assuming the self-cleaning window can be purchased for about the same price with no additional drawbacks (undesired outcomes).

The purpose of this technique is to assess the value of your current solutions against those of your competitors—and relative to an ideal state in which a theoretical solution could fulfill all desired outcomes and avoid all undesired outcomes. Such an idealized solution (ideal innovation) would meet all expectations, cost nothing, and have zero chance of harming the user, anyone else, or the environment.

Understanding the Value Quotient technique enables the innovator to identify opportunities—or value dimensions—that are ripe for exploration and exploitation (Exhibit 4.1). The extent to which you can increase value along these dimensions determines the extent to which you will be successful with an innovation project.

Steps

Scenario: An appliance maker is looking to develop a better solution for the job of washing clothes in the home environment, but doesn't fully understand how to do this or where to begin—or if any real opportunities

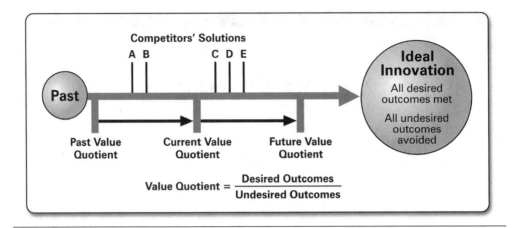

EXHIBIT 4.1 Value Continuum. Every product, service, or solution in the marketplace contains a certain degree of value relative to others. The goal is to fulfill desired outcomes to the greatest extent possible and avoid undesired outcomes to the greatest extent possible.

for innovation exist. Before delving too deeply into ideation, the innovation team wants to understand the opportunity space using the Value Quotient technique.

1. Agree on and Document the Job to be Done

The appliance company decides the JTBD is to *clean clothes at home.* See Jobs to be Done (Technique 1), Job Mapping (Technique 2), and Job Scoping (Technique 9) for more guidance on how to formulate and prioritize jobs for innovation.

2. Identify the Desired and Undesired Outcomes

For the job of cleaning clothes at home, Exhibit 4.2 lists a sampling of expected outcomes, desired and undesired, from both the provider's and customers' perspective. See Outcome Expectations (Technique 3) for more guidance on how to identify and document desired and undesired outcomes, as well as how to determine their relative importance.

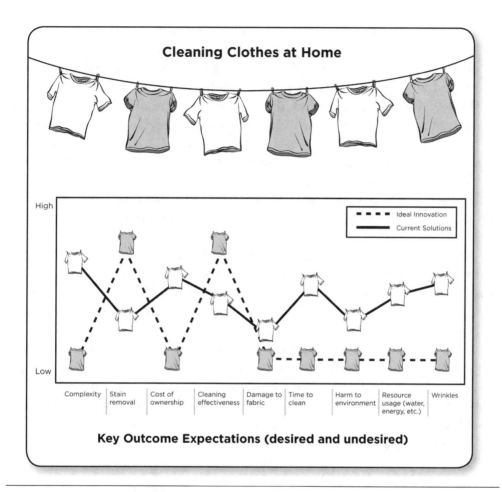

EXHIBIT 4.2   Value Analysis.

3. Plot the Ideal Innovation

For each important outcome expectation, plot the *ideal innovation* on a *value graph* using a scale from low to high as shown by the dotted line in Exhibit 4.2. This hypothetical exercise helps you imagine a state in which all desired outcomes are met and all undesired outcomes are avoided.

This state then becomes your innovation baseline; rather than starting from what you have (existing solution), you start with the perfect solution in mind and work backward. If you were to discover, develop, or otherwise hire a perfect solution for the JTBD, what would it be?

Coming back to our example, could a cleaning appliance wash all types of clothes in only one simple mode? Could all stains be removed from all clothes every time? Could clothes be cleaned without detergent? Could clothes not only be washed, but also come out of the system free of wrinkles?

Even beyond this, why wash clothes at all? Chinese engineers have already developed a process for making self-cleaning clothes using titanium dioxide—a very simple, nontoxic, and inexpensive chemical—along with such other chemicals as silver iodide. Clothes are dunked into a special concoction of nanoparticles, which become a self-cleaning mechanism when exposed to sunlight.

Other scientists have proposed infusing clothing fibers with bacteria that eat dirt, enabling the clothes to clean themselves in this manner. Self-cleaning clothes haven't yet been commercialized on a large scale, but it's interesting to consider how close we might be to ditching our laundry detergent.

There is a huge difference between starting an innovation discovery process with the ideal in mind, versus starting with whatever you do or offer customers today. The mind is like a rubber band, and the notion of the ideal innovation can only help stretch it. Therefore, whatever job to be done or outcome expectation you're trying to fulfill, start with the perfect solution in mind and work backward from there.

The ideal innovation concept is borrowed from the Theory of Inventive Problem Solving (TRIZ), which calls this perfect state the *ideal final result*. As a ratio, the value quotient approaches infinity, or a state where all benefits of a solution are achieved at zero cost and zero harm. In TRIZ terminology, this is called working *backward from perfect*, which forces the innovator to break through his or her psychological inertia into new, less limiting domains of thinking.

---

4. Plot Existing Solutions

After plotting the ideal innovation, the task is to plot existing solutions in the same manner according to the expected outcome dimensions. The key is to make plots in as many different ways as you want or need. You can plot your solutions against the ideal innovation or different competing solutions, or you can make your plots using different outcome expectations, or dimensions.

Play around with this tool (but seriously) to teach yourself with whom and what you are really competing, and to make yourself squarely confront how your current solution really stacks up.

Exhibit 4.2 illustrates the representative current state of all solutions based on using a machine and detergent to wash clothes at home—the existing standard. Our depiction of this state for each outcome dimension is based on back-of-the-napkin estimations for illustration purposes only. Note that current solutions usually fall short on outcome dimensions relative to the ideal.

5. Identify Opportunity Value Gaps

While every gap between what exists today and the ideal is an opportunity for innovation, it is most intelligent to determine which outcome dimensions are ripe for innovation. In doing this, look for any of the following three conditions based on an importance-satisfaction assessment; see Outcome Expectations (Technique 3) for details.

- *Condition 1:* Customers report the dimension is very important, but their satisfaction is low. This is an opportunity to raise the bar of desired benefits or outcomes offered.

- *Condition 2:* Customers report that the dimension is not very important, and they are satisfied. This is an opportunity to lower the bar of desired benefits or outcomes offered, and thereby, lower cost and increase accessibility to more customers (low-end disruption).

- *Condition 3:* There is no good solution so the customers cannot say whether they are satisfied. This is an opportunity to introduce a new solution that exceeds customer expectations and makes them say *wow*.

In our clothes-cleaning example, the outcome dimension of *time to clean* is a Condition 1 opportunity—customers find it very important but are largely dissatisfied. The dimension called *complexity* is a Condition 2 opportunity—customers are satisfied with current washing options and could even accept fewer choices or washing modes. Finally, the dimension of *wrinkles* is a Condition 3 example—customers don't expect that clothes could come out of their washing machines free of wrinkles, so if you can provide this, you will wow them.

6. Close the Value Gaps

Narrowing value gaps is a matter of ideating and developing superior solutions by moving through the innovation process and applying various techniques and tools. For example, Sanyo engineers received a patent (U.S. 7,296,444 B2) for an electric washing machine that generates water streams containing an electrolyzed liquid that cleans clothes without detergent. In doing so, this creates the potential to close several value gaps, including a reduction in the total cost of ownership, a reduction in harm to the environment, a reduction in resource usage, and a reduction in germs and bacteria left in clothes after washing.

Recognize that if you can move your solution closer to the ideal innovation and beyond any and all competitors, then you have successfully innovated. Much more importantly, recognize that if you cannot move your solution (or business model) materially closer to the ideal innovation, then you will fail at innovation.

Additional Example

We can get a glimpse of how innovation has played out along the value dimensions of choice, convenience, and cost by quickly examining the movie delivery industry. First, Blockbuster made it possible for people to simply travel to the local store and pick a movie from a very wide variety of selections. This was a far cry better (in terms of cost, convenience, and extent of selections) than relying only on what was playing at the theater or on TV.

Then, Netflix broke the mold with its mail-order business model. Customers didn't have to leave the comfort and convenience of their own homes; they could choose from thousands more titles than could fit in any brick-and-mortar store; and customers paid no late fees for holding a movie beyond any set period of time. Blockbuster was left for bankruptcy.

Even before Netflix became accustomed to its own success, it knew that streaming video would be the next innovation frontier—due in no small part to burgeoning Internet bandwidth. So, as of this writing in 2012, competition for streaming video and movies is rapidly coming to a boil.

Microsoft is involved with Netflix in delivering movies and video through such software as Silverlight and hardware as the Xbox. In September 2011, Dish bought Blockbuster for $320 million at a bankruptcy auction with plans to revitalize the dying brand as a provider of streamed movies. Amazon, Google, and Apple are all getting into the game as well—not to mention any number of large cable TV companies that are vying to acquire the rights for movie titles they can deliver to their massive customer bases.

Why the mad rush toward streaming movies and video content? Make a list of the outcome expectations from the customers' and providers' perspectives. Imagine a value analysis chart in your head. Customers gain even more convenience, more choices, and lower costs. On the other side, even though there is a cost associated with acquiring a new customer, providers can serve new customers at near zero incremental cost (due to the extremely low cost of pushing one more movie to one more customer through the network).

Ethnography

Observe your customers to uncover unarticulated needs.

Ethnography is a science that describes human social phenomena based on fieldwork and observation. Applied to the goal of innovation in business, ethnography is the practice of observing how customers try to get their *jobs done* by using your offerings, your competitors' offerings, or neither.

For example, before inventing Quicken software, Intuit observed people struggling to do the job of organizing and managing their personal finances. Even though professional-caliber accounting software was available at the time, many individuals were using computer spreadsheets or pencil and paper to accomplish this job. None of these approaches met the expectations of home users as well as Quicken does today.

By applying ethnography early in the innovation process, you may discover jobs and/or outcomes that customers have not articulated, especially in cases where existing solutions fail or fall short. For the best results, however, you will need to hire a trained ethnographer due to the discipline associated with collecting qualitative data in the field and accurately analyzing the findings.

Have you ever tried to complete a chore (like fixing a sink) that requires a flashlight? If you need both hands to complete the job, you end up holding the flashlight in your mouth or putting it down. Observing people in this predicament led Black & Decker to invent the snake light—a light that can hold itself.

Steps

1. Plan the Study

Planning your ethnographic study involves making a few important decisions, such as:

- *When will you observe people?* When they're purchasing your product or service, or when they're actually using it? If you're looking to uncover hidden jobs or customer expectations, then study people when they're using it. Observations at the time of purchase can be beneficial for discovering what appeals to people about the product/service price, reputation, packaging, and so on.

- *How will you observe people?* Observation can be covert—watching someone purchase a product or service without them knowing you are watching. Or it can be overt—standing in someone's kitchen watching them cook or going with them to buy a car.

- *Who will you observe?* If possible, observe both traditional and non-traditional consumers of the product or service. You can learn a lot by watching someone try to use something for the first time, or by interviewing someone who uses a different product to get the same job done.

- *Where will you observe people?* In their homes, places of business, or a public place? Remember, the point of ethnography is to observe people in their native environment, not in a lab or conference room as part of a focus group.

- *For how long will the ethnographic study take place, and how many people will you observe?* Will an ethnographic blitz, a one-week period of observation and interviews, suffice? Remember, you're trying to understand customer needs better, not gather statistical data, so the *quality* of participants, not the quantity is what matters most.

Ethnography uncovers not only conscious, but also subconscious emotional and biological needs. As such, it cannot be replaced by focus groups where participants provide primarily cognitive opinions.

---

2. Identify Participants

Identify specific participants and obtain their permission to be part of the study. Be sure to clearly convey to them the purpose of your study, what type of information you will be documenting, and how the results will be used. Even if you are observing people covertly in a store or restaurant, you'll still need to approach the owner for permission.

Ethnographers for Citigroup spent time watching how subway patrons paid for their rides. Based on the preferences they observed, Citigroup designed a key chain tag that could be easily swiped by riders as they pass through the turnstile, thus avoiding the need for passengers to fumble for tokens or take out their wallets in a crowded station.

---

3. Observe Participants

EXHIBIT 5.1 Collection of Information for an Ethnographic Study. This plethora of notes and images was gathered by Flow Interactive Ltd. for a client during an ethnographic study.

When you begin the ethnographic study, your primary task is to observe and take notes on how people interact with your product or service and what they think about it (Exhibit 5.1). As you do this, ask yourself these basic questions:

- Why is the person using this product/service? What's the job to be done? What are their expectations? When Kaiser Permanente set out to design a new hospital, an ethnographic study revealed that people who go to a hospital had many needs. In addition to the obvious—getting medical attention, visiting a patient—people sometimes required food, child care, or spiritual counseling.

- Are they using the product/service as designed, or in a way that is unexpected? For example, would companies that send unsolicited CDs through the mail be surprised to note how many people use them for drink coasters?

- How does the person appear to feel about the product/service? Are they pleased, surprised, frustrated, confused, or indifferent? What would they tell their friends and family?

- If you're observing a process or service, do people (both customers and employees) flow easily through the process? Are customers confused about where to go? Do they have to wait in long lines? Are employees tripping over each other trying to serve customers?

- Do cultural needs, barriers, or misunderstandings affect the use of the product/service? For example, Chinese appliance manufacturer Haier found through observation that some customers used its clothes washing machine to clean vegetables. This insight enabled them to create an appliance that excels at both jobs (cleaning clothes and washing vegetables).

During the study, it is imperative that you separate observation from interpretation. Like a courtroom juror, you should only be concerned with the facts while observing. There will be time later for analyzing the data you gathered and drawing conclusions.

Here's a list of recommended items to include in your field notes:

- Date, time, and place of observation.
- Specific facts, numbers, details of what happens at the site.
- Sensory impressions: sights, sounds, textures, smells, tastes.
- Personal responses to the fact of recording field notes.
- Specific words, phrases, summaries of conversations, and insider language.
- Questions about people or behaviors at the site for future investigation.
- Page numbers to help keep observations in order.

Source: Hammersly, "Ethnographic Research," Here We Are Blog, comment posted May 4, 2006, http://wearehere.wordpress.com/home/ethnographic-reasearch.

---

4. Interview Participants

Depending on your desired level of interaction with the participants, you may choose to interview them after observation. Although the key to ethnographic discovery is impartial observation, interviewing can provide additional insight if you keep these basics in mind:

- Ask open-ended questions that cannot easily be answered with *yes* or *no*. Also, don't try to limit participant responses to preordained categories by asking questions like, "How would you rate this product on a scale of 1 to 10?"
- Remain sensitive to the participant's beliefs, opinions, and concerns. If a question makes someone uncomfortable, don't force an answer.
- Ask permission to record or videotape the interview, which will allow you to review and categorize participant responses more easily.
- If you're not an experienced interviewer, practice on an associate, coworker, or friend—ideally, someone whom you don't know very well so you get a feel for what it's like to interview a stranger.

For more interview tips, see "A Synthesis of Ethnographic Research," by M. Genzuk, Ph.D., University of Southern California Center for Multilingual, Multicultural Research, www-bcf.usc.edu/~genzuk/Ethnographic_Research .html.

---

5. Collect Artifacts

Just as an anthropologist makes assumptions and draws conclusions about a culture via tangible artifacts, a company can draw conclusions about its products and services via the collection of behavioral artifacts. Obtain permission to take with you any items that coincide with your observations or provide additional information, including:

- Pictures or video of people using the product or service.
- Competitor or homemade items that accomplish the same job, or a tangential one, as your product or service.

- Participant-generated documentation such as homegrown manuals, cheat sheets, FAQs, and so on.
- Maps or diagrams of the process, along with notes about the flow of people or objects through the process.

Ethnographic observation often reveals ingenious solutions designed by customers in lieu of commercial solutions. In *Democratizing Innovation* (Cambridge, MA: MIT Press, 2006), MIT professor Eric Von Hippel encourages businesses to learn from user-centered innovations in their industry.

---

6. Analyze Data

Sort the data you gathered from the ethnographic study, including observations, interviews, and artifacts. Watch for patterns or trends that can be used to form one or more hypotheses. If you had a theory in mind before beginning the ethnographic study, review the data to see if it can be supported.

7. Verify Hypothesis

Once you have a hypothesis, follow up with the participants in a focus group or by survey to validate your theory. Alternatively, you could repeat the ethnographic study with a different group of people—just be sure to keep an open mind in case the new data doesn't support your theory.

8. Document Findings

Finally, it's helpful to prepare a written report that documents your conclusions and as much of the data as possible. This information may help others in the organization to better understand your customers, now or in the future.

Resources

If you want a primer for using ethnography to better understand customers, read:

Mariampolski, H. *Ethnography for Marketers: A Guide to Consumer Immersion.* New York: Sage Publications, 2006.

For an in-depth, but reader-friendly, approach to doing qualitative research, look to:

LeCompte, M. D., and J. J. Schensul. *Ethnographer's Toolkit* (7 Vols.). Walnut Creek, CA: AltaMira Press, 1999.

Scenario Planning

Paint visions of possible change.

Scenario planning (also known as scenario thinking) is a tool that helps you prepare for changes in such factors as demographics, politics, the economy, and industry environment. By identifying the status quo and how it will be affected by future events and uncertainty, scenario planning can better position an organization to transform and survive.

Scenarios are narratives that help us frame our thinking on how present circumstances will be affected by future change. Scenarios are not forecasts or extrapolations of current trends—they're simply interpretations of the impact of possible changes. Rather than trying to predict the future, scenarios help innovators understand the driving forces of change, how to prepare for it, and how to take advantage of it.

The output of scenario planning is not a company or personal to-do list, but rather, a general guide to contemplating change, cognizant of its associated risks. This technique is best performed in a team environment with the help of an expert scenario planning facilitator.

Scenario planning has been extensively used in such different industries as energy (Shell Corporation) and politics (evaluating the future of a post-apartheid South Africa).

Steps

Scenario: Healthy Bits is a small software company that develops patient-care software used by doctors and nurses on their handheld Windows CE PDAs (personal digital assistants). However, new devices and platforms are now leading the market, and Healthy Bits has fallen behind competing firms that do better at providing always-on, always-ready services working in concert with the latest technology.

1. Identify and Document a Scenario Project Proposal

The first step is to determine the focus and scope of the scenario planning exercise. The proposal should clarify the purpose of the project, its collaborators, and its expected time frame. Depending on the type of project under consideration, you might want to document specific expected outcomes and success measures. If your goal is to better understand and formulate a response to a specific change, it's best to be more precise. If you're investigating macroeconomic factors that may or may not impact your business, the specific outcomes can be less defined.

Healthy Bits provides software that runs on a niche, expensive platform (PDAs). Contemporary technology (such as iOS, Android, BlackBerry, and Windows Phone) is now leading the market and making Healthy Bits' hardware platform look dated. Customers now demand characteristics and functionality that Healthy Bits doesn't offer. As a niche provider, the company's territory is getting smaller as competing medical software firms sprout up.

Given this, Healthy Bits needs to investigate how it can leverage its core competencies—or develop new ones—to bring itself into a better competitive position.

Start earlier rather than later. Absorbing the reality shift that comes with unfamiliar business scenarios takes time. People need time to accept their changing world and prepare to adapt.

---

2. Identify Driving Forces Influencing Your Scenario Project

Make a list of the events, tendencies, sentiments, trends, and fads that will have an impact on your scenario project. These can be aspects that are internal to your business or industry, such as your competitors, suppliers, and trade partners. In turn, all of these are influenced by such macro factors as the economy, new social forces, politics, green environmental developments and regulations, and ever-changing technology trends.

Identifying these forces and factors encompasses a wide yet thorough analysis of your world that, in turn, helps you form a zeitgeist for your company—a feeling for what will characterize and constitute the era your company is in and is about to enter or, better yet, create.

You can use any number of Define techniques to help you make your list of future-shaping factors as relevant as possible to your current situation. See Jobs to be Done (Technique 1), Job Mapping (Technique 2), Outcome Expectations (Technique 3), and Value Quotient (Technique 4).

At the same time, you can use scenario planning to guide you in formulating your job to be done, or in scoping it to the right level—or in making yourself ready to innovate along the lines of certain outcome expectations that you think either are or will become more paramount than others to your customers.

You can also benefit from challenging prevailing beliefs using Discovery tools like Creative Challenge (Technique 17), SCAMPER (Technique 19), Provocation and Movement (Technique 24), and Six Thinking Modes (Technique 32). These may help you bring more creativity and diversity to your list of future-shaping forces and factors.

Scenario planning can be used as a preliminary strategic planning technique, to come up with much broader and further-reaching possible future states. For our purpose here in this book, our scope is more narrow and immediately focused on formulating a specific job to be done *during*, not before, the define stage of the D^4 innovation model.

---

3. Rank the Factors

Rank the factors identified in step 2 by their importance and level of uncertainty. The goal is to identify those factors considered to be most influential but also uncertain. To do this, simply take the forces, developments, and factors from step 2 and list them in two ranked groups, Certain Factors and Uncertain Factors. Exhibit 6.1 lists a number of factors identified by the Healthy Bits' innovation team and thought leaders.

Certain Factors

1. Adoption of mobile technology — smart phones, tablets.

2. Need to support "always available" data.

3. Consumer appetite for new technology.

4. ...

Uncertain Factors

1. Software competitors in the medical field.

2. New platforms and mobile devices.

3. Device capability unification.

4. Medical software regulation.

5. ...

EXHIBIT 6.1   Ranked Factors.

4. Develop a Framework to Discuss Possible Future Scenarios

The ranked factors in step 3 become a framework that serves as a contextual basis within which to discuss each possible future scenario. Note that the number of factors and the resulting individual scenarios will depend on your situation. For illustration purposes, Exhibit 6.2 involves taking only the top two factors from the list of uncertain factors in Exhibit 6.1. The certain factors in Exhibit 6.1 are so much immediate givens (not under debate) that they don't provide the best fodder for rendering scenario plans in this particular example.

You can see in Exhibit 6.2 that we combine these two factors in a quadrant fashion (representing a continuum in a more discrete fashion)—and then shortly characterize the combination at a very high level of detail.

Few Market Competitors	Few Market Competitors
Multiple new platforms and devices The niche nature of medical software and the burden of supporting a broad range of platforms prevents competitors from entering the market.	**Few new platforms and devices** Slow demand for new technology.
Many Market competitors	**Many Market Competitors**
Multiple new platforms and devices A thriving market attracts many new suppliers and vendors.	**Few new platforms and devices** Lucrative medical customers attract suppliers to over-service the market.

EXHIBIT 6.2   Conceptual Scenarios.

Instead of placing two factors from each category in a matrix, uncertain factors may be placed in a table for analysis. Rows and columns represent factors at opposite levels of influence (e.g., few versus many, high versus low). Cells in the table correspond to combinations of factors that may be ranked for a discussion of their relative impact and possible inclusion in scenario narratives.

5. Construct the Individual Scenarios

For each of the groups of factors identified (see Exhibit 6.2), write an unambiguous narrative that brings their collective influence together into a believable description of a potential future. Open-ended factors can be used to inspire narratives that highlight their result. For example, a scenario based on the expectation of a highly unregulated environment would yield a materially different narrative than one based on the opposite—a highly regulated environment. The certain factors in Exhibit 6.1 describe aspects of the future assumed to be common to all scenarios.

Exhibit 6.3 shows the Healthy Bits' scenario narratives, stated in somewhat of a cause-and-result format, where the cause is fleshed out in a more detailed narrative, and the summary result is captured in the headers. In turn, these headers and their associated narratives define the possible futures that need to be addressed (and barriers to surmount) with an action plan.

Providers Struggle to Keep up with Demand	Supplier Leads Market
• Few market competitors • Multiple new platforms and devices Open platforms and open source initiatives lead to a significant increase in the number of device types that need to be accommodated. Mobile software operating systems, such as Android and Windows Phone, are easily licensed and customized to serve a particular vendor's hardware. Consumers are spoiled for choice and expect software to be available on all platforms.	• Few new platforms and devices • Slow demand for new technology Medical service software is unattractive. Few players venture into the market. Stringent legislation and compliance requirements make it difficult and time-consuming to develop new solutions and bring them to market. Updates are few and far between due to slow approval processes. Demand is low, as hospitals make long-term buys and are unlikely to invest in newer technology.
Consumers Spoiled for Choice	**Niche Products Abound**
• Many market competitors • Multiple new platforms and devices It's a buyer's market: the client is always right and gets what it wants. Hardware and software platforms abound — each and every market segment is served and is quickly saturated. Service needs and preferences are subsumed into new developments and integration options.	• Many market competitors • Few new platforms and devices Many suppliers have the ability to deliver similar capability and results. To differentiate themselves, suppliers tend to deliver the same solutions with niche add-ons. Systems do not communicate and often include components that are unattractive to some clients.

EXHIBIT 6.3   Possible Futures.

6. Evaluate the Implications and Create an Action Plan

Using brainstorming, or any of the more advanced ideation techniques, evaluate the implications of each scenario and identify actions that would lead to success. Given the identified implications (or risk factors), what repercussions will they have given the scenario? For example, which resources would be plentiful, and which would be scarce? Based on the implications, which steps could be taken to ensure that your organization reacts appropriately and prevails?

Often, these actions will identify shortcomings in your current business and risk approach. Some action may also be common across multiple scenarios; this could either be a warning sign that your current business needs rethinking in order to maintain itself, or it may show that you are already exhibiting the necessary agility in the face of change.

Exhibit 6.4 shows the Healthy Bits' action plan.

Providers Struggle to Keep up with Demand	Supplier Leads Market
• Few market competitors • Multiple new platforms and devices **Implications** • Limited competition • Need to keep up with bleeding edge development • Constant platform-specific customization required **Actions** • Develop software with re-use in mind • Price delivery at premium rate to fund extensive development costs • Promote industry standards for software inter-operation	• Few new platforms and devices • Slow demand for new technology **Implications** • Developers with both technical and medical knowledge may be in short supply • Few employment opportunities • More expensive solutions • Heavy compliance and regulation **Actions** • Build strong relationships with existing clients • Aggressively seek low-end disruption opportunities, regardless of barriers
Consumers Spoiled for Choice	**Niche Products Abound**
• Many market competitors • Multiple new platforms and devices **Implications** • Significant competition • Bleeding edge development provides opportunity for differentiation to competitors **Actions** • Expand core offerings to discourage customer churn • Invest in systems development that differs significantly from rival offerings	• Many market competitors • Few new platforms and devices **Implications** • Aggressive competition • Specialized solutions common • Limited investment in new technology **Actions** • Diversify offerings by collaborating with other medical service providers • Lean out production and development to offer low-cost/open-source solutions

EXHIBIT 6.4 Implications and Actions.

7. Evaluate the Implications and Create an Action Plan

After completing the scenario planning steps, you'll be left with a stronger understanding of what the future may look like, as well as how you might equip yourself and your business to respond and survive. It's often useful to label each of your scenarios with a colloquial moniker, for quick identification and discussion. For example, referring to a "Goldilocks economy" immediately calls up a familiar environment where conditions are favorable (i.e., not too hot and not too cold).

The real world will not necessarily play out in the same way you envisioned it. Frequent evaluation and the identification of leading indicators will help you identify which of your scenarios are the most aligned with what is happening in the world. It may also be necessary to re-evaluate your scenarios if factors that had appeared quite relevant are no longer of concern (think of the effect the dotcom bust would have had on your economic forecasting expectations at the time!).

Resources

For more reading and knowledge, see:

Schwartz, P. *The Art of the Long View: Planning for the Future in an Uncertain World.* New York: Currency Doubleday, 1996.

Chermack, T. J. *Scenario Planning in Organizations: How to create, use and assess scenarios.* San Francisco, CA: Berrett-Koehler Publishers, Inc., 2011.

Lindgren, M., and Bandhold, H. *Scenario Planning: The link between future and strategy*, 2nd ed. New York: Palgrave Macmillan, 2009.

Heuristic Redefinition

Draw a picture of your system and its parts to focus ideation.

Heuristic redefinition is a visual approach for focusing and scoping an innovation project at the right level in a system. For example, if you're trying to make a more fuel-efficient vehicle, you would visually identify all the elements in the total vehicle system that affect fuel efficiency, not just the elements that impact a vehicle's engine.

Use heuristic redefinition when your innovation job to be done (JTBD) is not scoped well, or is broad rather than targeted in nature, and you need more specificity to take meaningful innovation action. This technique is very helpful to innovation leaders who are assembling their innovation project portfolios.

Steps

Scenario: Let's say a team called the Patient Crusaders is trying to make dental patients more at ease. The team's overall innovation job is to *reduce fear and increase comfort for our patients.*

1. Visualize the Overall System and Its Elements

The team should create an illustration of the system for meeting the JTBD, showing *all* of its major elements. Remember that any combination of functions can be considered a system or a subsystem, no matter how large or small. The waiting room at a dental office is a subsystem, and so is the dentist's tool tray.

Additional guidelines:

- Prepare your illustration in any medium, but try to keep it simple (nonelectronic) and openly visual to the team. Thus, a flipchart or dry erase board is probably most effective. Artist skills are not required!
- The more system elements you identify, the more likely you'll find a viable pathway to an innovation.
- To stimulate identification of system elements, the team should ask *what, when, where, who, why,* and *how* regarding the JTBD. Combine this technique with Functional Analysis (Technique 15) or Nine Windows (Technique 8) to bring as much system- and subsystem-defining horsepower as you can.

The Patient Crusaders ask the following questions to help define elements of the *reduce-fear-and-make-patients-feel-comfortable* system:

- *What is happening?* Patients are afraid of dental treatment, and find it stressful and uncomfortable, if not painful.
- *When does it happen?* Primarily during treatment, but the anxiety can begin before upcoming treatment.
- *Where does it happen?* Primarily at the dental office, secondarily in the patient's own mind before treatment.
- *To whom does it happen, or who causes it to happen?* Patients and the staff.
- *Why does it happen?* Either actual fear is manifested, or uncomfortable treatment methods are used, or both. Some of this is real, and some may be patient perception.
- *How does it happen?* Experiencing treatment, remembering past treatment, or hearing horror stories about others' experiences.

The Patient Crusaders drafted a picture that incorporated as many system elements as they could define. In the process, they made many drawings, had some debates, and finally aligned their thinking.

2. Label System Elements and How Each Relates to the JTBD

The task now is to label each system element in a way that characterizes its impact on the JTBD—whether positive or negative. Ask, "How does this element impact the JTBD or its associated outcome expectations?"

Consider relationships, connections, and influences between elements by asking:

- How are the elements related?
- What are the influences between elements?
- Do any natural or scientific laws apply?

The labeling process should be detailed and lively, with debate and discussion—and with a strong facilitator. The result is a revised illustration that labels all the system elements in terms of their relationships and influences on the JTBD.

The Patient Crusaders end up with a 10-element system for reducing fear and increasing patient comfort (Exhibit 7.1), including the following areas of focus:

1. The patient during treatment, who may be scared, anxious, or uncomfortable—or calm and feeling good about the visit.
2. A potential patient, anticipating an upcoming visit, may be looking forward to it, or dreading it.
3. The tangible results and benefits of a successful patient visit.
4. Dental staff and their skill level regarding pleasant, comfortable treatment.
5. Current process components (tools and techniques) that are perceived as *bad* by the average patient.
6. Current process components (tools and techniques) that are perceived as *good* by the average patient.
7. The interaction between staff and patient during treatment.
8. The waiting area at the dental office.
9. The clinical practice rooms.
10. Preventive techniques.

Often the big *aha* when applying heuristic redefinition is the many new problem statements, or lower-order JTBDs or job steps, that pop up as a result of dissecting the higher-order JTBD. Just when you thought you knew what you needed to do, heuristic redefinition can help you define this in a way that enables real innovation breakthrough at an actionable level.

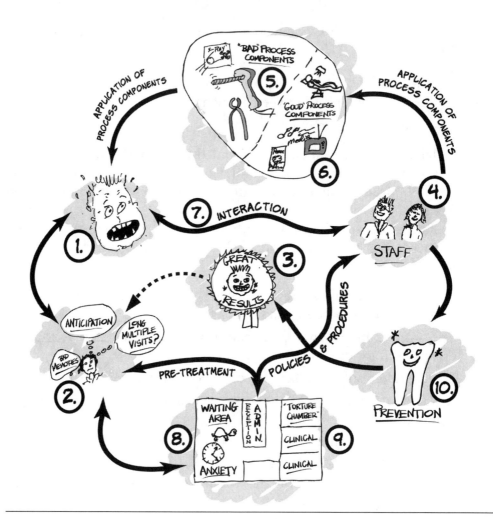

EXHIBIT 7.1   Reduce Fear and Increase Comfort at a Dental Office.

3. Create Problem Statements for Each Element

Now you are ready to translate each system element into its own job statement, or *scoped JTBD*. Starting with Element 1, ask how it can contribute to fulfilling the JTBD. For each element, ask, "How can we ensure that [Problem Statement] so that [JTBD] is accomplished according to customer hiring criteria?" (see Outcome Expectations, Technique 3).

Combine this technique with its counterparts, Job Mapping (Technique 2) and Job Scoping (Technique 9), if you need more help in crafting specific problem statements or job statements.

In essence, you are scoping in or scoping out for your innovation project. As you do this work, you'll be carefully investigating the relationship between each stated system element and its parent JTBD.

These problem statements (Exhibit 7.2) are now your guiding questions as you probe further into what parts of your system are ripest to yield innovation.

4. Pick the Best Elements for Innovation

This is essentially a prioritization activity using a devised rating scheme. First, enter your new problem statements into a matrix. Then rate each problem statement's impact on these three criteria:

1. Likelihood of solving the problem statement.
2. Ease of implementation.
3. Expected impact on the JTBD.

    The rating scheme is as follows:

    Good/High = 3
    Average/Medium = 2
    Poor/Low = 1

Totals are calculated by adding the numbers in all three criteria columns of the matrix, and the results are highly considered when looking for innovation focus areas. As long as there are no conflicts with company strategy or needs, these focus areas should be your best roads to innovation.

Some questions you can ask in this regard are:

- Does the problem statement support company strategy?
- Is the risk level too high or too low?
- Is it even worth pursuing?
- Is there the will and consensus to tackle the problem?

Good/High = 3 Average/Medium = 2 Poor/Low = 1 **Problem Statement:** **"How can we ensure that . . ."**	Likelihood of solving the problem statement	Ease of Implementation	Expected Impact on the JTBD	Total
1.	**The patient** experiences relief from anxiety, minimal discomfort, and shortest duration of treatment?	2	1	3	6
2.	A **patient anticipating upcoming treatment** is focused on the positive benefits of dental care and attains a positive outlook?	1	1	1	3
3.	The patient has confirmed awareness of the **positive outcomes** of their treatment, feels satisfied, and has no anxiety toward the next visit?	1	1	2	4
4.	The **dental staff** is skilled and competent in specific procedures and intent toward relieving patient fear and maximizing comfort?	3	2	3	8
5.	The standard practice treatment **tools, equipment, and materials** are selected and applied with patient anxiety and comfort in mind?	2	2	3	7
6.	**Additional "good" methods,** approaches, and equipment are utilized when applicable to reduce anxiety and enhance comfort?	2	2	3	7
7.	All **staff interaction with the patient** is conducive to elimination of anxiety, verifying comfort level, and ensuring understanding of the treatment benefits?	3	2	3	8
8.	The patient **waiting** time is minimal and the atmosphere is calming, encouraging, and positively instructional?	1	1	2	4
9.	**Treatment** time is minimal and the atmosphere is calming, comfortable, and encouraging?	3	2	2	7
10.	Post-treatment **preventative techniques** enhance treatment-benefits and build patient confidence?	2	1	1	4

EXHIBIT 7.2   Problem Statement Prioritization Matrix (Downloadable).

Copyright © 2012, BMGI. A blank version of this customized form is available for download at www .innovatorstoolkit.com.

Based on the prioritization matrix shown in Exhibit 7.2, the Patient Crusaders determined that the highest-scoring problem statements—4, 5, 6, and 7—were the best ones to pursue in coming up with an innovative solution for the JTBD. Some of the team's thinking was as follows:

- Statement 1 was really the focus of the entire effort and didn't really fit well as a problem statement. All other statements seemed to drive toward number 1.

- The team decided there was little it could do to influence statements 2 and 3 regarding the patient's anticipation of upcoming treatment and awareness of positive outcomes.

- Statements 8 and 10 seemed difficult to implement with minimal impact or likelihood of accomplishing the JTBD.

- The highest scoring statements were 4 and 7, and interestingly both involved staff. The team felt strongly that these should be pursued with rigor, and further discussion suggested that the two statements could be combined since they are closely related.

- Statements 5 and 6 were also closely related and scored similarly high. The team felt a problem statement (or scoped job statement) could be assimilated from these two that would involve improving the overall application of standard good-practice tools, equipment, and procedures.

- Statement 9 also scored high. However, the team felt that pursuing statements 4, 5, 6, and 7 would positively impact the issues of treatment time and atmosphere. Thus, they elected to forgo pursuing statement 9 in lieu of pursuing the others.

Before ideating further, the Patient Crusaders stopped to celebrate their success in framing their innovation challenge in a way that made it more actionable. But their work was far from over. By rolling this work forward into the next innovation phases, they ideated and refined their ideas for solving these problems until they converged on an innovative hospitality program, a set of new technologies, and a unique patient communication system. See KJ Method (Technique 30) for more details on how the Patient Crusaders prioritized their ideas for implementation.

The Heuristic Redefinition technique was developed by Dr. Helmut Schlick-supp, a German author and consultant who began researching and developing creativity methods several decades ago.

Additional Example

Say you want to make a house more energy efficient (a JTBD). But instead of tackling this problem as a whole, you could use heuristic redefinition to visually break the problem into smaller pieces. You could focus on any number of relevant system components: the house itself, its insulation, the sun outside, the surrounding trees, the windows, the shades or blinds, the awnings over the windows, major appliances, or the house's ventilation system. With this breakdown, you can see the whole system and begin to hone in on the part(s) that promise to yield the most innovation for the least amount of effort, time, and resources invested.

Resource

For more examples of heuristic redefinition see:

King, B., and H. Schlicksupp. *The Idea Edge: Transforming Creative Thought into Organizational Excellence*. Salem, NH: Goal/QPC, 1998.

Nine Windows

Looking at your opportunity through nine different lenses.

Nine windows is a technique that helps you examine the innovation opportunity across the dimensions of time (past, current, future) and scale (supersystem, system, subsystem). For example, suppose you're designing metal utensils that can be used on an airplane—but only for eating and not as a weapon. Instead of innovating the utensils themselves, you could focus your efforts on the raw materials that make up the utensils (subsystem), or even on the surrounding environment (supersystem).

The core of nine windows is a simple grid consisting of nine boxes, or windows. Filling in the boxes provides eight additional perspectives on the problem you've identified and helps you decide how and at what level to apply innovation. As such, you should leverage nine windows early in your project to better scope the innovation opportunity.

Steps

Scenario: To illustrate nine windows, let's say we run a construction and farm equipment rental store called "Git-er-dun." As a natural consequence of their work environments, our customers inevitably drag dirt, mud, and manure into the store. Therefore, our goal, or job to be done (JTBD), is to maintain clean floors inside the store, but why do this in some traditional way when we can innovate?

1. Prepare Nine Windows Grid

On a white board or flip chart, draw nine boxes arranged in a 3-by-3 matrix. Label the bottom row of boxes (from left to right): *Past, Present,* and *Future.* Label the far left boxes (from top to bottom): *Supersystem, System,* and *Subsystem* (Exhibit 8.1).

2. Fill in the Center Box

We call the center box *present system,* as this is our peg in the ground that serves as a reference point for constructing the remaining windows. To identify the present system, we must characterize the elements of our current solution for maintaining clean floors inside the store (the JTBD)—so we do this by populating the window with the words *floors, fan-dryers,* and *floor cleaning materials.*

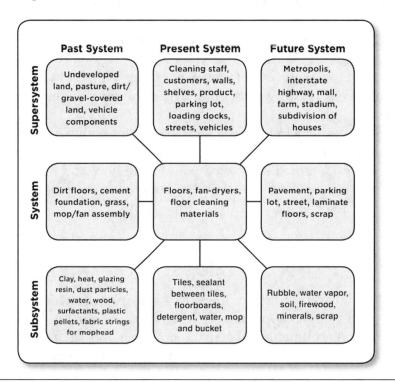

EXHIBIT 8.1   Nine Windows Architecture (Downloadable).

You can use words or images, or a combination of both, in the nine windows.

3. Identify Supersystem and Subsystem

In the present dimension (middle column), fill in the supersystem and subsystem boxes above and below the center box. You can write (or draw) more than one item in each box.

- The supersystem relates to how the system or object interacts with the surrounding environment. To complete this box, ask, "What larger system encompasses the system or object?" For the floors, the supersystem consists of the cleaning staff, customers, walls, shelves, product, parking lot, loading docks, streets, and vehicles.
- The subsystem breaks the present system or object down into the components and characteristics that constitute it. To complete this box ask, "What makes up the object in its present form?" For our Git-er-dun example, we have tiles, sealant between tiles, floorboards, detergent, water, mop, and bucket.

Nine windows is also known as *system operator* because it enables you to see how a system operates at both the macro (supersystem) and micro (subsystem) levels.

4. Determine Past and Future

Through brainstorming or observation, fill in the past and future boxes to the left and right of the center box. Don't limit yourself to just the immediate past or future. Instead, experiment with defining this temporal dimension in more than one way by asking:

- What did the system or object look like before its current incarnation, and what will it look like in the future?
- Where was the system or object before its present state, and where will it be in the future? The answer can range from a few seconds to years into the past or future.

- What happened to the system or object from its creation to its present form or function? What will happen after it ceases to function in the present?

- Before the present system or object existed, what was the previous solution for the JTBD? Also, focusing only on the components and characteristics of the present system, *regardless of the JTBD*, what could characterize or define a solution in the future?

In our teaching and consulting, we get a lot of questions about how far to go in scale. Should we stop short of the universe or atomic particles in our brainstorming? Generally, the answer is *yes*, and *yes*. Try to keep it realistic and pertinent to what you are trying to achieve. But, still, be arbitrary and nonjudgmental. Have fun with it and keep in mind that the nine windows only serve as triggers for idea generation, so you can't go wrong.

---

5. Complete the Grid

Fill in the four corners—the past and future states of the supersystem and the subsystem. You can complete these four boxes in any order. Although you don't have to fill in all the corners, it's worth spending a few minutes trying. If you get stuck, take a short break and return to the problem with a fresh mind.

6. Reassess Opportunity

After filling in the nine windows grid, reassess the innovation opportunity to determine if you should focus your efforts at the system, subsystem, or supersystem level, and in which temporal dimension. It might become obvious where to focus, or you might not have a clue. In either case, you'll want to take this final step of using the nine windows to generate real, specific solution ideas that you can implement immediately to create the future.

7. Generate Solution Ideas

Create a table with a row for each of the nine windows. List the window labels in column one and the words from the architecture in column two.

Use these words as triggers for generating solution ideas and list them in column three (Exhibit 8.2).

Generate solution ideas by asking:

- How can the system's inputs be modified to eliminate, reduce, or prevent a harmful function, event, or condition from impacting the output?
- How can the system's function be modified or completely changed to better achieve the JTBD or any of its associated outcome expectations?
- How can the system's output be modified in a corrective (after the problem has already occurred) or proactive (preventing the problem from occurring) way?

Additional Examples

Tesco, a British multinational grocery and merchandise company, is the third largest retailer in the world after Wal-Mart and Carrefour (a French company). But its size and maturity is no indication that the company does not or cannot innovate. With stores in 14 countries, Tesco is always looking to where it can next expand.

When it studied the South Korean market, Tesco asked itself an interesting question: Could we become the number one grocery retailer in this country *without increasing the number of stores*? Tesco's largest competitor in South Korea already had many more stores, and establishing new locations was riddled with all kinds of problems and constraints.

One huge factor that got Tesco thinking was the fact that Koreans are the second-most hardworking people in the world. They are tired after work and not in the mood to fight more traffic and store lines to acquire even the basic necessities, like food. So why not bring the store to the people? Why not look at the supersystem and ideate about how it could help the cause of innovating a new business model?

That's just what Tesco did. Under the brand name, Homeplus, it turned the boring walls of the train station into virtual grocery shelves. (See www.youtube.com/watch?v=nJVoYsBym88.) As this YouTube video shows, customers can stand in the train station while waiting for their ride and gaze at what is indistinguishable from real grocery shelves. They then use their

Window	Architecture (Trigger words)	Ideas Generated
Present System	Floors, fan-dryer, floor cleaning materials	(i) Robotic cleaner for floors. (ii) Customers wear slip-on booties before entering the store.
Present Subsystem	Tiles, sealant between tiles, floorboards, detergent, water, mop and bucket	(i) Grates instead of tiles to scrape off dirt and drop it onto dirt floors below the floorboards. (ii) Use electrostatic principles to remove dirt. Eliminating the need for water and detergent and hence the drying-fans.
Present Supersystem	Cleaning staff, customers, walls, shelves, product, parking lot, loading docks, streets, vehicles	(i) Drive-through product pick up. Customers stay in vehicle. (ii) Have the product displayed on the outside of the walls and transaction processing on the insides.
Past System	Dirt floors, cement foundation, grass, mop/fan assembly	(i) Leave dirt or grass floors even inside the store. (ii) Customers drive right through the store and collect product.
Future System	Pavement, parking lot, street, laminate floors, scrap	(i) Have the shelves placed outside, under tents. No need for flooring. (ii) Sticky coating on ground leading up to store entrance removes dirt from shoes before entering the store.
Past Subsystem	Clay, heat, glazing resin, dust particles, water, wood, surfactants, plastic pellets, fabric strings for mophead	(i) Coat the tiles with hydrophobic (water/dirt repulsion) material. Forces the dirt to stay on shoes. Customers take the dirt back with them.
Past Supersystem	Undeveloped land, pasture, dirt/gravel-covered land, vehicle components	(i) Abrasive grating all the way from the parking lot to the store entrance. Force a lot of the dirt off customers' shoes before entering the store.
Future Subsystem	Rubble, water vapor, soil, firewood, minerals, scrap	(i) Disposable tiles. Routinely "peel-off" and discard the floor. (ii) Routinely jets of air are streamed/puffed across the floor to clear the dirt automatically when there is a break in traffic.
Future Supersystem	Metropolis, water vapor, soil, firewood, minerals, scrap	(i) Delivery service. Take products to the customers with online order-taking.

EXHIBIT 8.2   Nine Windows Solution Ideas (Downloadable).

smart phones to scan wanted items, which are delivered to their homes as soon as or shortly after they arrive.

By innovating outward to the supersystem in a densely populated area (making the delivery function economically feasible), Tesco became number one in the online market and a very close number two in the offline market, at least in part due to the increased brand recognition from the virtual stores.

Another example of supersystem innovation is the increasing trend for growing food on rooftops, in parking lots, and inside people's homes. New Yorkers are growing food on their roofs, using either traditional soil methods or hydroponics that enable vegetables to be vertically stacked and grown with just water (no soil). Some restaurants are exploiting this technology and using the land around their buildings to grow their own fruit and vegetables.

A new company in San Diego, Home Town Farms, is planning to open its first growing and retail location—on an unused school property lot in an urban area. The company's CEO, Dan Gibbs, says: "We looked outside the traditional farming model, and the farm, to ask how we could innovate. We used hydro-organics as our base of growing technologies, and we just had to put two and two together and bring the high-efficient farm, and the food, to where people live."

Home Town Farms calls its model *Demand Farming: the ability to grow what people want where they consume it*. By using highly efficient growing systems where people live, the food requires 90 percent less fuel consumption, 85 percent less water to grow, 80 percent less fertilizer, and 70 percent less land. The result is higher quality and lower priced, locally grown, vine ripened, organic produce with no chemicals. Consumers will have the opportunity to eat the fresh produce within hours of when it's picked, giving them the highest nutritional value it can offer.

Job Scoping

Broaden or narrow your innovation focus.

Job scoping ensures that the innovation opportunity is effectively targeted at an actionable level. If the project scope seems too broad, job scoping helps you drill down a level by identifying obstacles that could keep you from achieving your goal. If the scope is too narrow, job scoping moves the focus up a level to explore the reason why (what for) you're working on the innovation problem in the first place. Whichever road you later follow, job scoping will help you see the innovation opportunity from a different point of view.

Scoping an innovation project is important because the way you define the opportunity, or the job to be done (JTBD), can make the difference between a run-of-the-mill solution and a truly innovative approach. A careful innovation practitioner will note some similarity between job scoping and the systems and spatial aspects of Nine Windows (Technique 8), and Heuristic Redefinition (Technique 7), in the analysis of broader and narrower issues. But the techniques differ mainly in job scoping's and heuristic redefinition's focus on problems versus nine window's focus on solutions.

Steps

Scenario: Interviews and preliminary Ethnographic studies (Technique 5) have shown that many business travelers struggle with the timeliness and ease of submitting expense reports (the JTBD) after completing a business trip. Many misplace their receipts, carry inconvenient adhesives for sticking receipts on blank sheets of paper, and struggle to organize receipts from multiple trips. How can we come up with an innovative solution that addresses the traveler's problem at the right level?

1. Frame the Current Focus

Using the job scoping format (Exhibit 9.1), write the innovation opportunity or JTBD in the center box. Use the preferred job statement format—an

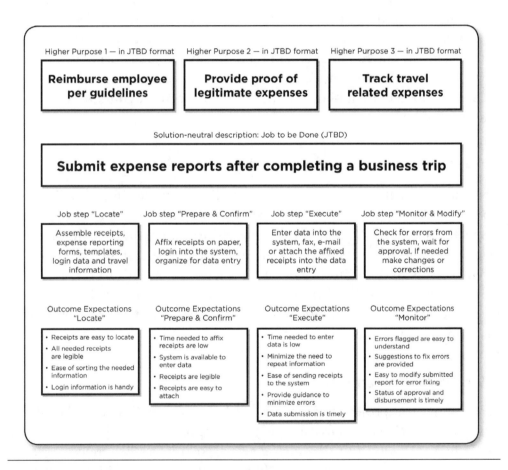

EXHIBIT 9.1 Job Scoping (Expense Submittal) (Downloadable).

action verb, followed by the object of the action and a contextual clarifier. See Jobs to be Done (Technique 1) for more information. In the case of your project, this job statement might read: "Submit expense reports after completing a business trip."

2. Identify the Job Steps

You can scope the opportunity down in two steps. First, develop the solution-independent job steps by applying Job Mapping (Technique 2). Write the steps of the job into the appropriate boxes. Our template shows several steps. For example, we need to locate and prepare receipts, we need accessories to organize receipts, and we need expense reimbursement system login details—before the reimbursement request can be made during the execute step. Through the job mapping activity, you may find that locating all receipts is done in an ad-hoc manner—so your project could be scoped on that need only.

3. Identify the Underlying Outcome Expectations

You can also drill down one more level by listing unmet Outcome Expecta-tions (see Technique 3) for any job steps. You would list these, too, in the respective boxes of the template. Using our example, maybe ethnographic evidence shows business travelers in airport lounges carrying boxes of clut-tered receipts and cutting adhesive tape with their teeth to organize and adhere them to a piece of paper. Such needs along the continuum of job steps and their associated outcome expectations present many possibilities for scoping your project.

4. Identify Higher Purposes

Next, scope the project focus up a level by asking, "What is the higher purpose?" or "Why (what for) are people trying to get this job done?" Instead of working on *submitting the expense report*, you may rather choose to scope your project on a higher purpose, like *provide proof of legitimate expenses* or *track travel related expenses*. There may be just one or multiple higher purposes (our template allows for up to three).

A project scoped on a higher purpose can end up yielding disruptive innovation (see growth strategies in Jobs to be Done, Technique 1)—especially when successfully commercializing solutions that do a job by themselves (like self-cleaning clothes as mentioned in Value Quotient, Technique 4) and/or solutions that use readily available resources (see Resource Optimization, Technique 14).

Should you choose not to scope your innovation project at that level, at least job scoping makes you aware that someone else might do it, thereby removing the need for travelers to hire such solutions as adhesive tape and compartments to house paper receipts.

5. Determine Project Focus

After applying job scoping, you may decide to change the focus of your innovation project to make it more actionable and impactful. Whatever scope you give the project, job scoping helps you clarify your alternatives and the choices you need to make.

Stakeholder Management

Get key influencers involved and on your side.

Stakeholder management helps you identify key stakeholders—people who have a vested interest in your innovation project—along with each person's level of support or resistance. Whether you're enhancing your existing products or services, adding something new to your offerings, or pioneering a breakthrough business model, you are in essence changing the status quo. Where there is change, there is pain, and where there is pain, there is resistance.

Resistance comes in all forms, from outright disagreement to subtle opposition, even subconscious sabotage. Stakeholder management helps you identify and understand the opposition your project may face so you can convert disbelievers into disciples—or at least minimize the damage they may cause. The Stakeholder Management technique includes three tools that will get you started, although formal change leadership training can take your skills in this area to a more effective level.

Steps

Scenario: In addition to using stakeholder management to gain support for an innovation project, you most certainly should leverage it when undertaking any large organizational initiative. For instance, imagine that your CEO feels strongly that innovation is the key to your company's growth, and charges you with leading an innovation deployment. Stakeholder management can help you identify who besides the CEO is in favor of the initiative so you can leverage supporters and move detractors in the right direction.

1. Identify Key Stakeholders

A *stakeholder diagnostic* identifies key stakeholders, along with their current level of support for the project (Exhibit 10.1). Most importantly, it documents how supportive you need each stakeholder to be to help make the project a success. As you complete the stakeholder diagnostic, keep the following in mind:

- *Key stakeholders:* These are individuals who have direct influence over the project, or who will be directly affected by it, and who can influence other stakeholders, employees, vendors, and even customers.
- *Role in organization:* List the stakeholder's title. Make sure that every affected organizational area is covered (including often neglected areas such as marketing or information technology).
- *Impact of project on stakeholder:* Estimate the impact of the project on each stakeholder. How much will the project change the way they work?
- *Power/Influence category:* This column tracks how much power the stakeholder has in the organization, relative to the influence they hold over the project. Skip it until step 3.
- *Current/Desired level of support:* Indicate what you perceive to be the stakeholder's *current* level of support for the project. Note: You'll determine the stakeholder's *desired* level of support in step 3.
- *Reasons for resistance or support:* Document why you believe the stakeholder is opposed to or in support of the project. If you're not sure why the person leans one way or the other, ask them.

Remember, the information uncovered in the stakeholder management process is confidential. It is only for use by the project leader and team.

---

2. Determine Stakeholder Power and Influence

Now that you know who your stakeholders are, and to what degree they support the project, you need to decide where to focus the majority of your stakeholder management efforts. Using a *power and influence map,* indicate where each stakeholder lies relative to their power in the organization and

Stakeholder Diagnostic

#	Key Stakeholder	Role in Organization	Impact of Project on Stakeholder (H, M, L)	Power/ Influence Category	Strongly Opposed	Opposed	Neutral	Supportive	Strongly Supportive	Reasons for Resistance or Support
1	W. Sateg	CEO	M	A					●	As CEO, believes that innovation is a key to the company's future growth.
2	K. Judge	CFO	L	A		● →		○		Satisfied with current product development process, believes major shift would affect profitability in short-term and alarm shareholders.
3	M. Rieger	VP Business Development	H	C		● →		○		Believes organization is suffering from initiative fatigue, management overwhelmed with day to day, sees significant resource limitations.
4	M. Owen	CIO	L	C			○			No obvious resistance, current IT systems are solid and can support the innovation deployment with few changes.
5	J. Stapleton	VP Research and Development	H	A		● →			○	Resistant because he sees innovation deployment as criticism of many years of R&D effort, fears loss of power and respect in organization.
6	K. Berger	VP Customer Relations	L	D				● →	○	As customer advocate, believes that any organization can always do more for the customer and innovation is one way to demonstrate it.
7	P. Smith	VP Marketing	M	B			● →	○		Limited awareness of innovation deployment vision, has solid network of grassroots team members.

(Callout: **Step 3** — with arrow pointing to the Strongly Opposed column.)

EXHIBIT 10.1 Stakeholder Diagnostic (Downloadable). This is a partial list of stakeholders for the innovation deployment example. An initiative of this type would likely have more stakeholders, depending on the size and structure of the organization.

their influence over the innovation project. On the map, each quadrant represents a specific power and influence ratio, as follows:

Quadrant A = *high* power and *high* influence

Quadrant B = *low* power and *high* influence

Quadrant C = *high* power and *low* influence

Quadrant D = *low* power and *low* influence

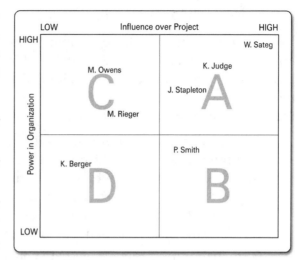

EXHIBIT 10.2 Power and Influence Map (Downloadable). Stakeholders in quadrant A have high power in the organization and a lot of influence over the project, making them the most important to manage.

In our example, M. Rieger has high power in the organization but less influence over the innovation deployment than most other stakeholders (Exhibit 10.2). Thus, any resistance on her part will be less consequential than those who have more control over the deployment.

3. Revisit Stakeholder Diagnostic

After filling out the power and influence matrix, return to the stakeholder diagnostic and fill in the remaining items:

- *Power/Influence category:* Enter the corresponding quadrant letter for each stakeholder (from step 2).
- *Desired level of support:* In the same area where you documented the stakeholders' current level of support, indicate the desired level of support (how supportive you need each stakeholder to be). This will depend on both the impact of the project on the stakeholder, as well as the stakeholder's level of power and influence (you'll want all the As to be *supportive* or *strongly supportive*).

4. Develop Plan to Reduce Resistance

Now that you know whose support you must gain, there are several approaches you can use (see the list that follows) to convert the most powerful and influential naysayers into advocates. The approach you take to move each stakeholder in the right direction will be based on many factors, including the reasons that spawned the resistance in the first place.

- *Education and communication:* If there is a lack of understanding about the project or its objectives, focus on upfront communication and education. In our example, the vice president of marketing could attend an innovation class or read more about the benefits of an innovation deployment. This would improve her support and she would also be able to help convey the benefits to others.

- *Participation and involvement:* If you have stakeholders with considerable power to resist, find ways for them to participate early and throughout the project. This gives them the opportunity to influence the project proactively instead of reactively. In our example, the very resistant vice president of research and development should definitely be involved early and remain a key player in the innovation deployment.

- *Facilitation and support:* If stakeholders are resisting the project due to fear and anxiety, provide extra facilitation and support. This could mean putting anxious stakeholders in touch with others who have gone through similar efforts—an approach that might convince our fictional CFO that an innovation program, if deployed properly, will raise profitability instead of threatening it.

- *Negotiation and agreement:* If a stakeholder or group will be negatively affected by the project, try to negotiate a compromise that will please both sides. For instance, you could work with the vice president of business development to prioritize and possibly reduce some of the daily workload so the innovation deployment resource needs can be met.

Common Reasons for Resistance

- *Misunderstanding:* Based on communication failures and inadequate information.

- *Low tolerance to change:* Based on job insecurity or lack of organizational stability.

- *Different assessments of the situation:* Based on disagreement over the advantages and disadvantages of the project or resulting change.

- *Parochial self-interest:* Based on concern over how the project or change will impact an individual's own interests.

		Who They Influence						
#	Key Stakeholder	1	2	3	4	5	6	7
1	W. Sateg, CEO	X	M	H	M	H	H	H
2	K. Judge, CFO	M	X	H	M	H	L	L
3	M. Rieger, VP Business Development	M	M	X	L	M	L	L
4	M. Owens, CIO	M	H	L	X	M	L	L
5	J. Stapleton, VP Reasarch and Development	L	L	M	L	X	L	M
6	K. Berger, VP Customer Relations	L	L	M	L	L	X	M
7	P. Smith, VP Marketing	L	L	L	L	L	M	X

EXHIBIT 10.3   Leverage Matrix (Downloadable).

Copyright © 2012, BMGI. A blank version of this customized form is available for download at www .innovatorstoolkit.com.

5. Complete a Leverage Matrix

A *leverage matrix* is used to rank the level of influence stakeholders have on each other. This comes in handy when, for instance, you need to move a stakeholder's support level from *opposed* to *supportive,* and you realize that another stakeholder can help move this person in the right direction.

Next to each name on the matrix, there is a number to the left. Corresponding numbers appear across the top of the matrix. For each stakeholder, move from left to right across the matrix and indicate how much influence the stakeholder in that row has on the other stakeholders (H = high; M = medium; L = low). For example, our fictional CEO (W. Sateg) has medium influence over stakeholders #2 (CFO) and #4 (CIO), but high influence over everyone else (Exhibit 10.3).

6. Update Documents as Needed

Stakeholder management is not a one-time check in the box. As you move through your project, it is important to update your approach based on new stakeholders and shifts in stakeholder support.

Resource

To learn more about stakeholder management and change leadership, read:

Kotter, J. *Leading Change*. Watertown, MA: Harvard Business School Press, 1996.

Cognitive Style

Leverage the diversity of your exploiters and explorers.

Cognitive style is an individual's preferred approach for solving problems and can be measured along a continuum from *adaptive* to *innovative*. While adaptors are more prone to improve the current system, innovators are critical of the current system, choosing to create entirely new products, processes, models, and solutions.

To run an innovation project from end to end, you always need the right mix of both adaptors and innovators—not just one type of person or the other, and not some set ratio of adaptors to innovators for all projects.

When all team members understand their own cognitive style, as well as the styles of other team members, the process of working together becomes much smoother and more productive—and you avoid unnecessary conflicts and delays. For example, a more adaptive team member who would ordinarily be frustrated with a more innovative team leader can, instead, understand the differences and use them to the team's advantage.

Background

Several factors affect a team's chemistry and success with innovation. *Motivation* is one factor, and there are known approaches for managing this. *Level* is another success factor, and it refers to (a) a person's current knowledge and/or skill and (b) a person's potential capacity for problem solving. We also have sound and established instruments (tests and IQ measurements, for example) for assessing these dimensions. Then there are *resources*—such as materials, money, machines, and tools—and these are typically well-known.

What's not typically known or understood is the critical aspect of team members' respective *cognitive styles*. Cognitive style researchers have proven that people who are more adaptive prefer to accept and work within the given paradigm; those who are more innovative prefer to solve problems by looking at them from new angles and perspectives (Exhibits 11.3 and 11.4).

It's also important to realize the relationship between preferred style and behavior. Actual behavior is a combination of preferred style and learned *coping behavior.* If you have a more adaptive style and you have to perform tasks that have few guidelines or established structures, you will need to resort to coping behavior, and this will create stress in the long-term. The converse is also true.

All innovation projects have steps that are adaptive and others that are innovative in nature. Therefore, you need a collaborative team with the appropriate motive, resources, cognitive level, and diversity of cognitive style. But research shows that people with differing cognitive styles struggle

EXHIBIT 11.1 Adaptors and Innovators Have Different Approaches to Solving Problems.

to get along—creating communication, trust and productivity issues. Therefore, make sure team members know and understand each other's cognitive styles so they can leverage each other's advantages and supplement each other's disadvantages at all stages of the innovation project.

Steps

Scenario: Let's assume you're assigned to a new cross-functional team tasked with developing a car that consumes carbon monoxide instead of producing it. Given the magnitude of the radical innovation required, it's advisable to select team members with diverse backgrounds, a variety of different skills, and a range of different cognitive styles.

1. Identify Potential Team Members

Choose team members with a variety of technical and nontechnical skills, experience, and motivation related to the specific job statement or JTBD (see Jobs to be Done, Technique 1).

2. Examine the Cognitive Style of Each Team Member

To determine the best fit for the task at hand, given the pool of potential candidates, be aware of the cognitive style that each team member brings to the task. You can do this in one of two ways:

1. Ask the following questions about the team members (in comparison to a reference person):

   - Does this person tend to question established rules, assumptions, and structures?
   - Does this person become frustrated or annoyed with details?
   - Does this person tend to have a steady stream of ideas without too much concern about how they're implemented?

   If the answers to the above questions are *yes*, then this person is more innovative than adaptive. If the answers are *no*, then the person is more adaptive.

2. If you want a more sophisticated way to determine cognitive style, use the *Kirton Adaption-Innovation (KAI) Inventory*, a highly validated and reliable psychometric instrument developed by psychologist Dr. Michael Kirton. Available at www.kaicentre.com, the KAI inventory works like this:

- An individual responds to a series of 33 statements by marking responses on a range from very easy to very hard.

- The KAI instrument is then scored by a certified facilitator to determine a primary KAI score and three KAI subscores. Primary KAI scores range on a normally distributed numerical scale from 32 (most adaptive) to 160 (most innovative), with a mean of 96. However, the observed range from worldwide data is 45 to 145 with a mean of 95. All scores are relative; there are no pure adaptors or pure innovators, so we often use the terms *more adaptive* and *more innovative* to describe the relationship between two people (Exhibit 11.2).

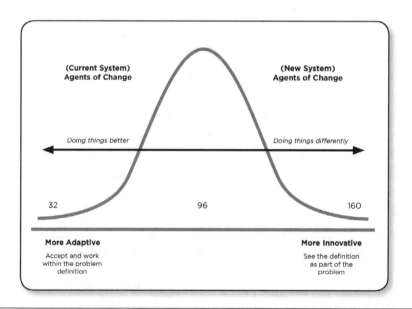

EXHIBIT 11.2 Cognitive Style Distribution Curve.

- A KAI facilitator then provides feedback to the individuals about the KAI instrument and highlights key insights about the scoring.
- The group is divided into smaller teams of participants with similar KAI scores; each team spends 15 minutes developing solutions to a specific problem that will be reported back to the group.
- Each team delivers a brief report summarizing their approach and the solutions generated.
- The facilitator highlights the differences between the different teams' styles, showing how the more adaptive team's approach differs from the more innovative team's approach.

Cognitive Style Insights

1. General

- All people are creative and solve problems.
- Cognitive *style* (adaptive or innovative) is different and unrelated to cognitive *level* (knowledge and capacity).
- There is no one best cognitive style.
- One's preferred cognitive style is genetically determined and stable over a lifetime.
- A group needs both adaptors and innovators to be effective over time.
- Forcing someone to work outside their preferred style (comfort zone) will cause stress; in the short-term this might be okay, but in the long-term it will lead to a breakdown in communication and reduction in productivity.

Don't mistake poor performance to always be a symptom of low problem-solving *level* or *motivation*. Instead of jumping to replace these team members, examine how you might reassign tasks to achieve better alignment with their preferred cognitive styles.

---

2. Adaptors

- The more adaptive tend to focus on improving the current system, even by leaps and bounds, *within the problem definition or paradigm.*

- Adaptors seek solutions in tried and understood ways. Adaptors are seen as precise, reliable, and methodical. They look at the problem and want to solve it efficiently.

- High adaptors tend to rarely challenge the rules and usually only do so when assured of support.

- Adaptors produce fewer ideas, but those ideas are more manageable, relevant, sound, and safe for immediate use. Expect a high success rate from these ideas.

EXHIBIT 11.3 Thomas Edison. Thomas Edison borrowed new paradigms discovered by others and preferred to perfect them methodically, systematically, and in a precise manner. Edison was more of an adaptor.

EXHIBIT 11.4 Albert Einstein. Albert Einstein questioned the existing Newtonian paradigm, which enabled him to discover the Theory of Relativity. Einstein was more of an innovator than an adaptor.

3. Innovators

- The more innovative tend to focus on doing things differently, often operating outside the parameters of the problem definition or current paradigm.
- Innovators are expected to question the assumptions behind the problem at hand, and will often manipulate and redefine it. They are seen by adaptors as undisciplined and prone to tangential thinking.
- Innovators tend to view rules and structures as limiting or hindering progress, and they want to solve problems in novel ways.
- High innovators produce many blue-sky ideas that they consider exciting, and they tolerate high idea failure rates.

4. Teamwork and Collaboration

- Adaptors execute details very well, according to plans; innovators often move forward with execution despite the details and in the absence of any substantive plans.

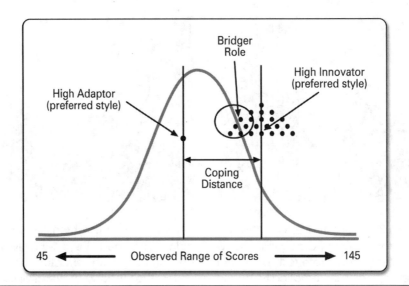

EXHIBIT 11.5   Role of the Bridger. A bridger is someone whose preferred cognitive style lies in between adaptors and innovators, and who plays the role of helping overcome communication and other barriers to progress.

- The larger the gap between people's cognitive styles, the harder it will be to collaborate, communicate, and solve problems.
- A *bridger* is a person who helps facilitate communication and teamwork between high adaptors and high innovators (Exhibit 11.5).
- Staffing innovation teams is a fluid activity that depends on the extent and nature of change required for any given project. It's also fluid in the sense that different stages of the innovation project require different people with different positions, skills, knowledge, and cognitive styles.

Resource

Kirton, M. J. *Adaption-Innovation: In the Context of Diversity and Change.* New York: Routledge, 2003.

Project Charter

Keep your innovation team focused and on track.

The Project charter keeps your innovation team focused and on track, and it ensures that you manage the risks associated with innovation closely, carefully, and effectively. You wouldn't start a business without a well-thought-out and carefully designed plan. And you shouldn't take on something as risky as innovation without clearly documenting your objectives, your key assumptions, the projected return on investment, and many other data points that ensure your team and other stakeholders remain on the same page.

Regardless of the degree of innovation you're hoping to accomplish, you should always make time for a project charter. It's important to note that the project charter is not a static document you finalize early on, but rather a dynamic technique that should be revisited, refined, and updated throughout the life of the project.

Project Charter and Innovation Financial Management (Technique 13) are two of the most important techniques in this book. After all, you can generate thousands of clever ideas, but if no one needs or wants what you have to offer then your time and money is wasted. Therefore, don't overlook the value of spending time up front, and throughout the project, continually verifying that your innovation is marketable, feasible, and able to bring your organization a profit.

Steps

Scenario: Pikes Peak Coffee owns 32 coffee shops in three Western states. For the past three quarters, the company has failed to deliver the type of growth that stockholders are accustomed to seeing. One idea to spur growth is to add a healthy, fresh breakfast item to the menu. Thus, the innovation project Operation Feeding Frenzy was begun to determine what type of breakfast offering would outperform the competition. We'll use the company's project charter to demonstrate this key technique (Exhibit 12.1).

1. Administrative Information

Document summary information that categorizes the innovation project including:

- *Project name:* Create a name for the project that allows people to clearly reference the effort. Instead of taking a purely literal approach, try coming up with a creative and inspiring name.
- *Type of innovation:* Categorize the focus of your innovation project as a product, process, or business model innovation.
- *Project leader:* The project leader should have experience in applying innovation techniques and facilitating change teams.
- *Innovation champion:* The champion (executive sponsor) removes organizational roadblocks and provides feedback during project tollgate reviews.
- *Methodology:* The D^4 methodology or other approach of your choosing.
- *Degree of innovation:* Categorize the degree of innovation associated with the project (incremental, substantial, or radical) based on the magnitude of the outcome or resulting change.
- *Date of completion:* Start with your best estimate based on phase and deliverable planning.

Innovation Project Charter

Project Name: Operation Feeding Frenzy
Type of Innovation: Product/Service

Project Leader: T. Nichols
Innovation Champion: A. Mahoney
Methodology: D4
Degree of Innovation: Substantial
Date of Completion: Jan. 1, 2013

(1)

Business Case: **(2)**
Pikes Peak Coffee (PPC) has consistently delivered double-digit growth since its inception, except for the last three quarters. While growth is the number-one priority, we believe the coffee market is saturated in the region. Research shows that about 35% of our competitors' sales come from food products, and 30% of these products are sold in the morning. This project will explore growth opportunities in the hot breakfast food business.

Job Statement: **(3)**
Eat a healthy breakfast on the go.

Customers: **(4)**
External: Coffee drinkers who want a hot, healthy breakfast on the way to work (primary); athletes, parents, students (secondary).
Internal: None.

Unmet Outcome Expectations: **(5)**
• Minimize the time needed to acquire breakfast in the busy morning.
• Increase the likelihood of eating a healthy breakfast.
• Increase the convenience of eating breakfast outside home.
• Minimize the mess generated from eating breakfast.
• Minimize the cost of buying breakfast out.

Competing Solutions: **(6)**
• Fast food chains that offer breakfast options.
• Microwaveable/homemade breakfast foods.
• Smoothies (breakfast through a straw).
• Restaurants that offer full-service, sit down breakfasts.
• Hotels that include breakfast in the price of a room for travelers.

Key Assumptions to be Tested: **(7)**
• 15% increase in revenue growth.
• Unit price of $4.95 for breakfast offering.
• Per store average volume of 80 sales per day.
• 40% contribution margin.
• Revenue from beverage sales will not be diminished by new offering.
• Customers will purchase breakfast from a coffee shop.
• Capital expenditure will be repaid in six months.
• New offering will not significantly impact coffee order cycle times.
• New offering will be distinct from competitions'.

• Expected Financial Impact: **(8)**
• 1st Qtr: $750,000 Rev./$300,000 net profit.
• 2nd Qtr: $1.2MM Rev./$480,000 net profit.
• 3rd Qtr: $1.3MM Rev./$520,000 net profit.
• 4th Qtr: $1.4MM Rev./$560,000 net profit.

Milestones/Timeline:	Scheduled	Actual	**(9)**
Define:	06-08-12		
Discover:	07-30-12		
Develop:	09-15-12		
Demonstrate:	01-01-13		

Project Investments		**(10)**
Define:	$5,000	
Discover:	$7,000	
Develop:	$10,000	
Demonstrate:	$30,000	
Commercialization:	$246,500	

Team: **(11)**
M. Chaw, A. Jones, D. McDonald, A. Perkins, S. Gonzalez, D. Roberts, E. Roberts

EXHIBIT 12.1   Innovation Project Charter (Downloadable). This is a template for an innovation project charter. As you move through the project, you will constantly revise this document.

2. Business Case

A business case is required to justify the allocation of time, money, and energy needed to make your innovation a successful venture. The business case should be a compelling summary for why the project is necessary and promising. Your business case can include any or all of the answers to the following questions:

- What's the business reason for undertaking this innovation project?
- How is the outcome aligned with or linked to strategic objectives?
- Is the idea financially viable and in what way will it contribute to profitable growth?
- Why is this an important opportunity and which customers (either internal or external) does it benefit?
- What is the expected return on investment for the project?
- Why should this project be a priority for the organization?

The business case is often based on initial assumptions (customers will buy this innovative offering from us, we will recoup our investment on this project, etc.). Just be sure to test these assumptions for validity as you move through the project. Otherwise, you may find out too late that they weren't sound.

---

3. Job Statement

A job statement is the job to be done (JTBD) summarized in a specific format: *verb* (eat), *object* (a healthy breakfast), *context* (on the go). Note that the job statement should be written from the customer's point of view, not the provider's (e.g., increase profits from new menu item). For more on this, see Jobs to be Done (Technique 1).

4. Customer

To build a robust project charter, it is important to identify the customers who will benefit from the innovation outcome. Segment your existing and potential customers by the job they're trying to accomplish instead of demographics, product line, geography, and so on. For example, the obvious target market for Pikes Peak Coffee's new offering is coffee drinkers who want a healthy breakfast on the way to work. Other customers might include athletes after their morning workout, parents returning from dropping the kids off at school, or students on the way to class.

5. Unmet Outcome Expectations

To ensure that your innovation will provide real value to customers, it's important to understand the major outcomes that are not currently satisfied by existing solutions. Use Outcome Expectations (Technique 3) to generate a list of expectations associated with the JTBD. Then, on the project charter, list the key unmet expectations. Use the format: *direction* (minimize), *measurement* (time needed to acquire), *object of action* (breakfast), and *context* (in the busy morning).

Consider using focus groups or Ethnography (Technique 5) to identify unarticulated outcome expectations.

6. Competing Solutions

Understanding the competitive landscape is essential for developing successful, profitable innovations. The key is to identify the current solutions for the JTBD (not just a list of who you think your competitors may be). Make a list of products, services, or processes that currently fulfill this job (well, poorly, or in between).

You can use Value Quotient (Technique 4) to compare and contrast competing solutions.

7. Key Assumptions to be Tested

Most business endeavors evolve from a series of assumptions related to functionality, outcomes, value, process, price, and so on. To identify which key assumptions need to be tested for your innovation, start by creating a comprehensive list of assumptions that are built into your idea. You can use the approach of Innovation Financial Management (Technique 13) to help with this task. Once you have a comprehensive list, prioritize your assumptions and select ones that will have the greatest impact on the success of the innovation. List these on the project charter.

Common Assumption Categories

- Availability of reasonable solutions.
- Price the customer is willing to pay for the innovation.
- How the business model can support the innovation.
- Supply chain logistics.
- Operational capabilities.
- Speed to scale-up.
- Cultural acceptance.
- Other strategic considerations.

Early in the innovation project, your ratio of verified knowledge to unverified assumptions will be low (there will be much you don't know). It's important to test and validate your assumptions as the project progresses. This increases your knowledge base, allowing you to make more informed decisions—and giving you the opportunity to abandon the innovation effort, if necessary, before you've reached your full investment.

8. Expected Financial Impact

Financial projections are often one of the most scrutinized aspects of an innovation project charter, especially when executives are trying to select which few innovation projects to fund. Almost all financial projections include estimates of revenue. Or, you can estimate *profitability* using Innovation Financial Management (Technique 13). Either way, the financial projections listed on the project charter should be estimated from the point your innovation will be available to customers, and should align with the company's current accounting periodicity (monthly, quarterly, annually).

Had Motorola tested its assumptions, maybe it could have avoided the billions lost on its Iridium (satellite phone) product. Perhaps Apple Computer could have curtailed its $350 million in losses on its handheld Newton device. Test your assumptions as rigorously and often as possible if you want to avoid innovation and business failures.

---

9. Milestones/Time Line

Establish milestones and time lines for your innovation project by identifying key deliverables. Milestones are often mapped against your innovation methodology (with a reviews at the end of specified phases). Or they could represent major steps toward the end result, such as *business case, feasibility, preliminary design, detailed design, pilot/prototype, prelaunch*, and *launch*.

10. Project Investments

To complete the initial project investment estimates, identify the cost of raw materials, people, training, time, capital expenditures, and other costs that will be required to bring your innovation to market. You can use Innovation Financial Management (Technique 13) to help you identify investment costs relative to your assumptions.

11. Team

To select your innovation project team members, start by identifying the combination of technical and change leadership skills that will be required to bring your innovation to market. The appropriate number of team members should be driven by the complexity and requirements of the innovation. You can also examine the candidates' problem-solving styles (see Cognitive Style, Technique 11) to ensure an effective and diverse mix.

Innovation Financial Management

Constantly improve your assumption-to-knowledge ratio.

The innovation financial management approach offers a clear advantage over traditional financial assessments. By forcing you to articulate your assumptions early in the innovation process, innovation financial management provides a systematic way to evaluate the feasibility of your innovation before putting too much time, money, and resources into it.

Consider the case of Euro Disney. When Walt Disney Company built the park, one key assumption was that visitors would spend an average of four days in an on-site hotel. The average turned out to be only two days. Alone, this inaccurate assumption does not account for Euro Disney's initially poor return on investment. But it can be coupled with a host of other unverified assumptions that cost the company nearly $1 billion in losses during its first two years.

Any innovation is risky. Innovation financial management reduces this risk by increasing the ratio of verified knowledge to unverified assumptions as the project unfolds. This learn-as-you-go approach ensures that you have the most accurate and updated information possible and enables you to confidently proceed or abandon the project at any point.

Background

Many innovation projects fail because the business lacks the right tools to understand markets, build brands, find customers, select employees, organize processes, and drive strategy. Traditional financial analysis tools, such as discounted cash flow and net present value, tend to distort the importance, the likelihood of success, and the value of investment in the innovation. These approaches build in certain assumptions that are rarely tested after the initial investment decision has been made.

Innovation financial management offers an alternative to these methods by identifying, tracking, and updating key assumptions, and linking the verification of these assumptions to the investment decision-making process.

Innovation financial management is an amalgamation of other proven financial management approaches. For more information, see:

McGrath, R. G., and I. C. MacMillan. "Discovery-Driven Planning." *Harvard Business Review,* July–August 1995.

Sykes, H. B., and D. Dunham. "Critical Assumption Planning: A Practical Tool for Managing Business Development Risk." *Journal of Business Venturing* 10, no. 6 (1995): 413–424.

Dewar, J. A., and C. H. Builder, et al. *Assumption-Based Planning: A Planning Tool for Very Uncertain Times.* Santa Monica, CA: RAND Corporation, 1993. www.rand.org/pubs/monograph_reports/2005/MR114.pdf.

The extent to which you can complete the innovation financial management documents early in the project depends on the level of innovation you hope to achieve. During incremental innovation, your initial ratio of knowledge to assumptions (Exhibit 13.1) will be higher than for substantial or radical innovation. In either case, you should update the relevant financial documents, as well as the project charter, as you uncover new data throughout the project.

Steps

Scenario: To demonstrate the basics of innovation financial management, we'll continue the Pikes Peak Coffee example from the Project Charter technique (Technique 12). The company can use this approach to determine the profitability of adding a healthy, portable breakfast offering to its menu.

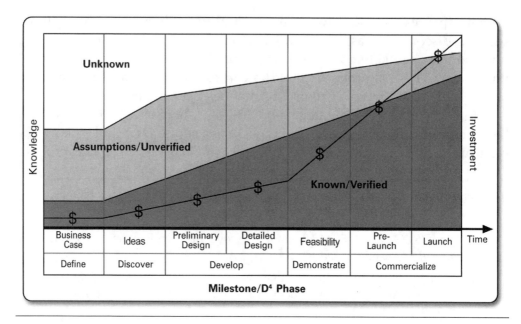

EXHIBIT 13.1   Knowledge/Investment Map. Early in the innovation project, there may be a low ratio of known/verified information compared to unverified assumptions and unknowns. Ideally, investment will also be low at this stage. As the project progresses, the level of verified knowledge should increase relative to the project investment.

1. Document Initial Assumptions

If you've completed a project charter, you've established the business case for your innovation. Innovation financial management takes over from here and begins with a list of what you know (verified knowledge), as well as what you need to find out (unverified assumptions and unknowns).

For example, Pikes Peak Coffee knows that it currently has 32 locations, and that if the innovative breakfast offering proves to be viable, it would be offered in all locations. What the company doesn't know yet is the details of the offering, the retail price, the demand, or the cost (materials, personnel, and new equipment). However, for each of these assumptions, innovation financial management encourages you to put forth an educated guess. The point is not to show what you know, but to learn as you go (Exhibit 13.2).

> Assumptions are factors you assume to be a certain way without enough evidence to prove or disprove your theory.

	Per Store	All Stores
Stores	1	32
Sales Volume	29,293	937,374
Unit Price	$ 4.95	$ 4.95
Revenue	$ 145,000	$ 4,640,000
Production Days	365	11,680
Daily Production Capacity	160	5,120
Employees/Store	1	32
Employees' Wages/Store	$ 22,500	$ 720,000
Material Cost per Unit	$ 1.63	$ 1.63
Paper Cost per Unit	$ 0.17	$ 0.17
Capital Cost	$ 8,500	$ 272,000
Equipment Life (years)	5	5
Allowable Overhead	$ 9,970	$ 319,046

EXHIBIT 13.2   Initial Assumptions (Downloadable).

2. Prepare Reverse Income Statement

Now that you've articulated some basic assumptions, the next step is to determine the amount of *profit* (not revenue) you want to generate as a direct result of your innovation. Determine the profit margin and amount of profit that would make the project worthwhile. Then, use a *reverse income statement* to calculate how much revenue you would need to reach this profit after subtracting your initial investment and any ongoing costs.

Pikes Peak Coffee, for example, hopes that adding a unique, healthy breakfast offering to its menu will net them an additional $1.8 MM profit annually across their 32 locations. A reverse income statement (Exhibit 13.3) shows that to meet this goal, annual revenue from the new offering (before costs) needs to be $4.6 MM.

A reverse income statement models the basic economics of the proposed innovation based on projected profit, not revenue.

Required Profit	$ 1,856,000
Required Contribution Margin	40%
Allowable Cost	$ 2,784,000
Required Revenue @ 40% ROS	$ 4,460,000

Revenue = Profit/Contribution Margin

EXHIBIT 13.3 Reverse Income Statement (Downloadable). To determine the Required Revenue (line 4), divide the Required Profit (line 1) by the Required Contribution Margin (line 2).

Copyright © 2012, BMGI. A blank version of this customized form is available for download at www .innovatorstoolkit.com.

3. Estimate Operating Specifications

	Per Store	All Stores
Sales		
Annual Sales Volume	29,293	937,376
Daily Sales Volume per Store	80	2,560
Production		
Annual Production Capacity	58,400	1,868,800
Daily Production Capacity	160	5,120
Stores	1	32
Expenses		
Workers Needed	1	32
Workers' Wages	22,500	720,000
Total Material Cost	47,850	1,531,200
Total Paper Cost	4,980	159,534
Marketing Cost	5%	5%
Capital		
Total Capital Cost	8,500	272,000
Annual Depreciation	1,700	54,400

EXHIBIT 13.4 Pro Forma Operations Specs (Downloadable). Pro forma operations specs document all specific and measurable costs required to implement the innovation.

Copyright © 2012, BMGI. A blank version of this customized form is available for download at www.innovatorstoolkit.com.

In addition to investment costs, ongoing operational costs will divert your innovation's revenue stream. Use *pro forma operations specs* (Exhibit 13.4) to identify and estimate overhead costs. Include estimates for wages and salaries, raw material and inventory cost, manufacturing costs, insurance, shipping, marketing and advertising, and whatever other annualized costs the innovation may incur above and beyond your current operating costs. Also include annual depreciation or any other factors that could impact the profitability of your innovation in an ongoing manner.

The APQC Process Classification Framework can be a useful tool when trying to articulate all the associated costs for the pro forma operations specs. You can download a copy at www.apqc.org/process-classification-framework.

4. Update Income Statement

After compiling the estimated operational costs, update the income statement (Exhibit 13.5) to see if your initial profit projections are still on target. For our coffee shop example, total costs will likely be less than predicted on the reverse income statement, which increases the amount of projected profit. Of course, had the pro forma operation specs predicted higher costs than the initial estimate, Pikes Peak Coffee would need to either reduce costs or increase revenue projections.

Required Revenue	$	4,640,000
Direct Costs		
Additional Employee Wages	$	720,000
Food Cost	$	1,531,200
Paper and Packaging	$	159,354
Equipment Depreciation	$	54,400
Direct Costs — Sub Total	$	2,464,954
Allowable Admin., Marketing Overhead	$	232,000
Total Costs	$	2,696,954
Projected Profit	$	1,943,046
Initial Required Profit	$	1,856,000

EXHIBIT 13.5 Updated Income Statement (Downloadable).

Copyright © 2012, BMGI. A blank version of this customized form is available for download at www.innovatorstoolkit.com.

5. Identify Critical Assumptions

Make a list of any critical assumptions that, if left unchecked, could seriously impact your innovation financially. Many of these you have already created for the income statements and operations specs. Include the following:

- Competition, market size, retail price, average order size, up-sell potential, and other revenue-related assumptions.
- Design time line/costs, prototyping/piloting expectations, testing time line, and other R&D cost assumptions.

- Production schedule/time line, sales cycle, material cost, shipping costs, inventory costs, salaries, wages, and other operating cost assumptions.
- Marketing, advertising, packaging, redesign, and other promotional cost assumptions.

Avoid These Dangerous Inherent Assumptions

- Customers always prefer technologically superior products and services.
- Customers don't know how to articulate their needs.
- Build a better mousetrap and the world will beat a path to my door.
- When customers hear about our new solutions, they will quit using existing solutions in favor of our solutions.
- Our solution is so superior that it will sell on its own without any extra effort.
- Distribution channels will promote our products and services over existing products and services they sell.
- We have the expertise and resources needed to create the solution and get it right the first time.
- Our competitors have no capability to match our plans.
- All stakeholders in our company will rally behind our new idea.
- We are the leader in our industry.

---

6. Link Assumptions to Milestones

Milestones are checkpoints that help you determine whether to continue on course or redirect your innovation effort. Make a list of milestones for your innovation. Include significant targets both during the innovation project and after. Then associate each milestone with the critical assumptions that must be verified before the checkpoint can be completed (Exhibit 13.6).

7. Test and Validate Assumptions

For each critical financial assumption, design a test that will prove it right or wrong. You could target the assumptions at each milestone before moving on to the next. Or, you may need to take a more granular approach and design a test that validates each assumption. Either way, make sure the

Milestone	Assumption	Test Plan
Business Case	15% increase in revenue growth Unit price of $4.95 for breakfast offering Per store average volume of 80 sales per day 40% contribution margin	Benchmark Competition
Discover and Design	Capital expenditure will be paid within 6 months New offering will be distinct from competition's	Explore Alternatives
Feasibility	Production capacity per store per day Capital cost of equipment Equipment life Production days Additional employees per store Additional employee wages Food cost Packaging cost	Identify Availability and Cost for Capital, Materials, and People
Pilot	Unit price Volume Food cost Packaging cost Revenue from new offering Test marketing costs New offering will not diminish revenue from beverage sales Customers will purchase breakfast from a coffee shop New offering will not significantly impact coffee order cycle times During pilot, operating costs will be offset by incremental revenues	Measure Performance of New Offering
Pre-launch	Unit price Revenue Profit margin Marketing and advertising costs	Analyze Collected Data and Update Business Plan
Launch	Marketing and advertising costs Success of pilot replication Growth rate Market size	Continuously Improve Operating Methods

EXHIBIT 13.6   Milestones and Assumptions (Downloadable).

Copyright © 2012, BMGI. A blank version of this customized form is available for download at www .innovatorstoolkit.com.

assumption is clearly stated and understood, and the data and method used to verify the assumption is sound.

Don't wait for the pilot or prototype phase to validate all your assumptions. Although many of Pikes Peak Coffee's assumptions will be tested during a three-month, three-store pilot of their new breakfast offering, many other key assumptions need to be tested both before and after the pilot (Exhibit 13.6).

8. Revisit Financials

As you proceed through the project milestones, testing your assumptions along the way, your knowledge increases regarding the innovation's potential. Thus, you should recalculate the income statement at each milestone. Depending on what you learn, you may also need to revisit the operations specs. Your critical assumptions list will also change as you validate your initial assumptions and develop new ones during the process.

If you're following the D^4 innovation process, verify that your assumptions have been validated (demonstrate feasibility) before entering your project into the company's innovation portfolio.

PART II

DISCOVER THE IDEAS

Successful innovation is about capitalizing on an opportunity to fulfill unmet customer expectations in a superior way. But finding that superior way is far from easy, because at the core of most opportunities lies a difficult problem. Customers, for instance, want wrinkle-free clothes but no current solution meets their expectation very well. This is an innovation problem as well as an opportunity.

In this second phase of the innovation process, your goal is to generate substantive ideas for closing outcome expectation gaps (or innovation opportunities) within the confines of a smartly scoped project. But first you'll want to *refine the opportunity* using the Resource Optimization, Functional Analysis, Trend Prediction, and Creative Challenge techniques.

Then, you need to bring out the best of what's in your mind and accelerate the creative process using the techniques of HIT Matrix, SCAM-PER, Brainwriting 6-3-5, Imaginary Brainstorming, Concept Tree, Random Stimulus, and Provocation and Movement. All of these techniques enable you to *leverage latent brainpower* beyond what resides in your immediate consciousness, or what can be surfaced with only classic brainstorming.

Still, the power of your team's collective mind might not be enough to ideate a sufficient innovation. The prescription is to *search knowledge bases* that exist outside your self, finding clues and direction. One knowledge base is the problem-solving wisdom held by other industries and enterprises nearby or far removed from your own—to wit, we offer the Forced Association technique, as it can get you across the barriers that stand between you and what you're seeking.

If this isn't enough, explore the collective experience of all inventors, as catalogued inside such techniques as Structured Abstraction, Separation

Principles, and Substance Field Analysis. Another knowledge base is the adaptive miracles of nature and nonhuman species that have proven their survival resiliency for an astoundingly longer period of time than humans have; the Biomimicry technique should be your source for exploring how nature's miracles can be put to use for innovation.

This phase of the innovation ends by filtering and narrowing ideas down to the few that are the *best candidates for further development and design*. See the KJ Method, Idea Sorting and Refinement, and Six Thinking Modes to help you converge on the ripest concepts for innovation.

Resource Optimization

Make sure you use all available resources.

Resource optimization is the use of existing resources to solve an innovation problem and increase the value of a solution relative to existing options. For instance, when manufacturers came up with reverse bottles (spout on bottom instead of top) for ketchup, shampoo, and other liquid substances, they used the free and available resource of gravity to solve the problem of getting every last drop out with ease and no frustration.

Use resource optimization when you need to come up with solution ideas that provide higher value than those in existence today—or when you need to refine and optimize a specific solution design. The key is to make sure you list as many resources as possible within and outside your immediate system or sphere of focus. After this, you can use any number of idea-generation techniques to figure out how your available resources can be applied to your inventive problem.

Background

In the vast majority of problematic situations where a creative idea is sorely needed, resource optimization is seldom if ever seriously considered. Most of the time, it never even makes the radar screen, because the typical approach is to throw money at a problem and fix it through adding complexity.

It's always easier to solve a problem through additive approaches rather than through elegant solutions that utilize readily available resources.

So what really is a resource? Machines, people, equipment, money? Yes. But what about the resources of gravity, air, vacuums, and even waste? This is where the creative part starts: using resources you never thought were available to position your innovation ahead of your competition.

Think of resources that are just hanging around waiting to solve a problem without a large outlay of time, effort, or expense. Heat from a car's engine is harnessed to keep passengers warm on a cold day. An empty wine bottle is used as a rolling pin. Gravity provides the centripetal force needed to keep a satellite in orbit.

This means you'll identify your system's immediately recognizable resources, but you'll also identify resources outside the system (supersystem), inside the system (subsystem) and even resources in the environment at large (like humidity, for instance).

An innovator also should consider resources that were available in the past or will be available in the future. For example, NASA engineers spent a lot of money trying to come up with a headlight for a lunar module. They had trouble creating the perfect interface between the glass lightbulb and the metal body holding it—until they realized they could use a future resource: Since the moon's atmosphere has vacuum properties, the engineers eradicated the need for a glass bulb at all.

Some resources to consider in solving innovation problems include:

- *Material resources,* such as waste, raw materials, modified materials, and inexpensive materials.
- *Time resources,* such as parallel operations and prefunction and postfunction work.
- *Information resources,* such as data usage, computer networks, public data, and information.
- *Field resources,* such as energy in the system (mechanical, thermal, chemical, electrical, magnetic, etc.) or energy in the environment (gravity, vacuums, light, wave movement, wind, geothermal, etc.).
- *Space resources,* such as empty spaces, nesting components, or dimension reconfiguration.
- *Function resources,* such as harmful functions that can be converted to good functions, or enhancing the secondary effects of functions.

Engineers participate in the activities that make the resources of nature available in a form beneficial to man and provide systems that will perform optimally and economically.

—L. M. K. Boelter, engineer, educator, and innovator

Steps

Scenario: Some resource optimization experts have proposed that every life on the *Titanic* could have been saved with the use of existing resources on the ship (Exhibit 14.1). That may very well be true, but clearly the crisis conditions prevented this from happening. The hope is that you won't find yourself in the middle of a crisis with your innovation project, and you'll always

EXHIBIT 14.1   The *Titanic*.

have time to explore how you can optimize your unused but available resources.

1. Formulate the Problem

What job, problem, or task creates the focus for your innovation effort? What are its associated customer and provider outcome expectations? Have you already created a project statement or job statement? See Jobs to be Done, Outcome Expectations, and Project Charter (Techniques 1, 3, and 12, respectively).

For the *Titanic* scenario, the job is to save all 2,223 people on board, even though there are only 1,178 available lifeboat seats. A rescue ship is on the way in approximately four hours, but the ship will sink in two hours if left to its own devices. Also, people will freeze in four minutes if exposed to the icy cold waters of the Atlantic Ocean.

2. Compose a List of Resources

Make an inventory of all resources at hand, leaving no stone unturned. First, list all the resources that are internal to your system; then list all resources that are external or outside of your system; then list all resources that are by-products of your internal and external resources. For the *Titanic*, we'll only list pertinent resources for illustration purposes (Exhibit 14.2), because we don't have the space to list every available resource on the approximately 883-foot long, 93-foot wide, 60-foot high, 46,328-ton ship.

3. Analyze the Resource List

The key to this step is to narrow the list of resources down to only those that have the most leverage or potential to change the system in a way that solves the inventive problem, without creating any unwanted side effects. When wanted changes are made in any system, those changes tend to create ancillary unwanted changes—so the fertile ground of innovation lies in those areas where you can make changes, or better utilize resources, without creating drawbacks elsewhere.

When looking for free resources to use, or looking to better utilize certain resources as a pathway to an innovation, complete the following equation: $y = f(x)$, substituting the desired outcome for the y variable and the proposed resource for the x variable. To achieve the expected outcome (y), the x resource must perform the function without added complications, cost, or undesired effects.

Some options for working with resources are:

- *Resource utilization:* Convert existing resources into new resources through the application of inventive fields (burn fuel to generate heat).
- *Resource accumulation:* Use a device or substance to increase the amount of a resource, and then release it (use a dam to accumulate water).
- *Resource combination:* Add one resource to another (add salt to water to affect buoyancy).

Date *April 10, 1912*	R.M.S. ★ Titanic	Destination *New York*
Time Resources Two hours to sink Four hours to rescue Four minutes to freeze **Natural Resources** Salt water Whales/other fish Iceberg **Team/People Resources** Passengers Crew Engineers Doctors Ship's chief engineer Ship's architect Ship's captain	**Material Resources** Life rafts Ship Tools Water Axes Cooking lard Steel Coal Clothes Kitchen utensils Band instruments Suitcases Rope Furniture Canvas Food Cars Car tires Rescue ships Bed mattresses Wood First aid kits Life preservers Bathtubs Deck chairs Garbage containers Blankets Maps	**Information Resources** Knowledge/skill sets Communication equipment/radio **Field Resources** Chemical (from coal) Thermal (engine heat) **Space Resources** Deck Empty spaces in bathtubs, suitcases, furniture, etc. **Function Resources** Engine Navigation system Steering system

EXHIBIT 14.2   Resources Aboard the *Titanic*.

- *Resource concentration:* Use a field to concentrate a resource to an effective level (microwave oven, laser for eye surgery).
- *Resource evolution:* Envision the evolution of a system—what resources might evolve and how (using plants to generate oxygen).
- *Resource scaling:* Change the scale or magnitude of a resource property (concentrated vaccine dilutes after injection).

Several uses of resources could be employed to possibly save all the lives on the *Titanic*. Teams of people could be organized to perform various functions, such as blocking the hole in the ship with clothes, garbage, mattresses, canvas, and so on, to delay the water-flooding rate. Also, teams could be formed to transport people from the ship to the iceberg, where they could stay warm enough until the rescue ship arrives. Other teams might create various floating devices using the ship's resources.

Additionally:

- Use lifeboats to shuttle people back and forth to the nearby iceberg.
- Use ropes and kitchen utensils to secure people to the iceberg.
- Keep people warm with mattresses and blankets.
- Use life preservers as a buffer between passengers and the iceberg to keep people warm and safe.
- Coat people's bodies with cooking lard to protect them from the icy cold waters and prevent hypothermia.
- Use empty suitcases and wooden furniture as mini lifeboats.
- Use car tires as flotation devices.
- Use engineering experience to devise and implement the rescue system.

Additional Examples

- Perhaps the most brilliant use of available resources was when the ground and flight crew of Apollo 13 devised a way to overcome severe electrical power and oxygen limitations to keep three astronauts alive and safely return them to earth. They did this by using the lunar module as a lifeboat in space and rigged an adapter system using materials in the spacecraft.

- General Electric's Jenbacher engines produce power for greenhouses, businesses, and homes using patented technologies. The same Jenbacher can run on a variety of gases, including natural gas but also gases from coal mines, sewage, and landfills. The Jenbacher was designed to harness these available resources that might otherwise be wasted.

- A power plant was emitting selenium, which is harmful if swallowed or breathed (waste). After the plant's engineers designed an expensive system for separating selenium, they realized something: Ragweed and cattails absorb selenium. With nature as their teacher, they created a pond and populated it with ragweed and cattails; then they dumped the selenium into the pond, where the ragweed and cattails absorbed it and bound it to their tissues. After this, the plants were harvested and sold as fertilizer to cotton and tobacco farmers.

Functional Analysis

Scrutinize your system for innovation.

Functional analysis is a process for assessing and improving system value—with a focus on retaining or increasing all useful functions, mitigating or eliminating all harmful functions, and improving inadequate functions. For example, a healthcare provider currently gives medicine to a patient at a clinic using a syringe-and-needle system; breaking these functions down into their parts (piston, cylinder, medicine, nurse, needle, patient) and functions (moves, guides, positions, penetrates) provides an opportunity to rethink and innovate the system.

Use functional analysis upstream in your ideation efforts to identify opportunities for improving the Value Quotient of your future solutions (see Technique 4). A simple functional analysis can be performed without the help of an engineer or expert. But for the details involved in complex systems, a value engineer or expert with experience is advisable, if not necessary—especially when dovetailing this technique with such other formidable techniques as Axiomatic Design (Technique 34) and Function Structure (Technique 35).

Background

Every system is composed of hundreds if not thousands of interfacing elements. Changes in any one subsystem, component, or even a process parameter can reverberate and set off a chain reaction of positive and/or negative consequences throughout the system. Without a thorough understanding of how all of the causal linkages impact each other, it's likely that any change will create a number of unintended consequences.

The work and value of functional analysis revolves around an information-rich *function diagram* that shows all the causal linkages in a system and indicates whether they are desired, undesired, or insufficient. Once the function diagram is complete, the following advantages accrue:

- It's easier to clarify the functions of an existing or proposed system, which feeds directly into solution ideation and development.

- It's easier to figure out where available resources can be employed to improve a system or solve a problem (also using Resource Optimization, Technique 14).

- It's easier to pinpoint and eliminate any *physical or technical contradictions*. See Structured Abstraction (Technique 26) and Separation Principles (Technique 27) for more.

- It's easier to flag any unneeded elements or functions through *trimming*, thereby reducing cost and moving the system closer to an ideal innovation.

The formulation of a problem is far more often essential than its solution, which may be merely a matter of mathematical or experimental skill.

—Albert Einstein

Steps

Scenario: Most people are familiar with the real estate transaction system whereby two agents facilitate a number of functions, including property listing, advertising, showing properties, offer and counteroffer negotiation, contracting, home inspection, title insurance, closing, and so on. How could this system become more value-oriented (innovative), and thereby increase desired outcomes and/or decrease undesired outcomes?

1. Gather Information and Define the Problem

Before creating a function diagram and performing a functional analysis, gather as much information about the system and problem as possible. The following questions can help:

- What is the primary useful function (the design intent) of the system, or the main job to be done (JTBD)?

- How do the elements of the system interact with each other?
- What resources are available to solve the problem?
- What constraints are there on the system? Are they necessary?
- What solutions have been attempted in the past and to what degree were they successful or not; if not successful, why not?

For our real estate example, we would like to complete the real estate transaction process more efficiently, especially pertaining to the services provided by agents working within a proprietary database (Multiple Listing System).

Use this technique to help assess system implications when applying Axiomatic Design (see Technique 34) to translate functional requirements into design parameters.

---

2. Develop a Functional Model of the System (Function Diagram)

What is a function? For our purposes, a function is defined as an activity, action, process, or condition that operates between two variables: (1) the input (independent) variable and (2) the output (dependent) variable. In between the input and output is a *value transformation*, because the function creates a sum of value (output) that is greater than the additive value of its parts (inputs). By virtue of the function, value is added.

While many functions are desired, some are undesired—or costly or harmful. Further, all functions in a system are either sufficient or insufficient in performing their duties, or value transformations. As well, functions are performed by elements or entities that reside either inside the system or outside the system, yielding certain results. Exhibit 15.1 summarizes the basic symbols and architecture involved in creating a function diagram.

The goal of a function diagram is to depict all pertinent functions in the system in a cause-and-effect style (using $y = f(x)$ to guide your thinking). The key agents in the system, inputs (x) and outputs (y), interact (f) to accomplish the system's objective.

Start by identifying the primary desired functions of the system, asking two questions with subsequent follow-on questions:

1. Does this function produce another function? If so, is the resulting function desired (and sufficient), undesired (harmful), or insufficient (needed but not good enough)?

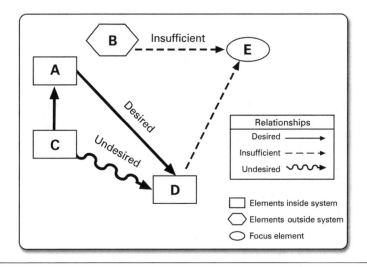

EXHIBIT 15.1   Function Diagram Symbols.

2. Is this function produced by another function? If so, is the producing function's impact desired, undesired, or insufficient?

These control questions then serve as the guide for linking the functions with the desired, undesired, or insufficient arrows as illustrated in Exhibit 15.1.

We've created a stylized, rough function diagram for the real-estate transaction process (Exhibit 15.2). The diagram identifies some functions but leaves others out, such as appraisal, title insurance, home inspection, contract preparation, advertising, county recording, securing a mortgage, obtaining mortgage insurance, obtaining homeowners insurance, and closing.

Looking at Exhibit 15.2, we see that some functions are desired, some are insufficient, and some are undesired. Real estate commissions, for example, are an undesired function because they do not represent the ideal innovation and because they add significant and unnecessary cost to the process.

3. Perform the Functional Analysis

Analyzing the model in a group setting is the best way to proceed with functional analysis. Essentially, the task is to review the function diagram and

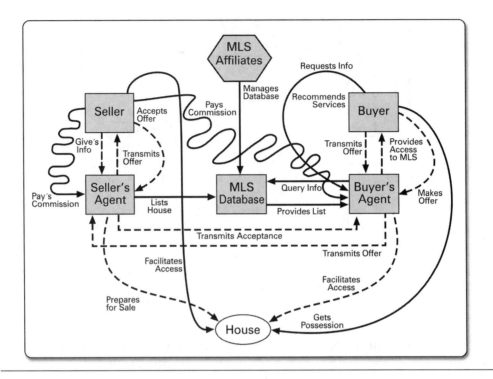

EXHIBIT 15.2 Simplified Function Diagram for Real Estate Transaction.

modify it in ways that will make the system more value-added. What desired functions can we increase? What undesired functions can we remove? What insufficient functions can be made sufficient? This requires exploratory use of any number of ideation techniques in this book.

> Use a Cause & Effect Diagram (Technique 56) to document all the important causal relationships in the system. After this, prioritize these relationships using a Cause & Effect Matrix (Technique 57). These then become the initial focus of an attempt to trim the system using a trimming worksheet.

One way to generate immediate ideas is to use a *trimming worksheet* (Exhibit 15.3). Populate the worksheet as shown:

- For all key functions, ask what the function is and identify its input and output.

Real estate transaction system

Provider	Function	Recipient	Is function desired, undesired, or insufficient?	Is function necessary?	Trimming Questions (to simplify system or reduce cost)	
					Could recipient do it by itself?	Could some other resource do it?
Seller agent	Enters data	MLS	Desired	Yes	Possibly — Using county records	Yes — Seller could enter into public Central Listing Authority, with controls
Buyer agent	Shows house	Buyer	Desired	Yes	Yes — Buyer could show house	Yes — Buyer and Seller can arrange showing
Buyer	Transfers offer	Buyer agent	Insufficient	Yes	No	Yes — Offers can exchange directly between seller-buyer, maybe with Internet
Buyer agent	Transfers offer	Seller agent	Insufficient	Yes	Yes — Could have only one agent involved	Yes — Offers can exchange directly between seller-buyer, maybe with Internet
Seller agent	Transfers offer	Seller	Insufficient	Yes	No	Yes — Offers can exchange directly between seller-buyer, maybe with Internet
Seller	Transfers counter	Seller agent	Desired	Yes	No	Yes — Offers can exchange directly between seller-buyer, maybe with Internet
Seller agent	Transfers offer	Buyer agent	Insufficient	Yes	Yes — Could have only one agent involved	Yes — Offers can exchange directly between seller-buyer, maybe with Internet
Buyer agent	Transfers counter	Buyer	Insufficient	Yes	Yes — Buyer could get from seller agent	Yes — Offers can exchange directly between seller-buyer, maybe with Internet
Seller	Pays commission	Seller and buyer agents	Undesired	No	No	No — Commissions paid; only fees for advertising, contract, etc.

EXHIBIT 15.3   Functional Analysis and Trimming Worksheet (Downloadable).

Copyright © 2012, BMGI. A blank version of this customized form is available for download at www.innovatorstoolkit.com.

- Indicate if the function is desired (and sufficient), undesired (harmful), or insufficient (needed but not good enough).
- Ask if the function is necessary. If so, then it becomes a candidate for trimming by asking two questions: (1) Could the recipient of the function do it by itself—*how*? (2) Could some other resource (in the system, preferably) perform the function—*how*?

The trimming questions are very important because they facilitate reducing the complexity of the system through elimination of unnecessary elements. This reduces system cost and improves value.

If the function isn't necessary, then it becomes a candidate for elimination.

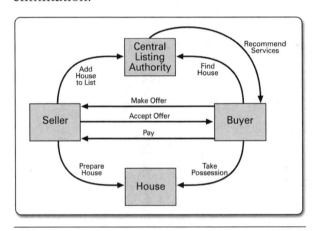

By trimming certain elements of the real estate transaction system, we can envision a cleaner, simpler, and less expensive system, depicted in Exhibit 15.4. Of course, this innovated system is stylized and simplified; in reality, the functional analysis would be much more detailed, showing all aspects of the real estate transaction, not just the listing, negotiation, and other functions shown.

EXHIBIT 15.4 Function Diagram for Real Estate Transaction Innovation.

In this envisioned agentless system, many resources could be available in the Central Listing Authority to sellers and buyers, and not just information about and pictures or video tours of available properties. Attorneys, title companies, appraisal companies, insurance companies, and lenders could advertise their services; at the same time, they could provide information about how to accomplish related functions, or jobs to be done.

For example, as a self-serve customer you could download an instruction set for doing a title search and for hiring a title company. Or, download a contract template that you can customize and use to exchange offers and counteroffers. Or, even hire a home-based real estate specialist who can coach you through the process for a small fee.

Trend Prediction

Learn from evolution's genetic code.

Trend prediction is a powerful knowledge-based technique that extrapolates how current systems will evolve in the future. Using this extrapolation, you can plan your own innovations. For instance, all systems are trending toward *decreased human involvement*—robotic functions in factories, automated information systems, the need for only one human (the customer) to be involved in trading a stock or booking an airline ticket online.

To apply this technique, you'll need an extensive understanding of about 35 known universal technology trends, each of which progresses toward increasingly valued and ideal innovation. While the knowledge and time required to apply this technique is formidable, it reveals the trends that underlie all product and service innovations, thereby vaccinating against the tendency to innovate insufficient solutions, or to innovate a new product or service at the wrong time.

Background

There are many ways you can predict trends in an industry, and there are numerous trend gurus whose work could be helpful. We like the work of Genrich Altshuller, the founder of the Theory of Inventive Problem Solving (TRIZ), because it's one of the most empirical approaches. We also favor the work of U.K.-based author Darrell Mann, who has built on Altshuller's paradigm of *systematic innovation* to refine it for further use.

The basic idea behind trend prediction is that evolution is not random but follows certain patterns and stages that can be predicted. If you know what these patterns and stages are, then you can solve difficult innovation problems and define technology-related strategic opportunities.

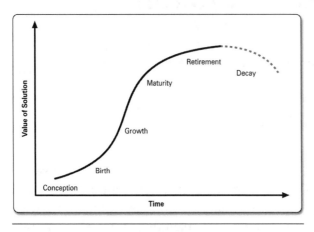

The basis for applying trend prediction is to understand the concept of *S-curves* as they operate in time, one giving way to the next as the new eclipses the old. Each S-curve moves slowly from conception to birth, then rapidly from birth to maturity, then slowly again from maturity to retirement. After this, the system or solution of focus tends to taper off and decay in value (Exhibit 16.1).

EXHIBIT 16.1   Classic S Curve.

This retirement/decay inflection point is determined by the market force generated by a newly developing system or solution—one that is clearly fueled by a breakthrough technology, process, or business model (Exhibit 16.2). Note that the target, or expected outcome, is beyond what the current system can deliver, so an innovation is required.

The legitimacy of trend prediction is derived from studying system dynamics contained in worldwide patent databases. When you understand the dynamics and principles involved in why and how systems, products, and services change over time, you have a secret weapon in ideating innovations.

There are thousands of examples of one S-curve eclipsing another. Employing new technologies along the way, we moved from the horse and buggy to the train to the car to the airplane to the space rocket. We moved from writing on stone to writing on paper to large-scale printing

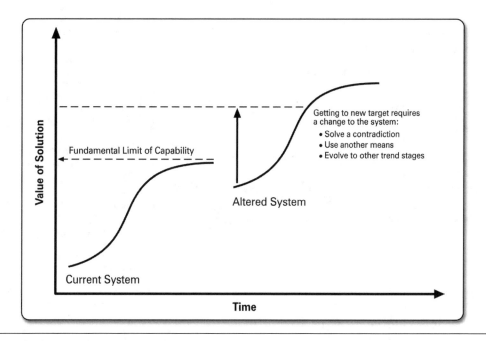

EXHIBIT 16.2   S-Curve Generations.

to all forms of digital communication. From the macro systems level to the smallest micro level, the trajectory of S-curves tells the story of an evolving world.

It's possible to examine a product, service, or system (solution) within the context of the 35 known universal, generic evolutionary trends—call them the chromosomes of innovation. Such an examination enables you to gauge your idea-generation efforts against established and undeniable historical patterns. It also enables you to:

- Avoid costly innovation missteps and consistently provide a superior customer experience.
- Prevent new disruptive shifts in technology from blindsiding your organization.

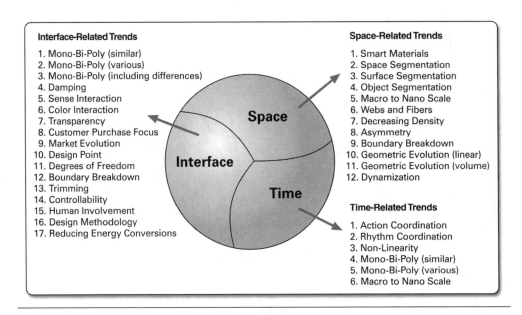

EXHIBIT 16.3 Technology Trends.

Source: Hands-On Systematic Innovation, by D. Mann, Clevedon, UK: IFR Press, 2007, www.systematic-innovation.com.

- Determine when it's necessary to shift your product strategy to a new technology platform.
- Create critical patent umbrellas under which to protect yourself against competitive attacks on your company's intellectual property.

The 35 trends of trend prediction are classified into three main categories as shown in Exhibit 16.3. These are the signposts of innovation, whether it involves pushing a solution along the continuum of a particular S-curve (incremental innovation), or replacing one S-curve with the next (radical, or breakthrough, innovation).

If an organization can fix its position on the life cycle curve (S-curve), and it has a sense of the slope of the curve, it has an excellent mechanism for determining where its technology is headed, and it can also determine the relative rapidity of that movement. Understanding this dynamic yields unique insight on how to direct product/service development and R&D processes, as well as how to proactively align core competencies with new technology imperatives.

In addition to *technology trends,* which operate at the product, service, and solution level, Altshuller, Mann, and others have also developed about 36 *business trends*—but these still represent a relatively new body of research and are yet to be rigorously validated.

Steps

1. Become Familiar with Technology Trends

Once you understand each of the 35 technology trends, you are ready to examine any of your products, services, or solutions from the lens of these established evolutionary patterns. The key is to know that each trend progresses along a scale of evolutionary potential, from a less evolved state into a more evolved state. One space-related trend is *dynamization,* which says that over time a system, product, or part will evolve from a rigid state to a flexible one, moving through several stages as shown in Exhibit 16.4.

Another universal trend is the tendency for systems to evolve from the *macro* to the *nano* scale. We see this trend in action when looking at the first early computers, which weighed about 27 tons and contained 17,468 vacuum tubes, 70,000 resistors, 10,000 capacitors, and around 5 million hand-soldered joints. IBM's ENIAC computer measured 8.5 feet by 3 feet by 80 feet. By comparison, today's notebook computers are quite small.

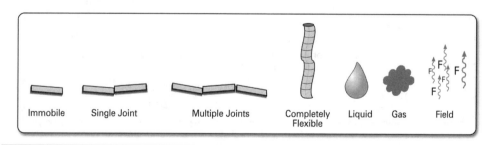

EXHIBIT 16.4 Dynamization Trend.

For an in-depth description of each evolutionary trend with examples, read *Hands-On Systematic Innovation,* by D. Mann, Clevedon, UK: IFR Press, 2007, www.systematic-innovation.com.

2. Determine Evolutionary Potential

You can use *radar charts* to set the stage for ideating better products and services. A radar chart is a visual way of depicting the state of a system, product, service, or solution relative to some other one, as shown in Exhibit 16.5. Note that we have constructed a fictitious example radar

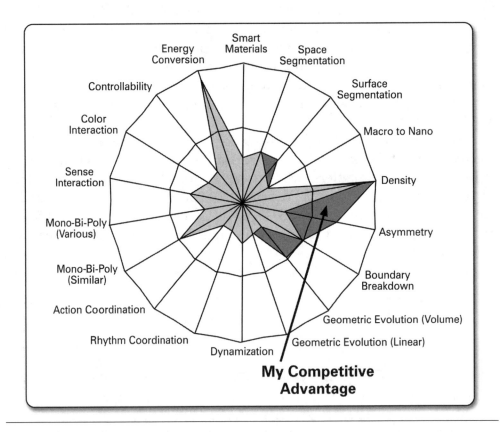

EXHIBIT 16.5 Radar Chart.

chart using 18 of the 35 technology trends. Each spoke of the radar chart represents evolutionary movement along the S-curve at progressive stages starting from the center point. The darkly shaded area represents the evolutionary potential of a solution that extends the current competitive reality more toward the ideal innovation (for more on this concept, see Value Quotient, Technique 4).

Predicting such evolutionary developments entails many technical or scientific considerations, as well as considerations related to feasibility, cost, time to invent, and anticipated customer reaction. This is when other techniques, such as Innovation Financial Management (Technique 13) and Outcome Expectations (Technique 3), come in handy.

3. Close Evolutionary Gaps

Although you can use trend prediction alone to carry an innovation idea through to a viable design, the difficult job of closing evolutionary gaps is made easier by using other ideation techniques in this book. This enables the innovator to make sure the very best ideas are surfaced and tested before spending time and resources developing new solutions.

Example

Scenario: Sparked by customer frustrations with lukewarm pizzas upon delivery, a group of scientists set out to develop a better solution for keeping pizzas hot and crisp during the delivery process. Relying on Trend Prediction to guide them, the scientists achieved their goal (see U.S. Patent Number 5,472,139).

The first task was to discover the evolutionary trends that might apply to this challenge or problem. After much research and due diligence, the research team converged on the trends of *surface segmentation* and *geometric evolution of linear constructions*. Both trends are shown in Exhibit 16.6, which depicts their progression through standard evolutionary stages.

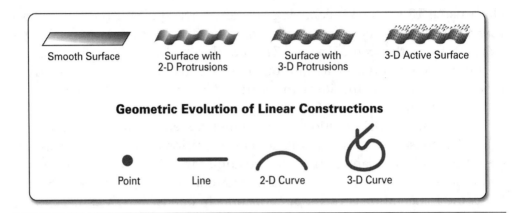

EXHIBIT 16.6   Surface Segmentation.

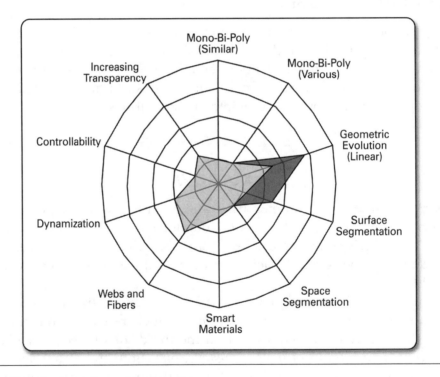

EXHIBIT 16.7   Evolution of a Pizza Box.

Accounting for all pertinent evolutionary trends, the team prepared a radar chart to depict its planned innovation. In doing so, the team expected it could move up one notch on the evolutionary scale for each of the two identified trends. In the case of surface segmentation, the new design moved from a line to a two-dimensional curve. As for the geometric evolution of linear constructions trend, the team calculated that it could move from a surface with two-dimensional protrusions to one that displays three-dimensional protrusions.

These evolutionary steps are depicted in Exhibit 16.7 relative to the space occupied by existing solutions at the time. The additionally shaded area shows the planned extent of evolutionary expansion.

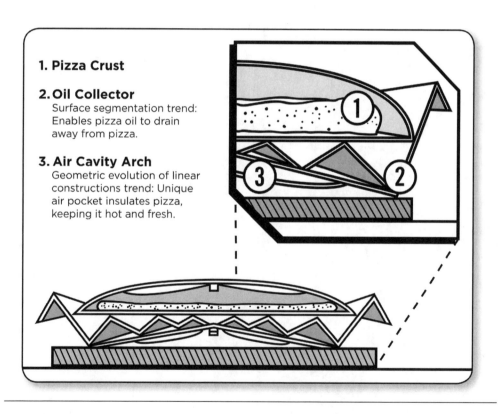

1. Pizza Crust

2. Oil Collector
Surface segmentation trend: Enables pizza oil to drain away from pizza.

3. Air Cavity Arch
Geometric evolution of linear constructions trend: Unique air pocket insulates pizza, keeping it hot and fresh.

EXHIBIT 16.8   New Pizza Box (U.S. Patent Number 5,472,139).

Traditionally, the pizza oils soak into the box and tend to cool the pizza off and make it soggy. Looking at the two identified trends, the scientists innovated a new, arched box bottom with air pockets. This created an insulation barrier and enabled oils to drain away from the pizza, thus meeting the expectation for *hot and crisp* better than any existing solution. Exhibit 16.8 shows the newly designed pizza box and its innovative elements.

Creative Challenge

Sacrifice the sacred cows.

The goal of creative challenge is to question the current solution for a particular job to be done (JTBD). If you think about it, the world is full of solutions that challenge the status quo. Electronic airline tickets are quickly replacing traditional paper tickets. E-mail and Internet marketing are threatening to usurp direct mail. Downloadable MP3s are making CDs unnecessary, just as CDs made cassettes and albums obsolete.

Creative challenge helps you investigate the necessity, validity, and uniqueness of the current solution or approach. As such, this technique can be extremely helpful during the idea-generation phase of your innovation project—and can give you the impetus you need to discard your current solutions in favor of ones that are more ideal.

Background

Creative challenge is not a rapid-fire brainstorming technique. Rather, it leverages a different approach called *E/R/A:*

- *E:* Can we *eliminate* some element of the current approach?
- *R:* What are the *reasons* for the current approach?
- *A:* Are there *alternatives* to the current approach?

Using E/R/A, you challenge the reigning beliefs, assumptions, and limitations relative to the status quo to create a list of innovative ideas that will increase your innovation's Value Quotient (see Technique 4).

125

You can follow up creative challenge with Functional Analysis (Technique 15) to improve insufficient functions or eliminate undesirable ones.

Steps

Scenario: Credit cards are arguably easier to carry and safer to use than cash, but they can still be lost or used by unauthorized parties. As a result, credit card lenders have accumulated millions of dollars in fraudulent charges, and consumers are at great risk of identity theft. But what if credit card lenders challenged the status quo in search of a new, fraud-free method of payment? Let's see how creative challenge could help them accomplish this job.

1. Select a Focus Topic

This can be an innovation opportunity, product, service, system, process, or business model. It can be anything you want to change or challenge. For our example, the goal is to create a type of credit that is easy to use but virtually impossible for identity thieves to steal.

You can creatively challenge any part of a process or system. Some hotels, for instance, now ask guests to reuse their towels rather than replacing them every day. The hotels didn't challenge the entire maid service, but just the part that uses excessive water and energy.

2. Investigate Current Solution

Create a SIPOC and/or Process Map (Techniques 50 and 51) to document the current solution's inputs, outputs, customers, and suppliers, and any associated processes. Use this information to make a list of the process steps, systems, subsystems, or components that are linked to the focus topic. For example, part of the process of using a credit card is carrying a physical card, which can be lost or stolen and subsequently used by identity thieves.

3. Identify Assumptions

Add to the list from step 2 all assumptions you take for granted about the current solution. Include factual data, physical characteristics, supporting ideas or philosophies, and limitations of the current solution. For the credit card example, some of our assumptions include:

- All credit cards are plastic, sized 85.60 × 53.98 mm, and have a magnetic strip or chip that holds data.
- Credit cards can be used in person, over the phone, or on the Internet to pay for goods and services.
- Consumers expect to have multiple credit cards, and to carry balances on more than one credit account.
- Extending credit must remain profitable for credit lenders.

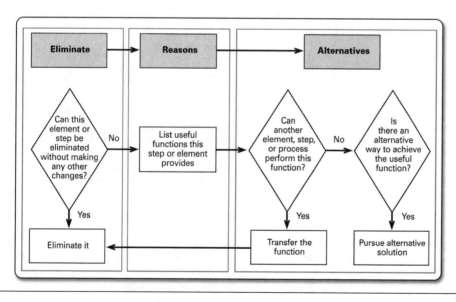

EXHIBIT 17.1   E/R/A Challenge Process.

Creative challenge is never an attack or criticism, but a method that questions current thinking to discover new ideas and directions.

4. Apply E/R/A

Apply the E/R/A challenge process (Exhibit 17.1) to each item on the list:

- *Eliminate:* Challenge the necessity of each process step, element, or assumption. Is it still necessary, or can it be eliminated without incurring any negative side effects?
- *Reason:* If the step, element, or assumption is necessary, what function or feature does it provide?

Process Step, Element, or Assumption	Eliminate Can this item be easily eliminated without negative consequences?	Reason Why can't we eliminate this item? What is the function or feature it provides?	Alternatives Are there alternative ways to provide this function or feature?
Credit cards must be carried with you in order to make purchases in person.	No	Credit card possession, and signature on card and receipt used to verify authorized use.	Use retinal scan, fingerprint, or smartphone application to verify identity and availability of funds in credit account.
Credit cards are plastic, sized 85.60 x 53.98 mm, and have a magnetic strip or chip that holds data.	No	Industry standard.	RFID chip in keychain or other small device (like smartphone) that securely carries credit account information.
Credit cards can be used in person, over the phone or on the Internet to pay for goods/services.	No	Easier to carry and use than alternative forms of payment (cash, checks).	Use smartphone application to charge items to account.
Consumers expect to have multiple credit cards and to carry balances on more than one credit account.	No	Lenders only extend a certain amount of credit per person to spread default risk across multiple borrowers.	Assign everyone a single credit account at birth, funded jointly by multiple lenders.
Extending credit must remain profitable for lenders.	No	It's a business.	Government-run, non-profit lending.

EXHIBIT 17.2 Creative Challenge Matrix (Downloadable).

- *Alternatives:* Challenge the uniqueness of the solution. Is this the only way to provide the needed feature/functionality, or are there alternatives?

Use a creative challenge matrix (Exhibit 17.2) to track your ideas and decisions for each item.

Never assume the current way is the only way. If you do, you'll never innovate a thing.

---

5. Compile Alternatives

After the E/R/A challenge process, make a list of the alternative ideas that you want to investigate further.

HIT Matrix

Compare existing solutions to spark new breakthroughs.

A HIT matrix compares the characteristics of two seemingly unrelated products or services to develop new ideas. What do you get when you combine the characteristics of a high-speed, wide-bandwidth Internet connection with a very high-definition viewing and audio device? Taking other characteristics into consideration (such as fiber optic cable, a boosted wireless signal, and high-quality earphones), you can get an awesome movie watching experience anywhere in your home.

HIT, short for Heuristic Ideation Technique, was developed by marketing professor Edward M. Tauber, who found that *new* products are typically a combination of characteristics from two or more *existing* products. HIT matrix is a simple but beneficial tool to jump-start your team's creativity in search of innovative ideas.

Steps

Scenario: In the very competitive travel industry, most businesses target a high volume of low-paying customers through cheap, no-frills service. However, Innovative Railways hopes to catch the attention of fewer, high-paying customers by offering a luxury experience for mid-distance business travelers. A HIT matrix will help Innovative Railways develop ideas for an innovative solution that fulfills customer expectations.

1. Select Existing Items

Choose two products, services, or brands that seem to have no apparent connection and are not already overtly combined. These could be offerings from your company, or from a competitor or another industry. Avoid items that are too close in meaning; coffee cup and drinking glass will produce fewer innovative ideas than drinking glass and bicycle (think CamelBak). The Innovative Railways team chose *luxury conference services* and *international first class travel*.

The opposite of heuristic ideation is *backward ideation,* which looks at the characteristics of *unsuccessful* products and brands to generate new ideas and solutions. For more information, use a Google search to see "Backward Ideation Technique for Generating New Product Ideas," by O. A. Mascarenhas, *Vikalpa* 8, no. 2 (1983).

---

2. List Characteristics

Brainstorm a list of characteristics related to the two items you selected in step 1. Ask yourself what the features or components are that make up the item. Also how, when, and why is the item used? Generate the same number of characteristics for each item (typically five to seven per item). If you have too many characteristics, use a Pugh Matrix (Technique 40) to narrow down the list.

Don't get too granular in your thinking. For example, if you're listing the features of a first-class airplane seat, some characteristics might be *ample legroom* or *reclines to a bed*. This leaves more opportunity for creativity than specifying that the seat has 10 inches more legroom than a coach class seat, or that the seat reclines to a 160-degree angle.

You don't have to be an expert on the items you select. However, it is important to understand the customer expectations associated with each item. For more information, see Outcome Expectations (Technique 3).

HIT Matrix		Luxury Conference Accomodations				
		Wireless Access	Spa Services	Personal Chef	Dedicated Concierge	Executive Lounge
International First Class Travel	Reclining Seats	Wireless Access Reclining Seats	Spa Services Reclining Seats	Personal Chef Reclining Seats	Dedicated Concierge Reclining Seats	Executive Lounge Reclining Seats
	In-Seat Chargers	Wireless Access In-Seat Chargers	Spa Services In-Seat Chargers	Personal Chef In-Seat Chargers	Dedicated Concierge In-Seat Chargers	Executive Lounge In-Seat Chargers
	Gourmet Meals	Wireless Access Gourmet Meals	Spa Services Gourmet Meals	Personal Chef Gourmet Meals	Dedicated Concierge Gourmet Meals	Executive Lounge Gourmet Meals
	Personal Attention	Wireless Access Personal Attention	Spa Services Personal Attention	Personal Chef Personal Attention	Dedicated Concierge Personal Attention	Executive Lounge Personal Attention
	Expedited Service	Wireless Access Expedited Service	Spa Services Expedited Service	Personal Chef Expedited Service	Dedicated Concierge Expedited Service	Executive Lounge Expedited Service

EXHIBIT 18.1 HIT Matrix (Downloadable).

Copyright © 2012, BMGI. A blank version of this customized form is available for download at www .innovatorstoolkit.com.

3. Populate HIT Matrix

In a HIT Matrix (Exhibit 18.1), list the characteristics from one item across the top, and the characteristics from the other item down the side. Then, pair one characteristic from each item until all cells are filled. In our example, we have the characteristics of luxury conference services (top) and international first class travel (side).

4. Qualify Ideas

Review each cell in the matrix and discuss the merits of joining the two characteristics. Eliminate cells that contain existing ideas or don't make sense (such as *spa services* and *in-seat chargers*). However, don't immediately discard ideas because they contain technical or physical contradictions; you may be able to get past the contradictions using Structured Abstraction (Technique 26) or Separation Principles (Technique 27).

5. Select Ideas

Identify all the paired characteristics that could become a potential solution. For instance, *personal chef* and *gourmet food* has potential, as does *dedicated concierge* and *personal attention*. Also, look for ideas that combine more than one characteristic, such as *executive lounge, wireless access, in-seat chargers,* and *personal attention*. Make a list of ideas for further exploration.

SCAMPER

Ask eight important questions.

The SCAMPER technique uses a set of directed questions to help you evolve your existing product, service, or solution into one that is superior (more ideal). For example, SCAMPER led to the combining of two shaving solution elements—the razor and the shaving cream—into a razor that holds cream in its handle and dispenses it as a person shaves. SCAMPER is most powerful when you have an idea or set of ideas, and you need to make them even better. It is especially helpful in mature markets where there are many competing solutions.

The SCAMPER acronym stands for:
- **S**ubstitute
- **C**ombine
- **A**dapt
- **M**odify/Mirror/Distort
- **P**ut to other purposes
- **E**liminate
- **R**earrange/Reverse

Steps

Scenario: A team was tasked with innovating the sales approach in an organization with 50 locations, keeping each abreast of the company's latest

133

products, technologies, policies, and procedures. The existing approach was to perform on-site training at each location once a quarter using several trainers. The team used the SCAMPER technique to generate ideas for improving the knowledge-transfer process.

1. Define the Job to be Done

Before you use this tool, it's best to make sure you have clarity on how the current process or product is used to achieve the job to be done (JTBD). Articulate the JTBD and the current approach for delivering its solution. Remind the team to stay focused on the JTBD, so that innovative solutions (with higher value quotients) can be generated, not just incremental improvements to current solutions. (For more information, see the Jobs to be Done, Outcome Expectations, and Value Quotient, Techniques 1, 3, and 4 respectively.)

Another variation of SCAMPER is SCAMMPERR (the double M to indicate Magnify and Minify and the double R to indicate Reverse and Rearrange).

---

2. Apply SCAMPER

As a group, discuss the SCAMPER questions one at a time, and list the team's ideas. Keep these tips in mind:

- Involve team members by using the simple rule of one idea per person per question.
- Use the questions as a trigger to generate ideas and don't get bogged down in answering each question. No one should criticize ideas or evaluate ideas during the exercise.
- It's not important that the ideas are associated directly with the question that originated the idea.
- Ideas may be repeated if they fit with several questions.

Exhibit 19.1 shows the ideas the team came up with for improving the sales training process.

S	Substitute	Think about substituting part of your product / service or process for something else. By looking for something to substitute, you can often come up with new ideas. **Typical questions:** What can I substitute to make an improvement? What if I swap this for that and see what happens? How can I substitute the place, time, materials or people? **Example:** Online training, chat sessions with the trainer, conference (video, audio), computer-based training, library (eLibrary, physical library), self study by employee, on-the-job training, recorded classroom (available 24/7, divided into slots, Anyone can attend any module twice, group discussion, mail-based training.
C	Combine	Think about combining two or more parts of your problem to create a different product / process or to enhance synergy. **Typical questions:** What materials, features, processes, people, products, or components can I combine? Where can I build synergy? **Example:** Combine classroom training with on-the-job training, library studies and trainer / conferences, self study and online trainer / conferences, combine locations (reduce number of locations), combine induction and training wherever possible, combine work with training, mix people (trained and untrained) then trained people will train untrained people.
A	Adapt	Think about which parts of the product / service or process could be adapted to remove the problem, or think how you could change the nature of the product / processes. **Typical questions:** What part of the product can I change? And in exchange for what? What if I were to change the characteristics of a component? **Example:** Notes change between participants, convert training material to drawings / flip charts, mix people (trained and untrained) - then trained people will train untrained people, video of one-training / one -trainer then replicate and distribute (reuse).
M	Modify	Think about changing all or part of the current solution to distort it in an unusual way. By forcing yourself to come up with new ways of working, you are often prompted into an alternative product, service, or process. **Typical questions:** What happens if I warp or exaggerate a feature or component? What will happen if I modify the process in some way? **Example:** Change training delivery media, classroom to computer-based training, classroom to audio / video training, on-the-job training, change mode of training, paper / pencil to web-based learning, reduce locations of training, increase batch size, intensive training, anytime training.
P	Put to other purposes	Think of how you might be able to put your current solution to other purposes, or think of what you could reuse from somewhere to solve your innovation problem. You might think of another way to meet your Job To Be Done or find another market for your product. **Typical questions:** What other market could I use this product in? Who or what else might be able to use it? **Example:** Use training material as reference in library, training in auditorium, training in movie / drama format, training in game / puzzle format, part training to set of people - then each set becomes internal trainer for the part it learned and trains others.
E	Eliminate	Think of what might happen if you eliminated various parts of the product / process / problem, and consider what you might do in that situation. This often leads you to consider different ways of tackling the problem. **Typical questions:** What would happen if I removed a component or part of it? How else would I achieve the solution without the normal way of doing it? **Example:** No classroom, training without classroom, no trainer, virtual trainer, eliminate time constraint, anytime training, video of one-training / one-trainer reuse - replicate the same.
R	Reverse	Think of what you would do if part of your problem / product / process worked in reverse or was done in a different order. What would you do if you had to do it in reverse? **Typical questions:** What if I did it the other way around? What if I reverse the order it is done or the way it is used? How would I achieve the opposite effect? **Example:** Learner is trainer, create trainer, create library, prepare training and trainer in-house.

EXHIBIT 19.1 SCAMPER Guidelines and Example (Innovate the Sales Approach) (Downloadable).

3. Review Ideas

Once the team has completed ideating after all the questions, review the list for duplications. Combine similar ideas, but don't discard any at this point. You can use a technique such as KJ Method (Technique 30) or Idea Sorting and Refinement (Technique 31) to select the very best ideas for further development.

Resource

Michalko, M. *Thinkertoys: A Handbook on Creative-Thinking Techniques*, 2nd ed. Berkeley, CA: Ten Speed Press, 2006.

Brainwriting 6-3-5

Encourage equal opportunity ideation.

Brainwriting 6-3-5 is a modified form of classic brainstorming that encourages equal participation from all team members using written rather than verbal idea generation. For instance, if half of your team wants to launch a new product line and the other half is resistant, brainwriting 6-3-5 would give team members a chance to express their ideas without commentary or criticism.

This technique is particularly helpful when the group is in danger of domination by certain participants, or when team members may hold back because of the group makeup. However, if you're looking for more outside-the-box ideas, other ideation techniques may be more powerful, such as Provocation and Movement (Technique 24) or Creative Challenge (Technique 17).

The name *brainwriting 6-3-5* comes from the practice of *six* people writing down *three* ideas in *five* minutes. In reality, the tool works fine with a slightly larger or smaller number of people.

Steps

Scenario: Say you have a website where customers can register for your company's online training courses. One problem you've noted is that 35 percent of the people who begin the registration process fail to complete it before leaving the site. Your team can use brainwriting 6-3-5 to list possible reasons for this behavior and discover ideas to alleviate it.

1. Choose Participants

If you have more than eight people, split them into equally divided groups. If you have less than four participants, use a different idea-generation approach such as Imaginary Brainstorming (Technique 21) or Random Stimulus (Technique 23). Either way, select a mixed team that includes people who are familiar with the issue at hand as well as outsiders who can promote a new perspective.

If there are tensions within the group, you can use brainwriting 6-3-5 to diffuse the emotional situation and encourage participation.

2. Generate Ideas—Round 1

Distribute a brainwriting 6-3-5 worksheet (see Exhibit 20.1) to each participant. In the first row of the worksheet, participants should write three potential ideas that might fulfill the job to be done (JTBD). Each person takes five minutes to write their ideas in silence (although it may take less time during the first few rounds). Remind team members to write legibly so that others can read their contributions.

Remember that brainwriting is conducted in silence, so no talking is allowed until all ideas have been recorded. This allows participants to interpret other ideas solely from what is recorded on the worksheet.

3. Generate Ideas—Round 2

When everyone completes three ideas, the worksheets are passed to the next person who can add three new ideas or build on the ideas listed. Either way, new responses should be written in the second row. Again, the allotted time is five minutes.

Instead of passing the sheets in a circle, participants can put completed sheets in the center of the table, and team members can pull from the center stack at their own pace.

Job to be Done: Reduce number of booking transactions not completed on our website		Date: 30-Oct-2013
		Team: 1
		Member: Elizabeth

1	2	3
Provide login before starting the process so customer can restart at the appropriate point.	Provide paper catalog with quick codes to identify course and use with client profile to make booking.	Send automated e-mail to find out why transaction wasn't completed and offer help.
Store user details locally so the system recognizes them.	Make website search function more accurate and user friendly.	Follow up with phone call on incomplete transactions.
Allow multiple customers to book the same course with minimum effort.	Allow customers to amend their course selection details rather than having to start again.	Provide a way to hold course bookings for 24 hours until payment is made.
Reduce the number of fields customers must complete.	Make website easier to use.	Provide customers with incentives (bonus materials or special pricing).
Allow customers to book multiple courses during the same transaction.	Simplify online ordering process.	Give discounts for bookings completed with a single transaction.
Provide user with booking history and list of incomplete transactions when they login.	Add a pop-up window to alert users that they are closing the browser without completing the transaction.	Recommend courses based on the user profile.

EXHIBIT 20.1 Brainwriting 6-3-5 (Downloadable).

Copyright © 2012, BMGI. A blank version of this customized form is available for download at www .innovatorstoolkit.com.

4. Continue Idea Generation

Repeat the idea generation cycle until every participant has written three ideas on every worksheet. If your team has six people, you should have generated 108 ideas. You can take time now to discuss, clarify, refine, and combine similar ideas, then make a list of ideas for further analysis using other Discover techniques.

Imaginary Brainstorming

Get silly for the sake of creativity.

Imaginary brainstorming helps distance you from practicalities that may be hindering your creativity. Say you are trying to *gain market share in Southeast Asia.* With imaginary brainstorming, you could replace *market share* with *exotic animals* and concentrate instead on *gaining exotic animals in Southeast Asia.* After brainstorming solutions for this imaginary scenario, you would come full circle and retrofit the resulting ideas to the original problem.

When you're struggling to develop innovative ideas around a particular area, imaginary brainstorming encourages a fun atmosphere where wild and crazy ideas can be put forward, and people can participate without intimately understanding the technicalities of the problem.

If you conduct classic brainstorming before imaginary brainstorming, you'll identify the most obvious and common ideas. Then you can encourage the team to go beyond these ideas during imaginary brainstorming.

Steps

Scenario: Pretend you're a professor in the history department of a local college. You and your colleagues are having difficulty getting students to submit their assignments on time. It's a topic at every weekly meeting, where the same ideas come up but never seem to work. Let's see how imaginary brainstorming can help your group generate new ideas for solving this dilemma.

1. Identify Real Problem Elements

Review the problem, or job to be done (JTBD), and identify the following key elements:

- What is happening? [action]
- Who or what is the recipient of the action? [object]
- Where is the action occurring/what is the scope? [context]
- Who is performing the action? [subject]

Looking at our history department example (persuade students to submit assignments on time), we can identify an action (persuade), an object (students), and a context (submit assignments on time). The subject (professors) is implied. Document your answers on an imaginary brainstorming worksheet (Exhibit 21.1).

2. Brainstorm Imaginary Elements

For each real element you identified in step 1, generate a few imaginary replacements. For instance, we could replace *students* with *gorillas, cyclists,* or *aliens. Submit assignments on time* could become *take out the trash* or *wash behind their ears.*

Classic brainstorming typically uncovers ideas near the surface of our consciousness. Imaginary brainstorming digs deeper by leveraging make-believe situations to trigger subconscious creativity.

---

3. Create an Imaginary Problem Statement (or JTBD)

Choose the *one* element you're having the most difficulty with and replace it to create an imaginary statement. In our example, we could replace *submit assignments on time* with an imaginary element and the problem becomes *get students to **wash behind their ears** on time.*

1. Real JTBD				
Persuade students to submit assignments on time				

2. Real Problem Elements			5. Imaginary Problem Ideas	6. Application to Real Problem
ACTION	What is happening?	Persuade	Have a public ear inspection	Call out students by name to hand over assignments in front of class
OBJECT	Who or what is the recipient of the action?	Students	Each student checks another students' ears for cleanliness	• Get students to complete assignments in groups • Have students "grade" each other's work
CONTEXT	Where is the action occuring and what is the scope?	Submit assignments on time	Provide attractive soap	• Start an assignments after school group in the school cafe with free refreshments • Reduce number of assignments
SUBJECT	Who is performing the action?	Professors	Have a clean ear competition	• Feature the best work in the school magazine • Have competitions aligned with specific assignments • Replace assignments with exams
3. Imaginary Elements			Provde awards to students that wash their ears regularly	• Give extra credit for work submitted on time
ACTION	What is happening?	Entertain, bribe, prevent	Show pictures of extremely dirty ears	Explain to students the consequences of not completing work (fail course, name posted on poor performing list in main hall)
OBJECT	Who or what is the recipient of the action?	Gorillas, cyclists, aliens	Provide synthetic examples of the smell and texture of dirty ears	Invite speakers who can show the value of a college education
CONTEXT	Where is the action occuring and what is the scope?	Take out the trash, wash behind their ears		
SUBJECT	Who is performing the action?	Singers, cats, soccer players		
4. Imaginary JTBD				
Persuade students to *wash behind their ears* on time				

EXHIBIT 21.1 Imaginary Brainstorming (Downloadable).

Only replace one element at a time so you can more readily translate your ideas back to the original problem statement, or JTBD.

4. Solve the Imaginary Problem

Now, brainstorm ways to solve the imaginary problem. For instance, if dirty ears were really an issue on campus you could *hold public ear inspections, provide scented soap in the bathrooms,* or *give awards to students with the cleanest ears.*

5. Apply Imaginary Ideas to the Real Problem

When you've thought of as many ideas as you can, try to relate each idea back to the original problem. It may help to sort your ideas into three categories:

1. Ideas that can be applied directly to the original problem without making any changes.
2. Ideas that need to be modified or altered before they are applied to the original problem.
3. Ideas that cannot be used or modified but may contain an element that could spark a new idea. Spend a few minutes on each idea no matter how unlikely it may seem.

If you don't end up with enough viable ideas, create another imaginary statement by replacing a different element and go through the steps again. Or, try another idea generation approach such as Creative Challenge (Technique 17) or Random Stimulus (Technique 23).

Concept Tree

Leverage current ideas to generate many ideas.

Concept tree starts with an idea and uses that idea to identify concepts, or connecting points, from which alternative ideas can be derived. For example, a perfume designer could explore the concept behind a new fragrance idea and subsequently create a way to naturally enhance a person's pheromones.

By using an existing idea as a source of inspiration for untapped ideas, concept tree can lead you to a unique approach to an old problem. It's also valuable if your original idea is too general, has too many limitations, or is not actionable.

Some call this technique a *concept fan,* or *concept abstraction and alternatives.* For more information, see "Generation of Alternatives" in *Lateral Thinking: Creativity Step by Step,* by E. de Bono (New York: Harper Paperbacks, 1973).

Steps

Scenario: Let's say we want to improve our company's image. We have a few broad ideas along these lines, but we can use the Concept Tree technique to generate many actionable ideas.

1. Agree on the Job to be Done

On a white board or flip chart, write the job to be done (JTBD). In our example, we are tasked with the rather broad job of improving the company's image. We could use Job Scoping (Technique 9) or Nine Windows

(Technique 8) to better define this job, but since we have a few general ideas for meeting this JTBD, let's see where the concept tree takes us.

2. List Ideas

Next, list your ideas for fulfilling the JTBD. So far in our example we have: *reduce environmental impact, give back to the community,* and *launch a PR campaign* (Exhibit 22.1).

Although the terms *idea* and *concept* are often used interchangeably, in the context of this technique they have different meanings. Concepts represent a general way of achieving your goal, while ideas are more specific and actionable.

3. Generate Concepts

For each original idea, brainstorm related but nonspecific concepts. Make sure that none of the concepts is the same as the original idea. For instance, if you're trying to *reduce environmental impact,* someone may suggest the concept of *going green,* which is really just another way of restating this idea.

4. Generate Alternative Ideas

For each concept you brainstormed, list new ideas that come to mind. This can be done in typical brainstorming fashion, but each idea must be related to a concept. If you need to add more concepts, do so. These, in turn, may generate new ideas.

Concepts are the connecting points between your original idea and the alternative ideas that the concept tree helps you generate.

5. Keep Going

Repeat steps 3 and 4 until the team runs out of concepts and ideas. If you started with more than one original idea (as in this example), don't forget to apply the concept tree to your other ideas. When you're finished, you should have a long list of ideas you can organize using a technique like KJ Method (Technique 30).

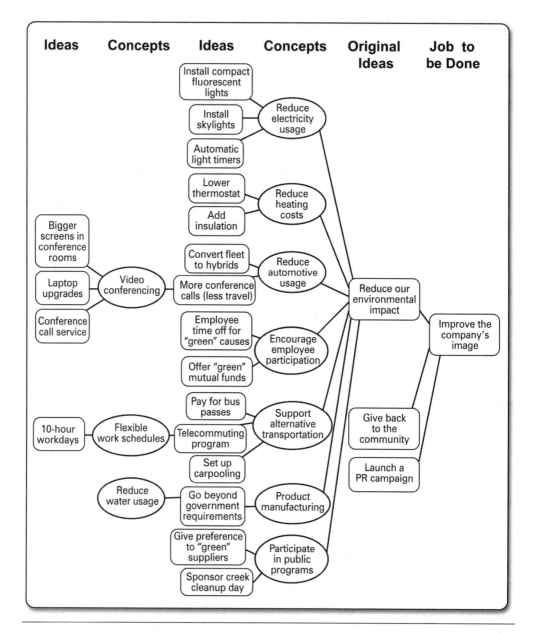

EXHIBIT 22.1 Concept Tree Format. In this example, we started with three general ideas for *improving the company's image.* Using the concept tree for only one of these ideas (*reduce environmental impact*), we generated 19 ideas that are more specific and actionable than our original ideas.

Random Stimulus

Use an unrelated picture or word to spawn new ideas.

During random stimulus, participants use free association in connection with an arbitrary word or image to generate new ideas. For example, looking at a picture of a racecar could bring to mind a racetrack, which in turn could help you think of a new way to desalinate water.

Techniques like random stimulus initially might seem too disconnected in the way they lead to new ideas, but this disconnection from one's mental inertia is exactly what is needed. Humans naturally establish logic patterns as they process information over time, so creative thinking actually becomes unnatural. The only way to spark it is to move away from these patterns, and using random stimulus is one way to do that.

A *random stimulus* can be any kind of signal—a word or image, even a sound or smell—that forces you to move your thoughts to a new place outside of your current focus and associations.

Steps

Scenario: Developing countries are increasing disposable income in more layers of society, and car companies are beginning to target this with new automobile offerings. Many of these offerings, such as the Tata Nano and the reintroduction of the Nissan Datsun brand, are designed for drivers with lower income levels. All of these new drivers are creating another opportunity in the marketplace—the need for car insurance.

1. Identify Jobs to be Done (JTBD) and Outcome Expectations

As a group, agree on the JTBD (see Technique 1) and any associated Outcome Expectations (see Technique 3). In our example, the job to be done is *insure an emerging population of low-income drivers in developing countries*. For this job, the desired customer expectations for the solution might include: *fast to buy and enact, simple to use (claims and service), lowest cost possible,* and *policy meets legal standards*. Undesired customer expectations might include *expensive policy with too many bells and whistles* and *waiting too long between when I buy a car to when I can drive it*.

On the provider side, desired outcome expectations include *obtaining new customer premiums* and *achieving higher customer satisfaction*. Undesired outcomes might be a *disproportional increase in accidents and claims, customers with risky driving habits,* and *customers who don't pay their premiums*.

These outcomes set the boundaries for the random stimulus idea-generation session.

You can use the Random Stimulus technique to generate solution ideas for a JTBD, or even for an outcome expectation (see Exhibit 23.3 for an example of the latter).

---

2. Select Random Stimulus

Choose a random word or image that is not directly related to the JTBD. If you select a word, choose a noun using one of these common methods (or a method of your own):

- Use a dictionary or thesaurus and randomly choose a page number and entry number (e.g., page 169 and entry 10, which would become your random word). Or, use a magazine or newspaper, randomly choosing a page number, paragraph, and word number.
- Refer to a random word list (Exhibit 23.1), choose a number, and then count down to that word on the list.

- You can also use random word generating software, such as the one at www.randomwordgenerator.com.

Use the list of 150 words in Exhibit 23.1 to spawn new and great ideas. But don't just pick your favorite word or image—randomness is key. The further the random stimulus is from the JTBD, the higher the chance of generating outside-the-box ideas.

If you want to use an *image,* choose one that clearly conveys an action and inspires positive emotions. Also, remember the following tips:

- Use real photos, preferably in color; color brings more emotions to mind. Don't use clip art or cartoons. These are already characterizations, and thus, may limit free association creativity.

- Avoid content that may be controversial, offensive, or depressing (e.g., pictures of war, nudity, funerals). Don't use embarrassing pictures of the participants.

- Good sources of photos are magazines and books on travel, movies, sports, current events, and nature.

---

tongue plastic wrench star gourmet money flashlight dice
windsurfer ribbon camera can pencil pin watermelon soda
tape necklace mold gutter jewel house gully fuel music
wastebasket X-ray cup paint lamb stomach rain telescope
knee pole champagne top beans angel student lips salmon
lungs gasoline tub fox chimney bikini prison tax igloo
fireplace ax smoke referee cork stream planet goldfish vines
bomb umbrella cone flood frog rib table chair towel window
locker toy podium saucer rainbow amoeba disk snail rice
grass fence horse shed leaves bird tractor Olympics straw
mirror chapter vacuum bread cyclone gravy emerald gang
pliers binoculars studio parakeet fingernail meadow bat curb
zipper gutter outlet elbow weeds paper wig road sauna cord
duck floor book announcer diaper cake flower sandwich lake
lightning candle crown jam fossil pet ruler circus plug coach
wallpaper ham envelope actor riot clay train television garage
stadium mold detective magazine medal refrigerator sonar car

EXHIBIT 23.1 Sample Random Word List.

For an automated random picture generator, visit www.brainstorming.co.uk/onlinetools/randompicture.html.

3. Brainstorm Associations

When you've chosen a random word or image, ask the team what associations the random stimulus brings to mind. We've picked the stimulus word *warehouse*, pulled from the front page of *The Wall Street Journal* on a specific day. This word, in turn, might be associated with the words *whistles*, *inventory*, *forklift*, *safety*, *radio frequency identification*, *distribution*, and *shelves*.

Record each association on a separate line radiating from the random word or image (Exhibit 23.2). Welcome every answer without judgment and without stopping to explore the idea further.

If you're using an image, ask participants what they see happening in the picture, as well as who, when, where, why, and how.

4. Generate Ideas

Discuss each association to determine how it could be realized as a tangible idea related to the JTBD (keeping the associated outcome expectations in mind). For instance, the association *forklift* might lead to the idea of bringing the insurer to the customer, meeting the desired customer outcome expectation, *fast to buy and enact*. Or the words *whistles*, *safety*, and *shelves* might spawn ideas and innovations around how the provider can avoid its undesired outcome expectation of getting stuck with customers who have *risky driving habits*.

It may seem difficult at first to see any connection between the association and the JTBD. The trick is to keep trying. In most cases someone will start the associations rolling, and such associations will eventually lead to innovative ideas. If not, choose another random stimulus and try again.

Of course, as much as possible, when engaged in the idea-generation part of random stimulus, strive to be creative and innovative. Bland, worn, or uncreative ideas that point to the past rather than to the future will surely defeat your purpose as an innovator.

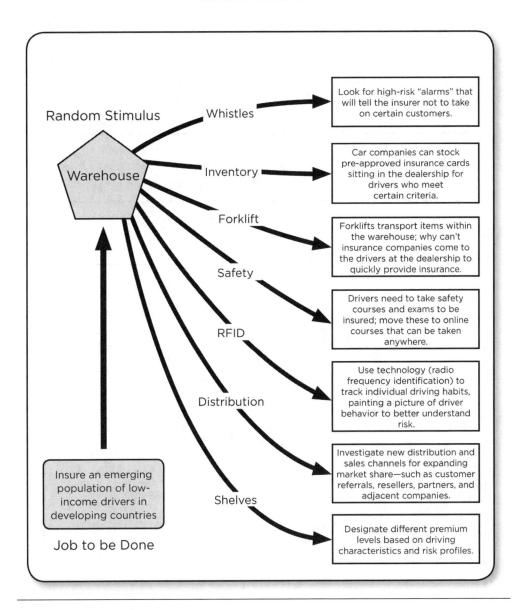

EXHIBIT 23.2   Random Stimulus Using a Word.

5. Review Ideas

When you're finished generating ideas, review the list. If you need additional ideas, repeat the steps with a different random stimulus. Or, try another idea generation technique such as Provocation and Movement (Technique 24).

Exhibit 23.3 shows another example of Random Stimulus using an image to generate new ideas for *minimize cost associated with activities,* which is an outcome expectation for the JTBD of *improve employee morale in operations.*

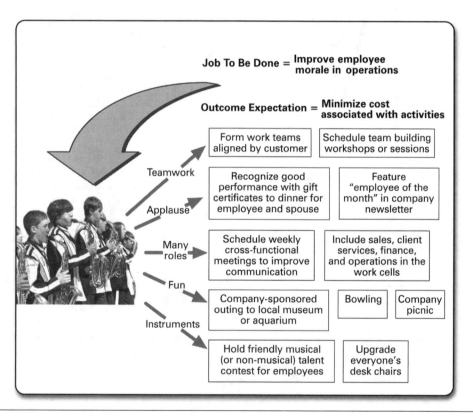

EXHIBIT 23.3   Random Stimulus Using an Image.

Provocation and Movement

Bust through the roadblocks in your thinking.

The overall idea of provocation and movement is to create a shocking statement that is strong enough to move people out of their *psychological inertia*—their tendency to think the way they've always thought. For example, "We need customers to generate revenue" is a statement one might take for granted. However, if we said, "We *don't* need customers to generate revenue," this provocation would certainly generate discussion that would point us in a different direction and generate new ideas.

As such, provocation and movement is one of the best tools for generating outside-the-box ideas—*if* you're open to questioning the status quo, imagining *what if*, and shocking yourself into a new reality.

Often, frustration is the initial force that creates a provocation and spurs movement toward a better product, service, or solution. The Diner's Club card, precursor to all credit cards, was born out of the frustration of always having to pay for a meal with cash. And no one should be surprised that, today, the world is making another huge evolution from conducting transactions with credit cards to conducting them with smart phones and tablet computers.

Steps

Scenario: The Private Pools company designs and builds Olympic-sized swimming pools for homeowners. Recently, the company has watched its profits plummet, thanks in part to an economic downturn in the housing

153

market. A cross-functional team hopes to use provocation and movement to discover an innovative way to expand the company's market share.

The goal of provocation and movement is to improve the satisfaction level of an outcome, or generate a solution that allows you to better fulfill a job to be done.

---

1. Select a Focus

Choose a focus topic—a product, service, process, or business model for which you need ideas. Make a list of the current features, characteristics, and aspects of the focus topic. To create the list, you can use brainstorming, or an approach like Creative Challenge (Technique 17).

If at first the idea is not absurd, then there is no hope for it.

—Albert Einstein

---

2. Create Reality Statement

Choose one item from the list of features and craft a statement that represents the current reality. Often, this statement reflects a poorly satisfied customer expectation, or a job the solution has trouble fulfilling. Or, it could be something taken for granted or rarely questioned. The Private Pools team, for example, chose the statement: *Private swimming pools require a large outdoor area.* Bypassing this traditional notion could extend the reach of the company's product to people who don't have large backyards, or who live in a climate with cold winters.

Provocation is the stepping stone that allows you to carve out useful ideas from illogical thoughts, while keeping an eye on your innovation's value quotient (see Value Quotient, Technique 4, for more on this concept).

---

3. Develop Provocation

Based on the current reality statement, generate several Provocative Thought (PT) statements that depart from the current reality in an unusual, fanciful, absurd, or otherwise illogical manner (Exhibit 24.1). Just remember to take this *provocation* at face value and suspend judgment. This is not the time to question the validity of the statements, or to block the free flow of radical creativity. In general, PT statements fall into four categories:

1. *Negation:* Counteracts the current reality with an opposite statement.
2. *Reversal:* Reverses the action of the current reality statement.
3. *Exaggeration:* Takes the current reality to an incredible or extreme state (in either direction).
4. *Dream:* Imagines how the current reality would be different *if only* ...

In psychological circles, extreme negation is considered a form of insanity (Cotard's syndrome). In the world of innovation, however, a little insanity can be a good thing if it leads you in the direction of never-before-imagined solutions for your job to be done.

---

4. Generate Ideas from Movement

The provocative thoughts you generated in step 3 should have the team thinking outside its normal frame of reference. The next step is to make these PT statements more realistic and feasible by applying one or more *movement* techniques to each statement. Movement techniques can be categorized as follows:

- *Moment to moment:* Visualize what would happen if the provocative thought were put into effect. For example, if every home in America had a swimming pool (Dream PT), then the market for pools would expand dramatically and the price would be significantly reduced. Correspondingly, the use of public pools would decrease.
- *Extract a concept:* Determine the concept behind the provocative thought and use this as the basis to generate new ideas. For instance, the team could use its Reversal PT (a large outdoor area requires a swimming pool) to extract the concept of building pools in large outdoor areas such as front yards, rooftops, and parks.
- *Focus on differences:* Make a list of differences between the provocative thought and the current reality. For instance, the differences between a private swimming pool and a bathtub (Exaggeration PT) include

Current Reality		Provocation		Movement	Ideas
Private swimming pools require a large outdoor area.	Negation	A private swimming pool does *not* require a large outdoor area.	Extract a Concept	Pools do not have to cover an area on the ground.	Develop a small pool with big pool functionality.
	Reversal	A large outdoor area requires a private swimming pool.	Extract a Concept	Build pools in large outdoor areas such as front yards, rooftops, and parks.	Create a "tube" of water to swim in.
	Exaggeration	A private swimming pool only requires as much space as a bathtub.	Focus on Differences	Outdoor vs. indoor Large area vs. small area Deep vs. shallow Standing water vs. flowing	Have a conversion kit to make a swimming pool an ice rink in winter. Design a water tub that allows for practice of specific strokes.
	Dream	What if every home in America had a private swimming pool?	Moment to Moment	Market for pools would expand dramatically; price would be significantly reduced; use of public pools would decrease.	Design roof pools.

EXHIBIT 24.1 Provocation and Movement (Downloadable).

Copyright © 2012, BMGI. A blank version of this customized form is available for download at www.innovatorstoolkit.com.

outdoor versus indoor, large area versus small, deep versus shallow, standing water versus flowing (from the faucet). One or more of these differences could lead the team to think about swimming pools in a completely new way.

Provocative thoughts will always sound impossible, stupid, crazy, or ridiculous if not attached to some operative movement that can achieve the proposed radical idea.

---

5. Review Ideas

As a result of applying movement to the PT statements, you should have a list of innovative ideas to explore further. Your ideas may be ready-made solutions. More than likely, however, provocation and movement may have pushed you to the boundaries of what is possible. In this case, you may need to leverage Structured Abstraction (Technique 26) or Separation Principles (Technique 27) to help you overcome any physical or technical contradictions inherent in your ideas.

Real Life Example

Dr. G. Venkataswamy (1918 to 2006) was an ophthalmologist and eye surgeon who committed his long and storied life to eradicating blindness (and deafness) in his home country, India. Just one way in which Dr. Venkataswamy made his dream a reality was to pioneer a new way of performing cataract surgery; he employed the principles of mass production and commoditization to drive the cost of surgery down from $300 in India to under $50. (The cost for cataract surgery in the United States is about $2,500).

To make such radical changes and perfect his system and methods, Dr. Venkataswamy constantly prodded and relentlessly challenged the assumptions, equipment, and procedures of the day. He was guided by only one question: How can we make critical eye care accessible to millions of impoverished people, most of whom make less than $2 per day?

The doctor provoked and jolted the status quo throughout the years, opening his first hospital (Aravind eye clinic) in 1977 with 30 beds. As of 2011,

Aravind's eye care facilities had served more than 32 million outpatients and performed 4 million surgeries through its eight hospitals (with 4,000 beds total), 40 vision centers in rural areas, and seven community eye clinics.

In fiscal year 2011 alone, the Aravind system handled more than 2.6 million outpatient visits and performed an estimated 300,000 surgeries.

We shouldn't be surprised that the Aravind model is the target of examination for healthcare authorities and systems around the world. What if we could similarly commoditize some, most, or all healthcare and surgical procedures across the board? For starters, some are already developing an alternative to complex, high-cost operations like heart bypass surgery; while the typical U.S. cost for such a procedure is around $50,000, the equivalent in India is $2,000.

Resource

For more on the provocation and movement approach, see:

deBono, E. *Serious Creativity Using the Power of Lateral Thinking to Create New Ideas*. New York: HarperBusiness, 1993.

Forced Association

Hone in on solutions from other industries.

Forced association encourages you to escape the current paradigm—whether that is today's product, your own industry, or your own problem-solving approach—and discover solutions from seemingly unrelated fields.

Some of the most significant advancements in history have come as a result of learning from and applying solutions from other industries. For example, in the mid-1400s, the last critical component of the mass printing press—the part that transfers the image from the metal type to the paper—was adapted from the winemaking industry's wine press.

To expand your perspective, you can immerse yourself in a variety of industries, disciplines, hobbies, and cultures (such as volunteering in a hospital or working abroad in a new culture). You can build a team with a collective makeup that gives you a broader reach across multiple industries and viewpoints. Or, you can use forced association to proactively push yourself and your team outside of your paradigm to find an instance where your problem has been solved before.

The success of open innovation communities such as NineSigma, InnoCentive, and AlliedMindStorm.com demonstrate the value of going outside your industry to find the missing link you need to solve your own innovation problem.

Steps

Scenario: A dairy farm in Eastvale, California, is experiencing increased demand for their number two product: fertilizer (courtesy of the farm's dairy cows). The only problem is that the untreated fertilizer contains significant water content, making it heavier to ship and unattractive to buyers since it's not ready to apply. The farmers need to find a way to remove excess water and moisture from the fertilizer.

EXHIBIT 25.1 Holstein cows at a dairy farm in Eastvale, California, graze during the day on feed designed to keep them healthy so they can produce more quality milk. Their waste is used for fertilizer on the farm and sold on the market for other agriculture and landscaping needs.

1. Identify the Problem

The first step is to agree on the problem you're trying to solve. In the dairy farm example, the farmers identified the need to *remove excess water and moisture from the fertilizer.*

2. Abstract the Core Function

To prepare a problem for forced association, you must abstract the core function from the problem. In other words, you must simplify and remove any industry jargon from the problem statement so you can focus on the function only. For example, the dairy farmers could make their problem more generic by removing the words *excess* and *moisture* and replacing *fertilizer* with *a substance*. Thus, the simplified problem statement would be *remove water from a substance.*

Other examples include:

Specific problem: Prevent ink from drying out in inkjet cartridges.

Generic problem: Prevent liquid from evaporating.

Specific problem: Produce an inexpensive, lightweight, and comfortable clothing material that is impervious to damage (wear and tear, holes, rips, snags, etc.).

Generic problem: Make a lightweight yet strong substance.

Specific problem: Design a sprinkler system that senses when the ground is dry and automatically turns itself on.

Generic problem: Measure moisture level and activate or deactivate a system.

Specific problem: Reduce cooling fan noise in personal computers.

Generic problem: Reduce noise associated with working parts.

3. Reference a Function Database or Function Benchmark

If the problem is non-technical, then ask who is good at this generic process. If the problem is technical, you can use a function database, such as is found at http://function.creax.com, to find known solutions to your technical problem. You may need to further simplify the problem statement for the software.

The dairy farmers selected a function of *remove* and a form of *liquid*, and the database returned more than a dozen methods by which water can be removed from a substance—including centrifuge, distillation, electrostatics, hydrophilics, osmosis, and resonance. Each of these methods can be applied back to the problem to determine whether it might be applicable in finding a solution.

4. Investigate Solutions from Other Industries

The goal of forced association is to investigate the methods that other industries have used to solve the problem at hand. If the problem is technical and the function database (step 3) provided some possible approaches, you can use these methods to help you target industries where they're employed. When it comes to our dairy farmers removing water from a substance, their list of other industries where this problem was solved included the following:

- During baseball games on rainy days, the grounds crew has to remove water from the field. There are two ways this is accomplished. First, they try to prevent moisture from accumulating by covering the field with a tarp. Second, they dry the excess moisture by adding absorbing clay to the soil and using roller squeegees in the outfield.

- The Dyson Airblade hand dryer uses two extremely small openings that blow air up to 400 miles per hour onto your hands, drying them in about 12 seconds. (www.dysonairblade.com/technology/dysontech.asp)

- Juice producers have developed a process for frozen concentrate that removes most of the moisture or water content from the juice. One of the main ways of removing water from the juice is the use of hydrophilic compounds, literally meaning *water-loving*.

- A wet Chihuahua shakes itself vigorously to fling the water from its fur as soon as it gets out of a bath or comes inside from the rain.

The Forced Association technique strives, as does Structured Abstraction (Technique 26), to find solutions outside one's familiar knowledge domain. If your problem isn't highly technical in nature, try forced association first. If it is, you may be better off starting with structured abstraction. Or, look to nature for a solution (See Biomimicry, Technique 29).

---

5. Explore Analogous Solutions for Applicability

After completing steps 3 and 4, you should have a comprehensive list of potential solutions to your problem. Now, the problem-solving team can rely on its industry expertise and determine how feasible each solution might be for the problem at hand.

In our example, the dairy farmers discovered several ideas from other industries that might hold the key to helping them remove excess moisture and water from fertilizer:

- Covering the area with a tarp
- Applying absorbing clay
- Using roller squeegees
- Blowing air at high speed
- Adding hydrophilic compounds
- Shaking furiously

The tarp is not applicable because the moisture is inherent in the fertilizer, and feeding the cows absorbing clay seems like an unlikely solution. Blowing high-speed air at the fertilizer will make quite a mess, and while shaking the manure in some sort of container might be feasible, this would require a capital investment.

However, the roller squeegee idea and the hydrophilic compound solutions seem to be analogous, and the farmers believe they would be relatively simple and low-cost to attempt. In the end, the dairy farmers applied the hydrophilic compound solution from the orange juice industry and were happy with the results.

Additional Example

In the late 90s, General Motors management was tasked with the responsibility to cut warranty costs by a billion dollars. GM noticed that they incur a large amount of warranty cost when mistakes are introduced accidentally into vehicles during new vehicle launch. It took GM 70 days to catch these accidentally introduced errors. To generate a breakthrough solution, GM asked: Who is best at catching errors that are accidentally introduced? They noticed that the Centers for Disease Control and Prevention (CDC) often can find the root cause of food poisoning within 72 hours. By studying the process used by CDC in Atlanta, and by using analogy, GM generated multiple ideas to solve their problem.

Structured Abstraction

Guide your innovation using 40 proven principles.

Structured abstraction is used to resolve a *technical contradiction*—two variables that are in conflict with each other. For example, you want to produce a car with more horsepower (A), but doing so entails a loss of fuel efficiency (B). You want to improve critical system factor A, but the actions involved in doing that cause factor B to degrade, and you need to avoid the trade-off.

The Structured Abstraction technique comes in handy when you've identified a functional contradiction that stands in the way of an innovation—and when other ideation techniques have fallen short. Because structured abstraction is deeply grounded in science, engineering, and the Theory of Inventive Problem Solving (TRIZ), it's best to seek the help of an expert when using this technique.

You'll also need a copy of the book *Matrix 2003: Updating the TRIZ Contradiction Matrix* to apply this technique. See the Resources at the end of this chapter for specifics about where to get the book.

Although this technique has been available and used for about 50 years, none of its inventors gave it a formal name. Most in the TRIZ field refer to this technique as the *contradiction matrix,* because the matrix is where all the research comes together and is displayed for use by innovators. We obviously prefer the name *structured abstraction* because it gets to the heart of what the innovator is doing as he or she applies this technique: engaging in abstract thought within a structured framework and process.

Background

TRIZ was conceived and developed by Russian scientists and engineers starting in 1946, and to this day, continues its evolution and influence in business. Because TRIZ is based on empirical research (global patent databases), we could say that a die-hard TRIZ practitioner would advise any worrisome innovator to *relax*. More than 90 percent of all innovation problems that engineers face have been solved at least in some industry at some time in some place.

But the nearly impossible difficulty is in filtering through the millions of inventions and innovations to discover who's had a problem, or problems, similar to yours in the past (there are millions of registered patents in the world). Then, even if you could somehow find patented inventions that solved a problem or problems similar to yours, how would you characterize the solutions in a way that could help you solve your specific problem in your specific field?

The Origin of TRIZ and Structured Abstraction

These same questions fueled extensive research in Russia, spearheaded by one Genrich Altshuller, the father of TRIZ who, along with mostly other Russian cohorts, spent about three decades sifting through, analyzing, and categorizing the world's database of about 2 million patents at the time (late 1940s to late 1970s). Thanks to this great effort, innovators have been using structured abstraction and other TRIZ tools to better understand and greatly expedite the innovation process.

The reader of this chapter should know that we're deviating from many decades of classic TRIZ by presenting an important (and arguably overdue) evolution based on the extensive work of Darrell Mann and his research organization in the U.K. This evolution entails changing the way certain *problem parameters* are worded, the grouping and sequence in which the problem parameters are presented in the contradiction matrix, and the addition of nine new problem parameters. (Read the Steps section below for complete clarification of the terms, *problem parameters*, and *contradiction matrix*.)

Here's how the technique was developed and set up from the outset. The early researchers sifted through the world's patents, examining them for the technical contradictions they solved. In doing so, they were able to identify 39 generic problem parameters, or *conflict parameters*—harmful or useful features of the technical contradictions at hand.

With this work accomplished, the early researchers also developed the *40 inventive principles*. Short and succinct—but extremely powerful—one or more of these 40 principles underlie the millions of resolved technical contradictions in our world that innovators quickly patent to protect their solutions from competitors.

Exhibit 26.1 shows an overview of the structured abstraction problem-solving process by which one moves from a specific technical contradiction at hand (innovation problem) to a generic contradiction; then, using the contradiction matrix, an innovator can identify the generic inventive principles that are likely to solve the specific problem. With further creative brainstorming, development work, and highly guided trial and error, a specific innovative solution can be found for the specific technical contradiction.

Recent Developments

While Structured Abstraction has informed and helped countless innovators over the past 50 years, *the system was still incomplete*. There were many cells (well over 200 out of 1,482) in the contradiction matrix (a very large

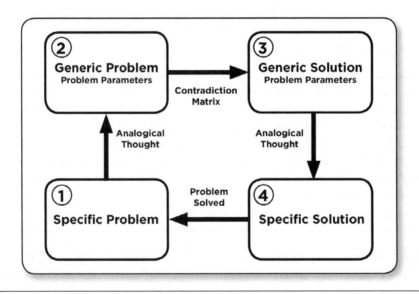

EXHIBIT 26.1 Problem-Solving Algorithm.

spreadsheet) where no inventive principles emerged as reliably helpful, leaving the innovator where he or she doesn't want to be: in the dark. If this paragraph sounds like Greek to you, it will become much clearer as you read on through the Steps portion further on.

You might not be surprised to know that structured abstraction is becoming customized for certain sectors, like software development, in an effort to achieve innovation simplicity and greater problem-solving efficacy. Some corporations have developed their own customized lists of problem parameters, essentially removing certain parameters that aren't relevant to the type of environment in which the corporation operates. (Think law firm or bank versus R&D organization for a chemical company).

From 2000 to 2003, a group of researchers led by Darrell Mann in the United Kingdom examined 150,000 patents, all dated after 1985 (Darrell Mann, Simon Dewulf, Boris Zlotin, and Alla Zusman). In doing so, they solved the problem of the empty cells in the classic contradiction matrix (no inventive principles in the spreadsheet cells for certain cross-referenced problem parameters).

As an explanation for why such gaps or invention holes existed with which to begin, Mann offers this:

> ... it is evident from the original contradiction matrix—and specifically the *Amount of information* parameter (for which the matrix contains many blank entries)—that the growth of the matrix is a story of a gradually unfolding world of innovation in which new parameters become important in the design process. Issues like safety, noise, and environmental factors, for example, are considered to be much more important today than they were during the 1970s.
>
> —"Updating the Contradiction Matrix," by Darrell Mann, Simon Dewulf,
> undated paper, www.systematic-innovation.com/Articles/02,%2003,%2004/
> Jan03-Updating%20the%20Contradiction%20Matrix.pdf.

In essence, the work of Mann and the rest has made the Structured Abstraction technique more robust and useful than ever before. And we recognize that Mann's organization has also extended its analysis far beyond this work in 2003, having embodied much of it in a worked titled *Matrix 2010*, but we use the 2003 matrix here because it is in the public domain and we can offer the entire matrix as a free download, whereas the 2010 matrix has to be purchased.

Having said this, we should be very clear: Without Genrich Altshuller and his colleagues, it is doubtful that this powerful technique would exist today. Altshuller imagined the initial vision that innovation could be systematized in an analogical way, and he is solely responsible for leading the way in making that vision a workable reality for innovators.

Steps

1. Identify the Contradiction

How do you identify a technical contradiction? More often than not, technical contradictions are evident and well known within any field of endeavor or technology. Engineers and technicians familiar with a system understand the conflicting dynamics that give rise to technical contradictions.

To identify and characterize a technical contradiction, think in terms of two related variables, or parts of a system or process. When you improve one of the variables, say *increase the speed of a car,* that action causes another variable to deteriorate, like *lower gas mileage.* Whatever your innovation challenge, it's likely to entail at least one if not many technical contradictions.

2. Abstract the Problem

After the contradiction and its improving and degrading elements have been identified, your next step is to translate each element into its associated problem parameter (make the problem generic). There are 48 such parameters in the revised TRIZ system, as shown in Exhibit 26.2.

In making your translations, ask this: What is the fundamental nature of each side of the conflict? This is an exercise in abstract thinking because you have to reframe each of your contradictory elements in terms of one of the 48 problem parameters.

For example, let's say you need more heat in a system, but that heat makes the system less safe. Referencing the 48 problem parameters, you can translate the need for heat into the parameter of *temperature* (number 22), and you can translate the negative impact on safety into the generalized parameter of *other harmful effects generated by the system* (number 31).

Or maybe your system needs more airflow, but more airflow undesirably cools the surface. The need for more airflow references to general parameter number 7, *volume of a moving object,* while the cooling of the surface references to parameter number 22, *temperature.*

1.	Weight of Moving Object	25.	Loss of Substance
2.	Weight of Stationary Object	26.	Loss of Time
3.	Length/Angle of Moving Object	27.	Loss of Energy
4.	Length/Angle of Stationary object	28.	Loss of Information
5.	Area of Moving Object	29.	Noise
6.	Area of Stationary Object	30.	Harmful Emissions
7.	Volume of Moving Object	31.	Other Harmful Effects Generated by System
8.	Volume of Stationary Object	32.	Adaptability/Versatility
9.	Shape	33.	Compatibility/Connectability
10.	Amount of Substance	34.	Trainability/Operability/Controllability
11.	Amount of Information	35.	Reliability/Robustness
12.	Duration of Action of Moving Object	36.	Repairability
13.	Duration of Action of Stationary Object	37.	Security
14.	Speed	38.	Safety/Vulnerability
15.	Force/Torque	39.	Aesthetics/Appearance
16.	Energy Used by Moving Object	40.	Other Harmful Effects Acting on System
17.	Energy Used by Stationary Object	41.	Manufacturability
18.	Power	42.	Manufacture Precision/Consistency
19.	Stress/Pressure	43.	Automation
20.	Strength	44.	Productivity
21.	Stability	45.	System Complexity
22.	Temperature	46.	Control Complexity
23.	Illumination Intensity	47.	Ability to Detect/Measure
24.	Function Efficiency	48.	Measurement Precision

EXHIBIT 26.2   48 Problem Parameters.

You can get a good rundown and explanation of the original, classic 39 problem parameters in just about any text covering TRIZ, most TRIZ curricula, and innumerable destinations online. If, however, you're focused on where TRIZ is headed in the future, see the work of Darrell Mann at www.systematic-innovation.com.

---

3. Converge on Inventive Principles

This step entails using a *contradiction matrix* (Exhibit 26.3), which cross-references the 48 problem parameters against themselves, yielding a total of 2,304 cells in the matrix—or 2,304 different types of contradictions (48 × 48 = 2,304). After taking away the 48 instances in which a problem parameter conflicts with itself, you are left with 2,256 usable cells in the contradiction matrix.

All you have to do is identify your generic useful feature (parameter), as well as your generic harmful feature; then, go to the contradiction

	Problem Parameters (48 Total)		
Harmful Feature / Useful Feature	17 Energy used by stationary object	22 Temperature	26 Loss of time
7 Volume of a moving object	35, 38, 33, 19	10, 39, 18, 31	10,19,2,6,34
20 Strength	35, 14, 17, 4	35, 40, 9, 31	19,3,10,5
32 Adaptability or versatility	35, 16, 1, 19, 3	35, 5, 19, 36	28,15,29,35
	Inventive Principles (40 Total)		

Problem Parameters (48 Total) appears along the left side vertically.

EXHIBIT 26.3   Contradiction Matrix Cross Section (Downloadable).

Copyright © 2012, BMGI. A blank version of this customized form is available for download at www.innovatorstoolkit .com.

matrix cell that resides at their intersection. Inside that cell, you'll find any of *40 inventive principles* (Exhibit 26.4), by which you can solve your contradiction.

The key to the 40 inventive principles is that they were derived from an extensive analysis and categorization of patented innovations numbering in the millions. In each and every case, the patented innovations employed at least one of the 40 inventive principles to solve some identified technical contradiction. This is why some call these 40 principles the genetic code of innovation, and why **TRIZ** experts will tell you that someone else in another field at another time has already solved your contradiction.

> For more specific examples of the 40 inventive principles, visit www.triz-journal.com/archives/contradiction_matrix. You'll find much more detail than what we provide you here—giving you more substance to consider when thinking about how you might apply any inventive principle to solve your specific innovation problem. You'll also find a series of articles that illuminate the meaning and application of the inventive principles in a wide variety of fields, including architecture, chemistry, education, finance, microelectronics, service operations management, and more.

The cells of the contradiction matrix display four or five inventive principles that can help you solve any contradiction. If you're in the consumer products business, for instance, the solution you need may have been already found and applied in the space industry, or in agriculture, or in any number of other fields. All you have to do is navigate your way through the technical contradiction algorithm to the inventive principle(s) you need.

For example, if you need the volume of airflow to go up but the surface temperature to stay constant, what do you do? According to the contradiction matrix (Exhibit 26.3), you go to inventive principles 10, 39, 18, and 31, because when you cross-reference these parameters, that's what the contradiction matrix gives you.

When you look up inventive principles 10, 39, 18, and 31 (see Exhibit 26.4), you get the following, in respective order: *preliminary action, inert atmosphere, mechanical vibration,* and *porous materials.* You now have four important clues for solving the airflow/surface temperature contradiction.

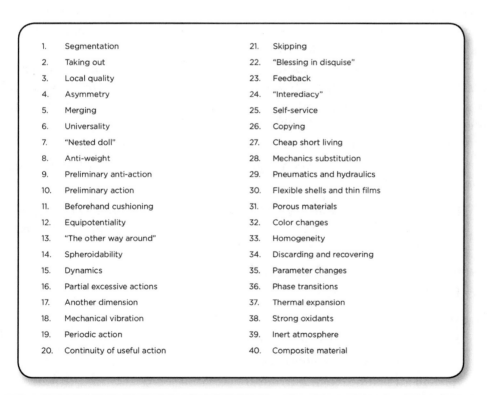

1.	Segmentation	21.	Skipping
2.	Taking out	22.	"Blessing in disguise"
3.	Local quality	23.	Feedback
4.	Asymmetry	24.	"Interediacy"
5.	Merging	25.	Self-service
6.	Universality	26.	Copying
7.	"Nested doll"	27.	Cheap short living
8.	Anti-weight	28.	Mechanics substitution
9.	Preliminary anti-action	29.	Pneumatics and hydraulics
10.	Preliminary action	30.	Flexible shells and thin films
11.	Beforehand cushioning	31.	Porous materials
12.	Equipotentiality	32.	Color changes
13.	"The other way around"	33.	Homogeneity
14.	Spheroidability	34.	Discarding and recovering
15.	Dynamics	35.	Parameter changes
16.	Partial excessive actions	36.	Phase transitions
17.	Another dimension	37.	Thermal expansion
18.	Mechanical vibration	38.	Strong oxidants
19.	Periodic action	39.	Inert atmosphere
20.	Continuity of useful action	40.	Composite material

EXHIBIT 26.4   *40 Inventive Principles.*

4. Apply the Inventive Principles

Now comes the moment of truth—actually applying the inventive principle(s) to solve your technical contradiction. This requires good analogical thinking skills because you have to consider the identified inventive principles as a guide for coming up with a specific solution to your original specific problem or technical contradiction.

This is obviously an exercise that not only requires analogical thinking, but also requires deep and intimate subject matter expertise. As always, the danger is in becoming a victim to your own psychological inertia by dismissing any inventive principle as preposterous before giving it serious consideration. If you're skilled at abstract thought, and you put your existing mind-set aside, you just might find the innovative solution you seek.

Resources

See the book, *Matrix 2003: Updating the TRIZ Contradiction Matrix*, by Darrell Mann, Simon Dewulf, Boris Zlotin, and Alla Zusman, www.aitriz.org (General Store/Books). The book, *Matrix 2010*, is also now available, but we use *Matrix 2003* in our work with clients.

For an immediate explanation of why and how the contradiction matrix was updated, see the paper, *Updating the Contradiction Matrix*, by Darrell (Systematic Innovation) and Simon Dewulf (CREAX), www.systematic-innovation.com/Articles/02,%2003,%2004/Jan03-Updating%20the%20 Contradiction%20Matrix.pdf.

Portions of material in this technique have been reprinted with permission from:

> D. Silverstein, N. DeCarlo, and M. Slocum. *Insourcing Innovation: How to Achieve Competitive Excellence Using TRIZ*. Boca Raton, FL: Auerbach, 2007.

If you need the help of a TRIZ expert, contact:

> BMGI (www.bmgi.com).

Or, you can find other articles, blogs, resources, and experts at:

> Real Innovation (www.realinnovation.com)
>
> TRIZ Journal (www.triz-journal.com)
>
> Altshuller Institute (www.aitriz.org)

Separation Principles

Split your innovation problem in four ways.

Separation principles help when some *physical contradiction* stands between you and an innovation, and you need to resolve the conflict with minimal or no trade-off. For example, you need the water in the system to be hot for some functions but cold for others. Or you want all the information to make a good management decision, but you don't want all the information because you don't have time to sift through it.

Use the Separation Principles technique when you've identified a physical contradiction, and when other ideation techniques may have fallen short of resolving it. You may need the help of an expert to apply separation principles, depending on the nature of your innovation project and its difficulty level.

The separation principles come from the Theory of Inventive Problem Solving (TRIZ), and they are defined a little differently by different experts. For simplicity, we characterize the separation principles by separating contradictory properties in *time, space, scale,* and *condition.*

Steps

1. Identify the Physical Contradiction

The key action here is to figure out which variable, system, or part of a system conflicts with itself. If this is not readily apparent, identify what you want to maximize and why you also want to minimize or eliminate that factor as well. Here are some examples of physical contradictions:

- We need tire rotation to provide steering and to avoid skidding under icy or wet conditions that require extreme braking to stop the vehicle. But we don't want tire rotation because the vehicle must stop.
- We need landing gear on planes for easy takeoff and landing, but we don't want landing gear because it causes drag.
- Engineers want a large window in a spaceship to see out, but they don't want the window because it adds extra weight to the spaceship.
- We want options when searching for flights online, but we don't want options because they consume too much time to review.

2. Consider Separation Heuristics

The four separation principles—time, space, scale, and condition—can be applied in an endless number of circumstances. To help you determine which principle could resolve your physical contradiction, consider the following:

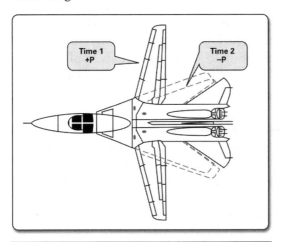

- *Separation in time:* The strategy for this principle is that at Time 1, the variable has property (+P), and at Time 2 it has property (–P). For example, a modern fighter jet has to be maneuverable during landing as well as in combat situations. The requirements of the wing geometry are radically different in each scenario. At low speeds (Time 1) the best wing geometry is unswept (+P), while at high speeds (Time 2) it is swept (–P). These contradictory requirements are resolved through the invention of variable sweep wing geometry (Exhibit 27.1).

EXHIBIT 27.1 Separation in Time (between system and components).

- *Separation in space:* The strategy for this principle is that at Place 1, the variable has property (+P), and at Place 2 it has property (–P). Classic examples of this principle include coffee pots, teapots, and thermos bottles. Taken further, this principle is at the heart of a new technology called holographic conferencing. Using this technology, for example, a holographic image of an executive in Bangalore, India, can be seen by an audience talking with another executive in San Jose, California. Both people have human properties in one space and holographic properties in the other space.

- *Separation in scale:* This separation strategy is applied to the system and its components, whereby the entire system has property (+P), and the component has property (–P), as illustrated in Exhibit 27.2. Another example is a chain, which is flexible at the system level but each link in the chain is rigid.

```
NO          NO      NO NO  NO  NO     NO NO  NO  NO
NO          NO      NO NO  NO  NO     NO NO  NO  NO
NO          NO      NO                NO
NO          NO      NO                NO
NO NO NO NO         NO NO  NO  NO     NO  NO  NO NO
NO NO NO NO         NO NO  NO  NO     NO  NO  NO NO
      NO            NO                         NO
      NO            NO                         NO
      NO            NO NO  NO  NO     NO  NO  NO NO
      NO            NO NO  NO  NO     NO  NO  NO NO
```

EXHIBIT 27.2   Separation in Scale.

- *Separation upon conditions:* This separation strategy entails that the system under Condition 1 exhibits property (+P), and under Condition 2, it exhibits property (–P). An excellent example is transitions lenses with a light-sensitive photochromic coating. The lenses are light or dark depending on the amount of UV radiation present (Exhibit 27.3).

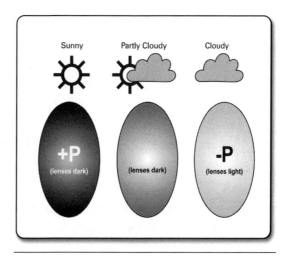

EXHIBIT 27.3   Separation in Condition.

3. Resolve Physical Contradiction

First, carry forward the contradictory element or characteristic of your physical contradiction from step 2. This is the characteristic X that must meet the self-opposing requirements.

Next, define the time period of the physical contradiction as:

- T1: before the event.
- T2: during the event.
- T3: after the event.

After this, complete logic statements A and B:

A: To (improve, retain) the useful action of (state the useful action), X must be (present, large, hot, etc.) during T (1, 2, or 3).

B: To eliminate the harmful action of (state the harmful action), X must be (absent, small, cold, etc.) during T (1, 2, or 3).

In statement **A**, X could be (present, large, hot, etc.), which means that in statement **B**, X would be (absent, small, cold, etc.).

Now, write the Physical Contradiction:

X must be_____ during time T_____ and
X must be_____ during time T_____.

Then, choose a separation principle (time, space, scale, or condition) to apply and solve the contradiction.

Example

Scenario: In electroplating, the rate of deposition of metal is increased when the plating solution is warm. The shelf life of the solution, however, is reduced dramatically with the increased temperature. It is necessary to increase the rate of deposition with minimal degradation to the solution. How can this be done?

1. The Problem

- The electroplating solution bath needs to be hot and cold.
- The characteristic is *temperature* of the solution bath.
- Time period is T1, T2, T3.

  A. To increase the rate of deposition, the solution bath must be hot during T2 (actual electroplating).

  B. To preserve the shelf life, the solution bath should be cold during T1 (before electroplating), T2, and T3 (after electroplating).

2. The Physical Contradiction

- Solution bath temperature should be hot during time T2 (electroplating).
- Solution bath temperature should be cold during time T1, T2, T3.

3. The Separation

- Separation of opposite requirements in *space*.

4. The Resources

- *Heat,* space, equipment.

5. The Solution

- Heat the parts—temperature is hot at the interface, and cold everywhere else.

Additional Example—Manager Working in an Office

- Manager Beth wants information so she can have control, but she doesn't want information because she has too much already. *Solution*: Use periodic management reviews to separate the information in *time*.
- Beth also needs to work on a critical project, but doesn't want to work on a critical project because she has people tugging at her in the office. *Solution*: She works offsite for two days, thereby separating in *space*.

- Beth is still overwhelmed with work so she co-opts several of her colleagues into taking on certain tasks. She has separated in *scale* to solve her problem. Some call this delegation.

- To reduce the volume and complexity of issues due her attention, Beth requests that any item not affecting more than 20 people not be brought before her for consideration—she has separated in *condition*.

Resources

The TRIZ Journal is packed with resources, papers, and commentary. A quick search on the site for *Separation Principles* will yield some good information.

TRIZ Journal (www.triz-journal.com).

Substance Field Analysis

Learn how substances interact with fields to form solutions.

Substance field analysis (SFA) is a way to model an existing system with the intent of identifying its deficiencies, then addressing them using innovative strategies. There are five strategies that can be used to address the inadequacies of the system. One of the five SFA strategies, for instance, could prompt an engineer to add a luminophore substance to the refrigerant substance in a cooling system, thereby making leaks visible that would otherwise go undetected.

This technique comes in handy when the innovation opportunity is (1) well-defined and (2) contains at least one deficiency in the system. In some cases, you may need the help of an expert to apply this tool—unless, of course, you have the applicable knowledge and skills. Or, if your problem is simple enough, what we give you here should be sufficient.

Background

TRIZ (the Theory of Inventive Problem Solving) practitioners usually apply SFA in conjunction with the *76 Standard Solutions*, a compilation of just that: 76 standard solutions that are organized into five classes. But this classical categorization scheme can be onerous and difficult to understand and apply—for most people who aren't engineers by trade and well versed in TRIZ techniques. Even engineers admit that this technique can be complex. In addition, the SFA modeling conventions vary among TRIZ practitioners.

Iouri Belski, TRIZ Master (Diploma No 75), and professor of thinking and problem solving at Royal Melbourne Institute of Technology, took this difficulty to heart when he focused exclusively on standardizing the conventions and rules for creating the substance field (or su-field) models; he created five foundational strategies to address deficiencies in a system.

Any system can be modeled as a set of substances and fields interacting with each other. By carefully studying the way substances (objects-S_1; subjects-S_2) interact through some energy field, one can identify opportunities to improve the system. Interactions causing conflict or harm, or interactions that don't achieve the job to be done sufficiently, are analyzed to find innovative improvements.

The basic, or fundamental, interaction of a well-functioning system is represented through a basic triad (see Exhibit 28.1).

The **object** S_1 (e.g., nail) is *passive*, and is affected by the actions of the **subject** S_2 (e.g., hammer) through the **field** F_1 (e.g., mechanical energy). Substances can refer to any part, material, component, person, or the environment. The source of energy in the system can be such physical fields as mechanical, thermal, chemical, electrical, magnetic, and gravitational—or any number of such fields as light, acoustic, olfactory, and so on. Substance interactions in triads are depicted using arrows characterizing the nature of the interaction.

The combination of S_1, S_2, F_1, as well as their interactions, constitutes the minimum required information to represent a complete system (Exhibit 28.1). The action of driving in a nail illustrates a minimum su-field triad. Your hand transmits energy to a hammer (S_2), which, in turn, transmits a mechanical field (F_{1mech}) to the nail (S_1), as depicted by the arrow going from S_2 to F_{1mech} and F_{1mech} to S_1. The arrow depicted at the bottom

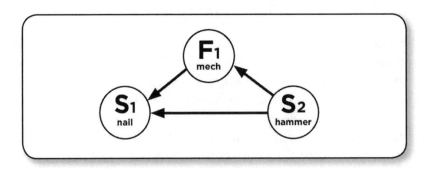

EXHIBIT 28.1   A Well-Functioning Basic Triad.

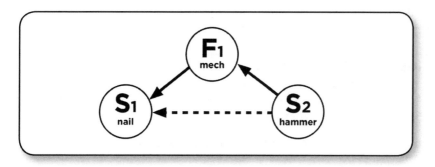

EXHIBIT 28.2   Su-Field Model of an Insufficient System.

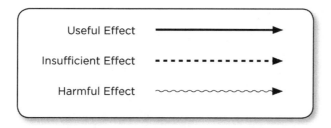

EXHIBIT 28.3   Su-Field Energy Transfer Options.

of the model going from S_2 to S_1 is our *perception* of the result. The dashed arrow shown in Exhibit 28.2 represents an insufficient result (e.g., hammer bending or crushing the nail).

As shown in Exhibit 28.3 another typical result is a harmful transformation (depicted by the curly arrow) based on our perception.

More complex systems are typically represented by many more substance and field interactions. In this case, each triad is analyzed independently and its ideal solutions can be combined with other triad solutions to improve the system as a whole.

Attributed to professor Belski, Table 28.1 shows many different fields and what results from their interaction with substances.

Each problem that I solved became a rule, which served afterward to solve other problems.

—René Descartes

TABLE 28.1   Sources of Field Energy

Fields	Substance Interactions
Mechanical	Gravitation, collisions, friction, direct contact, vibration, resonance, shocks, waves, gas/fluid dynamics, wind, compression, vacuum, mechanical treatment and processing, deformation, mixing, additives, explosion.
Acoustic	Sound, ultrasound, infrasound, cavitation.
Thermal	Heating, cooling, insulation, thermal expansion, phase/state change, endo- and exothermic reactions, fire, burning, heat radiation, convection.
Chemical	Reactions, reactants, elements, compounds, catalysts, inhibitors, indicators (pH), dissolving, crystallization, polymerization, odor, taste, color change.
Electric	Electrostatic charges, conductors, insulators, electric field, current, superconductivity, electrolysis, piezo-electrics, ionization, electrical discharge, sparks.
Magnetic	Magnetic field, forces and particles, induction, electromagnetic waves (X-ray, microwaves, etc.), optics, vision, color/translucence change, image.
Intermolecular	Subatomic (nano) particles, capillary, pores, nuclear reactions, radiation, fusion, emission, laser, intermolecular interaction, surface effects, evaporation.
Biological	Microbes, bacteria, living organisms, plants, fungi, cells, enzymes.

Source: Iouri Belski, TRIZ4U, www.triz4u.com

Analyzing Substance-Field Problems

Successful application of su-field analysis is predicated on identifying a substance field interaction scenario (or scenarios), where the $S_1 \rightarrow F_1 \rightarrow S_2$ interaction is sufficient, insufficient, or harmful. The analysis process proceeds as follows:

- List *all* the substances involved in the conflict scenario. Often, not all the listed substances will be relevant to the new solution. When seeking new solutions, you should introduce new substances and/or fields to fulfill a desired function or improve/innovate an existing function.

- Draw a complete su-field model. The model relates *all* substances in terms of their field interactions and clarifies the nature of these interactions (i.e., useful, harmful, etc.). This process can result in multiple problem triads.

- For each problem triad, construct a *model solution* by converting the problem triad using each of the solution strategies.

- Identify *solution ideas* using the field energy reference in Table 28.1. Although they may not always appear relevant, consider all field types to ensure novel ideas aren't overlooked.

- Consider all ideas to find the most applicable solutions to your innovation problem (technical or physical contradiction).

The Five Solution Strategies

Each of the five solution strategies offers a suggestion to lead your thoughts around what a potential solution to a problem triad may be. The strategies should be applied to each of the triads identified. Consider the following common household task:

Removing dust from a floor.

Per the previous section, we start by listing all the substances involved. In this case, the only substance we want to interact with is dust. Our initial su-field model is rather simple (see Exhibit 28.4).

The conflict starts out with dust on a floor. It isn't wanted and won't go away by itself.

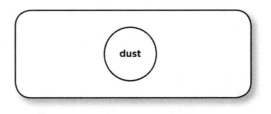

EXHIBIT 28.4   Initial Su-Field Model.

Conflict triads can also be written out in words to ensure they are clearly understood.

Solution Strategy 1

Add a substance (S_2), which generates a field (F_1), which influences S_1. The trivial solution is represented in Exhibit 28.5. Next, we consider each of the fields in Table 28.1 for inspiration to find a solution.

Mechanical: Through direct contact with a broom (S_2), a mechanical action (F_{mech}) will collect all the dust in a specified location. Through the use of a vacuum field, all the dust could be collected.

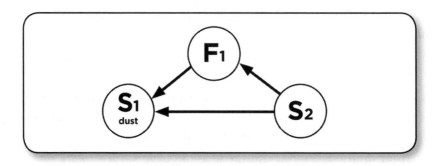

EXHIBIT 28.5   Solution Strategy 1: Model Solution.

Acoustic: One could conceivably create a device (S_2) that produces acoustic waves ($F_{acoustic}$) to blow away or attract the dust from the floor.

Thermal: Thermal reactions ($F_{thermal}$) can conceivably burn or consume the dust from the floor. Another possibility is to use a combination of thermo-mechanical devices that vacuum the dust, and then thermally decompose it.

Chemical: Dust could be dissolved ($F_{chemical}$) in a liquid that makes it easier to collect. Dust could be mixed with a substance that crystallizes and makes it easier to collect. The current method using a mop is a combination of a mechanical device combined with chemical actions.

Electric: Through the application of an electric field, dust particles may be ionized and then collected using a device with an opposite charge. P&G's product Swiffer is based on this core idea of using electrostatic forces to attract dust. It uses no detergent or water to clean dust from floor.

Magnetic: In theory, one could take advantage of the magnetic properties of dust and create a system to attract the dust away from the floor. It requires further research and validation.

Intermolecular: By taking advantage of the intermolecular properties of the dust particles, a device may be conceived to remove dust from the floor.

Biological: A dust-consuming microbe may be introduced (be sure that it doesn't consume anything else!).

Due to space constraints, not all possible ideas are explored here, but a complete analysis ought to include all possibilities. Novel solutions often lurk in the most unexpected places.

Solution Strategy 1 introduced both a new substance (S_2) and new field (F_1). The rule also applies if we have an existing S_2 and F_1 in place, which

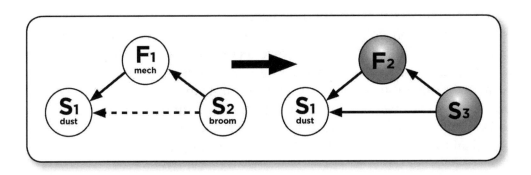

EXHIBIT 28.6 Solution Strategy 1.

introduces a conflict situation, such as a broom that doesn't collect all dust (see Exhibit 28.6). Formulating the problem like this pushes us to seek a solution that requires a new substance and a new field interaction.

The remaining solution strategies aim to help the practitioner explore ways in which existing conflict triads may be improved, while keeping the existing subject (S_1) and object (S_2) in place.

Solution Strategy 2

Object (S_2)'s capacity to generate a field (F_1) may be improved by the introduction of an additional substance (S_3), which generates a field (F_2), which modifies S_2 (Exhibit 28.7).

Practically, this implies the addition of a new substance that will generate a field that will affect the broom, improving its ability to mechanically collect dust. To generate ideas, consider *all* fields listed in Table 28.1.

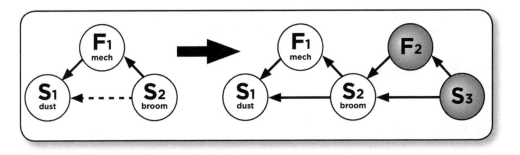

EXHIBIT 28.7 Solution Strategy 2.

Some suggestions might not necessarily make sense. For example, adding a heat source (thermal) to the broom might not initially lead to a practical idea. But could that improve its dust collection abilities? Perhaps a heat source might make it easier for persistent dust to come unglued from the floor or to destroy the dust by burning it. A statically charged broom (electric) would attract dust particulate (and the field would have to be applied with a new substance)—so might adding a particle-clumping chemical to the broom head (and the same for applying the chemical field).

Solution Strategy 3

Object (S_2)'s ability to interact with subject (S_1) can be improved by adding a new substance (S_3) that generates a field (F_2), affecting S_1 (see Exhibit 28.8).

In Strategy 2, we operated on the broom (S_2, the subject) with a third substance and a second field. In Strategy 3, we operate on the dust (S_1, the object) with a third substance and a second field.

So what field and associated substance could be added to dust such that it becomes easier to collect? Wet dust would employ gravity (mechanical), and a new substance, to make it easier to sweep up. Introducing a substance, and a new field (magnetic) to change the color of the dust, might make it easier to collect—easier to see what you missed.

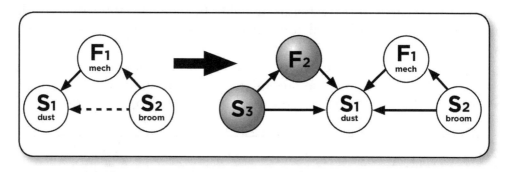

EXHIBIT 28.8   Solution Strategy 3.

Solution Strategy 4

Solution Strategy 4 is when you add a new substance (S_3), and a new field (F_2), in between the subject (S_2) and the object (S_1) to affect either one of

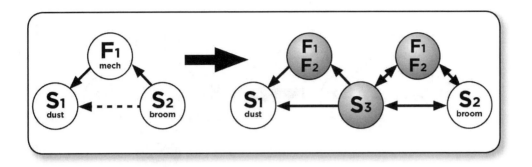

EXHIBIT 28.9   Solution Strategy 4.

them. When S_2 is affected by the new field (F_2), field F_1 affects substance S_3, and the effect of F_1 is applied to S_1, removing the conflict. When S_1 is affected by the new field (F_2), the interaction of field F_1 is improved to remove the conflict (see Exhibit 28.9).

What substance or field can be introduced in between dust and broom to improve collection? Compressed air may be used to blow dust into a corner where it's easier to sweep up (mechanical). Since dust particulates are small, sweeping them up with a broom makes it easy for individual particles to pass through the bristles of the broom. Covering the broom with a cloth to capture particles will improve the collection (mechanical). Another idea is to use the vacuum or jet of air guiding the dust toward the broom to improve collection efficiency.

Solution Strategy 5

Solution Strategy 5 calls for the introduction of a new field (F_2) interacting with both object S_1 *and* subject S_2 to improve the problem triad, as depicted in Exhibit 28.10.

The new field (F_2) might have an effect on S_1 and S_2—concurrently, or one after the other. Both possibilities should be considered to ensure that an innovation opportunity is not overlooked or discounted.

An idea under this scheme is to statically charge the dust particles using an electric field, and to also charge the broom material with the electrical opposite charge so dust will get attracted toward the broom.

Given the formulation above and the energy described in Table 28.1 at the beginning of this chapter, it may look like Strategy 5 would introduce

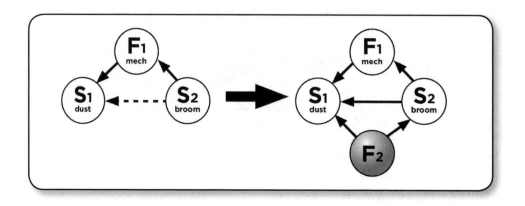

EXHIBIT 28.10   Solution Strategy 5.

suggestions that would overlap quite a bit with Strategies 1 through 4. It does, however, present an additional point of view that hasn't been considered before and shouldn't be ignored. Any idea could be a game changer!

Applying the five simple strategies enables the practitioner of su-field analysis to discover many new ideas for solving persistent problems, even though they haven't mastered the nuances of the 76 standard solutions.

Resources

For a more complete treatment of the five solution strategies see:

Belski, I. *Improve Your Thinking: Substance-Field Analysis*. Melbourne, Australia, 2007.

Some organizations that may be able to help are:

Altshuller Institute (www.aitriz.org).

BMGI (www.bmgi.com).

European TRIZ Association (www.etria.net).

TRIZ Journal (www.triz-journal.com).

TRIZ4U (www.triz4u.com).

Biomimicry

Seek nature's eons of experience to find answers.

Biomimicry (or biomimetics) is the process of learning from and then emulating nature's ingenious solutions to complex problems. Imagine making high-end audio speakers based on a cricket that uses its burrow to amplify sound. Or drawing inspiration from a boxfish to develop a concept car with 60 percent less drag. Or creating self-assembling fibers, like those produced by spiders, that are five times as strong as steel.

These real-life applications of biomimicry only scratch the surface of this fascinating approach. Nature has spent billions of years designing and perfecting systems and processes, excelling at finding optimal solutions under conflicting constraints and demanding requirements. Science and engineering have similar goals: optimal results with minimal input and minimal use of resources. If you have to solve a problem, chances are nature already did it.

Although biomimicry is often applied by those trained to observe nature at its most fundamental level, it doesn't necessarily require doing expensive, time-consuming research. Many examples of nature's problem-solving abilities are available for the casual researcher. The scope of this book prevents us from offering a comprehensive education in biomimicry, but we can offer some general guidelines for learning from nature and leveraging its vast bank of knowledge.

Steps

1. Change Your Perspective

Using other techniques in this book, you have already scoped the JTBD (see Jobs to be Done, Technique 1) and identified associated Outcome Expectations (see Technique 3). Now, ask, "What would nature do to solve this problem?" In doing so, you realize that nature isn't the environment in which your design will live; instead, it's a model on which to base your design. This subtle shift is important if you want to draw inspiration from nature and follow its guiding principles:

- Nature runs on sunlight.
- Nature uses only the energy it needs.
- Nature fits form to function.
- Nature recycles everything.
- Nature rewards cooperation.
- Nature banks on diversity.
- Nature demands local expertise.
- Nature curbs excesses from within.
- Nature taps the power of limits (see J. Benyus, *Biomimicry: Innovation Inspired by Nature*, New York: William Morrow, 1997).

Nature's designs are organic. They make optimal use of the resources and energy available, only produce recyclable waste, and integrate with existing natural life cycles.

---

2. Explore Existing Knowledge

Biomimicry has a rich body of literature, written by experts on every topic imaginable. Much of this information can be found online. Don't hesitate to make contact with experts; collaboration with professionals from different fields can yield inspiring solutions.

One body of exploratory computer science, now collectively known as Computational Swarm Intelligence, solves complex optimization problems by mimicking the flocking behavior of birds and the foraging behavior of ants (see A. Engelbrecht, *Fundamentals of Computational Swarm Intelligence*, Hoboken, NJ: John Wiley & Sons, 2006).

3. Plan a Field Trip

If you can't find a solution to your problem in an existing knowledge base, you'll need to take a field trip (or several). Here's where someone experienced in biomimicry can point you in the right direction. At the very least, you'll need to identify an organism, ecosystem, or process that has solved a problem similar to yours, and then go where you can study the solution in its natural environment. Remember that solution ideas might be found in nonobvious environments. For example, if you need a way to dry out humid air, you can look in the tropics, or you can go to the desert where cockroaches drink water from the air.

If you put the history of the planet on a calendar year, bacteria arrived in March. Other species followed. The human species came at 11:45 p.m. on the *last day of the year*. Clearly, we have a lot to learn from the way natural species have evolved, adapted, and innovated themselves to survive their own unique challenges and problems.

4. Observe and Learn

Once you're in the field, there are many ways to gather inspiration for your own design. Just remember that nature's solutions are often nonobvious and intricate, while at the same time functionally simple. Take time to immerse yourself. Patient study will uncover functionality you may never have considered. As you observe, keep these tips in mind:

- *Look for Metaphors:* Nature offers many metaphors that can be applied to a variety of artificially constructed systems. For instance, some termites regulate airflow through their mounds to keep the internal temperature and humidity near constant (Exhibit 29.1). A similar principle has been used in the design of high-rise buildings in Harare (Zimbabwe) and London (England), leading to significant reductions in environmental control costs.

EXHIBIT 29.1 Termite Mound.
A termite mound can seem eerily like a skyscraper, especially when you consider the mound's efficient regulation of airflow, temperature, and humidity.

- *Identify Anti-Solutions:* When you think about how nature might solve a problem, also consider how nature might *not* solve it. For instance, manufacturing protective shielding for military applications requires metal to be molded at high temperatures, which consumes massive amounts of energy. On the other hand, nacre (mother of pearl) is just as strong, yet it grows organically and requires no excessive consumption of resources.

- *Consider Extremes:* Explore how nature has solved your problem by going to one extreme or another. Desert beetles, for example, use a hydrophilic (water-attracting) shell to channel water to where it is wanted. On the contrary, lotus leaves keep water from building up where it isn't wanted using a hydrophobic (water-repelling) design (Exhibit 29.2).

- *Examine Interactions:* Everything in nature interacts with its environment. When you have identified a source of inspiration, consider its impact on other elements in nature. For instance, animals share

EXHIBIT 29.2 Lotus Leaf. The leaf repels water, a feature that is often sought after in man-made solutions.

resources, such as watering holes, but use the resource at different times to avoid conflicts. Man-made creations can also take advantage of interaction and reuse. One example is the design of many hybrid vehicles that are powered by batteries that are recharged during braking.

Are you drawing inspiration from an organism, a process, or an ecosystem? In any of these cases, you'll need to understand the system in detail to be able to mimic it successfully and without negative consequences.

5. Document Solution Ideas

As a result of exploring nature's genius, you should have one or more ideas you can investigate further.

Additional Example

Wired.co.uk writer Mark Brown wrote a blog (April 27, 2012) about researchers at MIT who have "engineered a new type of glass which eliminates glare and reflections, doesn't fog up, and causes water droplets to bounce off like tiny rubber balls." The surface texture of the glass, Brown says, was inspired by lotus leaves and moth eyes. Today, the manufacturing process for making this new glass is expensive, but "the nanotexture wonder glass could one day crop up on the screens of smartphones and televisions, solar panels, car windshields, and even windows in buildings."

It all depends on further real-world testing, Brown says, to find out just how resilient the new glass can be to raindrops in a strong downpour, wind-driven pollen, grit, sweat, fog, and overt finger-prodding by overzealous smartphone users. To date, the promise of the glass is "calculated, not tested."

Source: www.wired.co.uk/news/archive/2012-04/27/mit-fog-free-glass.

Resources

Here are a few of the best websites for biomimicry examples, case studies, resources, and expert help:

> *Bioinspiration & Biomimetics Journal* (http://stacks.iop.org/bioinsp).
>
> Biomimicry Database (http://database.portal.modwest.com).
>
> Biomimicry Institute (www.biomimicryinstitute.org).

For a fascinating presentation on biomimicry, see:

> "Janine Benyus: 12 Sustainable Design Ideas from Nature," www.ted.com/index.php/talks/view/id/18.

KJ Method

Group and organize ideas by their natural affinities.

KJ method provides a way to organize and refine your innovation ideas, sparking further dialogue and achieving consensus about which ideas are worth developing. Also known as an *affinity diagram*, KJ method works best when you have more ideas than you can readily handle or process in your mind.

Usually, KJ method directs participants to *generate* ideas via classic brainstorming. However, given the many other powerful ideation tools in this book, we recommend you use KJ method to help you organize and prioritize the highly creative and innovative ideas you've already generated.

KJ method was named after Jiro Kawakita, a man of many talents who was a professor of cultural anthropology in Japan. After extensive field research in Nepal during the 1960s, Kawakita developed KJ method to improve the integration and categorization of qualitative data around such factors as the environment, population, relationships, hierarchy, and religion.

Steps

Scenario: Let's see how KJ method helped the Patient Crusaders team organize and prioritize their ideas for making dental patients more comfortable and less afraid during treatment (also see Heuristic Redefinition, Technique 7).

A team of six to eight people is optimum for KJ method. Fewer than this can make prioritization too subjective; more than this can make it difficult to gain consensus.

1. Prepare Ideas

Write each idea you've come up with on a sticky note, and place the ideas randomly on a white board or large wall space. Also, post the Job to be Done (see Technique 1) and associated Outcome Expectations (see Technique 3) so the team can keep these in mind.

2. Categorize Ideas

As a group, sort the ideas into related categories based on functionality, features, implementation, outcome, or whatever grouping makes sense (there are no right or wrong categories). Ideas that don't fit into a particular category can be saved off to the side. Place similar ideas on top of each other so you can see how many unique ideas there are.

Participants should be discouraged from discussing ideas, except for clarification, until voting occurs in step 4. Otherwise, you risk wasting time on ideas that won't be pursued in the end.

3. Label Categories

Review the idea groupings, and agree on a label for each one that represents the theme or concept behind the ideas in that group. Labels should be short, like *Dental Technology* or *Patient Communication.* No two categories should have the same or similar labels—if they do, combine the categories. As labels emerge, you may need to split some groups into multiple categories, or move ideas around to fit better with the category logic (Exhibit 30.1).

Labeling categories helps the team evaluate the suggestions from a thematic or system perspective. Plus, if the categories translate to *concepts,* the team can generate additional ideas using Idea Sorting and Refinement (Technique 31).

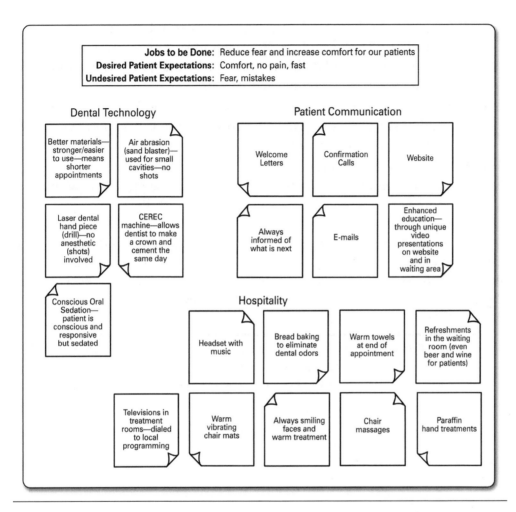

EXHIBIT 30.1   KJ Method (Affinity Diagram). The Patient Crusaders team organized their existing ideas into three categories.

4. Vote on Ideas

KJ method is a technique for both categorizing and prioritizing ideas. The latter is usually accomplished by having team members vote on the ideas they find most promising. There are several ways to approach voting, including:

- Give each team member three to five votes to place on the same idea or on multiple ideas. The ideas with the most votes merit further discussion and/or development.

- Have team members assign a percentage (totaling 100 percent per person) to one or more ideas. For each idea that receives a vote, add up the percentages and divide the answer by the number of people who voted to determine a weighted score.
- Discuss each idea and try to build consensus around the strongest ones. Although this does take longer than voting, it tends to generate stronger buy-in for ideas in the long run.
- If you have many different *categories,* vote on these first to see if there are any that can be eliminated. Then, vote on specific ideas within the remaining categories.

The Patient Crusaders team voted to implement a few of the simple and inexpensive ideas right away, including *welcome letters, confirmation calls,* and *warm towels at the end of the appointment.* They ranked several other ideas as potentially feasible solutions and will revisit these at a later date.

If you still have too many ideas after using KJ method, use a Pugh Matrix (Technique 40) to help you prioritize them.

Idea Sorting and Refinement

Organize and shape ideas to improve their yield.

Idea sorting and refinement is a simple and effective way to make your ideas more practical and viable, as well as more appealing to those who are funding the innovation project (your stakeholders). After you've generated dozens of ideas for a better battery, do you just throw out the notion of making the battery biodegradable, or can you find some value in this?

What about your other ideas? Are they immediately applicable or do you need to overcome some constraints, such as cost, time, resources, or perception? Idea sorting and refinement can help you answer these questions and subsequently choose the best ideas from your list for further development.

> You would not think much of a farmer who took a lot of trouble to sow a crop but only bothered to harvest a quarter of the crop. Yet that is exactly what most people do with the output of a creative thinking session.
>
> —Edward de Bono

Steps—Sorting

Scenario: Let's say that your organization has a new innovation deployment. Your team has generated a list of ideas for publicizing the program's success both internally and externally. You can use idea sorting and refinement to organize and further refine these ideas.

1. Categorize Existing Ideas

Take the list of ideas you've already come up with and place them into the following categories on an idea-sorting matrix (Exhibit 31.1):

- *Broad Concept:* Theory or notion that links one or more concepts.
- *Concepts:* General approaches or methods.
- *Specific Ideas:* Valuable, practical, and usable ideas.
- *Beginning Ideas:* Interesting starter ideas but not yet actionable.

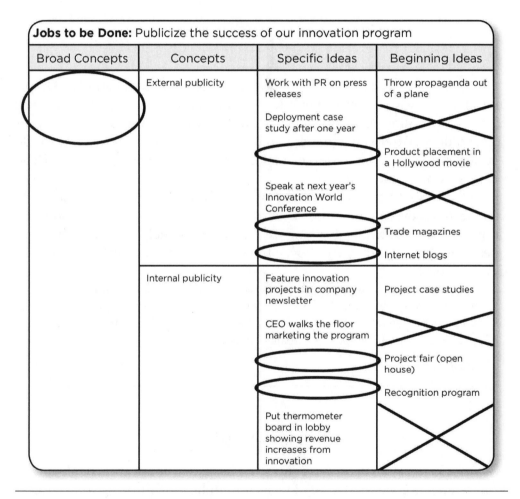

EXHIBIT 31.1   Idea Sorting—Before (Downloadable).

For instance, ideas for publicizing your innovation deployment might include writing case studies, generating press releases, holding project fairs, and featuring one of your innovative products in a Hollywood movie. Some of these ideas are specific and actionable, while others need work.

A *concept* links a group of ideas together, whereas a *broad concept* brings all the concepts under one umbrella. Both concepts and broad concepts are subjective—there is no right or wrong answer as long as the answer serves the job to be done.

---

2. Increase Idea Yield

Increase the yield of ideas and concepts by filling in any blanks on the idea sorting matrix. Can you turn a beginning idea into a specific idea? Try to do this for all beginning ideas. If you get stuck, flag the idea for later refinement (see steps below). Also, consider if you have articulated all the concepts and broad concepts behind the idea. Filling in these blanks may help you view the innovation opportunity from a different perspective, leading to more ideas (Exhibit 31.2).

You don't need to fill in any blanks in the *Beginning Ideas* column, unless you think of more to add.

Steps—Refinement

Scenario: Idea refinement takes an unpromising idea, then operationalizes and reinforces it into a practical and valuable idea. For example, one fanciful idea for publicizing your company's innovation program is placing one of your new products in a Hollywood movie. Although this may seem unattainable at first, operationalizing and reinforcing the idea might make it possible, or it may bring to mind associated ideas that are more realistic.

1. List the Idea Constraints

Choose an idea that has inherent constraints (cost, legality, time lines, technical feasibility, etc.). List all the constraints relative to the idea.

Jobs to be Done: Publicize the success of our innovation program			
Broad Concepts	Concepts	Specific Ideas	Beginning Ideas
Demonstrate that innovation can be scaleable, reliable, and repeatable	External publicity	Work with PR on press releases	Throw propaganda out of a plane
		Deployment case study after one year	
		???	Product placement in a Hollywood movie
		Speak at next year's Innovation World Conference	
		Submit article to *IndustryWeek*	Trade magazines
		Deployment leader posts 2–3 innovation blogs per week	Internet blogs
	Internal publicity	Feature innovation projects in company newsletter	Project case studies
		CEO walks the floor marketing the program	
		Annual fair features most successful projects	Project fair (open house)
		Project leaders invited to group lunch with CEO	Recognition program
		Put thermometer board in lobby showing revenue increases from innovation	

EXHIBIT 31.2 Idea Sorting—After (Downloadable). For the innovation deployment example, we added four specific ideas spawned from associated beginning ideas, and also filled in the broad concept.

One benefit of idea refinement is that it allows the innovation team to tailor the proposed ideas to fit specific organizational strategies. For example, if company policy is not to make any products that are lethal if accidentally ingested, you may need to *operationalize* your ideas to make sure they fit this requirement.

2. Operationalize the Idea

Brainstorm ways you could overcome each constraint (Exhibit 31.3). Don't pass judgment on any suggestions; some will be viable, while others may spark different ideas down the road. Let your creativity shape and transform the original idea into a more viable option.

Jobs to be Done: Publicize the success of our innovation program
Idea: Product placement in a Hollywood movie

Idea Constraints	Shape the Idea
We dont't know anyone in Hollywood	Call the producers directly
	Work with independent producers
	Ask our employees if they know someone in Hollywood
Product placement costs a lot of money	Enter contests sponsored by movie companies
	Create a YouTube video
Mismatch between product market and movie audience	Get product placement in company training videos
	Bring the movie to consumer homes (Pay-per-view, DVD)
	Sponsor screening of the movie for clients or potential clients
	Create an animated cartoon featuring the product
Need publicity sooner rather than later	Create a YouTube video
	Advertise in movie theaters

EXHIBIT 31.3   Idea Refinement—Operationalize the Idea (Downloadable).

Operationalizing an idea helps you overcome constraints that make the idea implausible. *Reinforcing* an idea leads you to make the idea more appealing to stakeholder groups.

---

3. Strengthen and Reinforce the Idea

Now, take the same idea and reinforce it by making it more appealing to stakeholders. Instead of listing individual stakeholders, identify a few groups

Jobs to be Done: Publicize the success of our innovation program
Idea: Product placement in a Hollywood movie

Stakeholder	Point of View	Reinforce the Idea
Executives	Understand WIIFM (What's in it for me?)	Show the potential for high-profile publicity
	Understand ROI (return on investment)	Gather the data that shows ROI
	How much control do I have over this?	Personal screening before the movie is complete
	Who else is doing this already?	Arrange benchmarks with competitors
	Why isn't anyone else doing this?	Pilot the idea and replicate if it works
	How does this link to the company strategy?	Do a strategic planning review with an expert
Managers	What are the resources needed from me?	Offer a part as a walk-on or extra in the movie
	How much will it cost?	Gather costs from the ROI developed for the executives
	How much control do I have over the finished placement?	Personalized preview
	Why do/don't you want to feature my product?	Design a time line or schedule for all major projects
Employees	How much extra work is this going to be for me?	Offer a part as a walk-on or extra in the movie
	How are we going to be compensated?	Offer overtime and free to tickets to movie
	Why do/don't you want to feature my product?	Design a time line or schedule for all major projects
	How is this going to help with my personal development?	Participants in the project can add this to their resumes

---

EXHIBIT 31.4   Idea Refinement—Reinforce the Idea (Downloadable).

segmented by organizational level, customer type, or whatever makes sense. For each group, make a list of the stakeholders' point of view relative to the idea. In other words, what are the wants and needs of the stakeholders in that group? What do you think their concerns and objections will be? Then, generate ways to improve the idea so that it meets the needs (or addresses the objections) of each stakeholder group (Exhibit 31.4).

When you've finished idea sorting and refinement, you should have increased the yield of viable ideas that can become solutions for your innovation opportunity. You can further evaluate these ideas using techniques like Six Thinking Modes (Technique 32) or Pugh Matrix (Technique 40).

Six Thinking Modes[*]

Evaluate your solution ideas in six different ways.

Six thinking modes leverages different points of view to help your team evaluate its best ideas. The approach works especially well with controversial ideas, such as innovative new business models, because it makes time for objectivity and subjectivity, as well as for evaluating the pros and cons of the proposed solution.

Although you can use six thinking modes to generate ideas, it works equally well after you've narrowed down the list of ideas to a couple of viable options. It can be tricky to keep the group on track, so you may consider additional training in this technique, or bringing in an experienced facilitator.

Background

Six thinking modes is a lateral thinking exercise pioneered by Edward de Bono in the 1980s. During the exercise, team members adopt (role-play) a metaphorical hat that represents a mode of thinking (Exhibit 32.1):

1. *Black* is judgmental, warning of difficulties, dangers, and pitfalls.
2. *Yellow* remains optimistic, probing for the positive value and benefits of the idea.

[*] This Six Thinking Modes technique is based on the original work of Edward de Bono, who holds a registered trademark for "Six Thinking Hats." BMGI has no affiliation, nor has received any sponsorship or approval from de Bono.

3. *White* calls for information known or needed, is emotionally neutral, and seeks the facts.

4. *Red* articulates emotion, feelings, and hunches, without explanation or judgment.

5. *Green* encourages creative thinking, focusing on new ideas, possibilities, and alternatives.

6. *Blue* represents process-based thinking, and is worn by the facilitator at all times.

Each color represents a different orientation to solving problems. Thus, if everyone on the team is in white mode, all comments and suggestions must be factual or based on data. During this time, no emotional (red mode), judgmental (black mode), optimistic (yellow mode), or outlandish (green mode) thoughts are allowed.

Although six thinking modes can be a lot of fun, it's also empowering because it makes use of every team member's intelligence and experience, and encourages constructive criticism. As a result, the team's performance and results are strengthened.

Steps

Scenario: GreenJeans Software sells computer programs to track household income and expenses. The company is looking to grow its market share, and wants to explore the feasibility of offering its service via the Internet. While most team members are in favor of this idea, they need to convince upper management that the service can be offered securely, and that it can be reliably supported with minimal restructuring.

1. Assign Facilitator and Establish Ground Rules

Always in blue thinking mode, the facilitator's role is to remain neutral and guide participants through the exercise. Before beginning, the facilitator should explain any ground rules, such as:

- Reason for the meeting, which includes a recap of the Job to be Done or JTBD (see Technique 1), its associated Outcome Expectations

EXHIBIT 32.1   Thinking Modes. Each color represents a different orientation to solving problems.

(see Technique 3), and the key idea(s) the team will evaluate using six thinking modes.

- Perspective of each thinking mode.
- Order in which the modes will be utilized. Note that the order depends on the topic you're discussing, participant familiarity with the topic and each other, and the type of problem you're trying to solve.
- Time allotted in each mode. Typically one to five minutes per mode works well—except for the red mode, which should be limited to one minute or less.

Regardless of the sequence of modes, the facilitator must keep the team moving. Remember, the key is to view the idea from any number of six different perspectives and not to remain fixated on any one point of view.

---

2. Assign a Scribe

Ask someone who will not participate in the exercise to take notes. Since the exercise is entirely verbal, this role is important for documenting the group's discussion and the outcome. Alternatively, you could provide a pad of sticky notes to each participant, and ask them to post their comments on a flip chart or white board as the exercise proceeds.

3. Designate the Thinking Modes and Sequence

Not all thinking modes apply to all problems, and not all modes are necessarily useful to all teams. Therefore, it's important for the team facilitator to (1) select all the applicable modes and (2) design the sequence in which the modes will be used by the team. In doing this, the facilitator relies on his or her direct experience with the problem and team members at hand. If he or she has limited direct experience, modes and sequences can still be planned based on general experience in working with innovation teams and a firm grasp of the task at hand.

Not all thinking modes were created equal—depending on how and when you're using them. Some teams need just one of the modes at one time. Other teams need a combination of modes, in a certain sequence, to achieve their purposes. Still others need just a couple of modes, even picked at random, to help them solve innovation problems.

For example, a team with a history of generating a lot of useless, far-fetched ideas might benefit greatly from thinking in the white and yellow modes. White will help ground the team with better or more accurate knowledge; yellow will force the team to at least envision, if not document, more details about how its ideas will actually solve the problem or fulfill the JTBD and outcome expectations.

Other teams might have the challenge to generate new ideas in pure ideation mode. In this case, a good facilitator might avoid all modes except the green and the blue. Green, recall, is about new ideas, the more creative the better; blue is about the idea-generation process, which is always necessary when it comes to innovation.

A few more suggestions: Lean on the white, yellow, and black modes for teams that need to make breakthroughs in complex technology environments. Use the white mode for teams that don't have consensus or clear procedures for how their work gets done (no documented process). Rely on the blue mode, followed by the red mode, for emotionally packed problems. Rely on all the modes when you need to further evaluate and make decisions about already developed ideas.

4. Implement Session

Depending on its composition and its task, any number of modes, in any sequence, are employed to guide the team through idea discovery and development. As indicated previously, every team has a facilitator that engages in blue-mode thinking from the very beginning to the very end of each session.

For our example, the GreenJeans Software team will sequence the modes in order of: white, yellow, black, green, red, and blue. Following is a little more about each mode and what to consider while engaged in it.

- **White**

The white mode represents objectivity. Participants must stick to factual information, including making notes of any additional information needed to evaluate the proposed idea. Key questions for the group to consider include:

- Why do we think this idea will fulfill the JTBD or meet the targeted outcome expectations?
- What data do we have in support of the idea?
- What information do we need before we can move forward?

During white mode discussion, for the new online service, the GreenJeans team reviews the proposed specifications and recommended modifications to the company's existing infrastructure.

When in white mode, don't get sidetracked with fact checking or arguments about whether something is true—validity can be confirmed later.

- **Yellow**

Yellow mode thinking explores the positive aspects of the idea. In addition to articulating the value of the proposed solution, the yellow mode can result in a refined vision that takes the idea in a new direction. Key questions include:

- What are the benefits of this idea?
- Why do we like this idea?
- What's the best possible scenario that could result from implementing this idea?

For example, an online service for tracking household expenses could lead GreenJeans Software to abandon its packaged applications, drastically reducing manufacturing and distribution costs. This could also differentiate GreenJeans from its competition if the service remains on the cutting edge of web-based technology.

The six thinking modes are about just that: thinking modes and how they relate to behavior. The modes have no relation to people or categories of people; we can all learn to think in any of the modes and approach a problem from any of the six different perspectives.

- **Black**

  Use the black mode to uncover risks and expose adverse outcomes that could result from implementing the idea. Caution, logic, and critical thinking are the keys to making the black mode session effective. A few critical questions include:

  - What's the downside to this idea?
  - What are the idea's weaknesses?
  - What could go wrong if we implement this idea?

  In our example, the GreenJeans team discusses security and cost concerns while in the black mode. Since these concerns are also held by management, the discussion serves a dual purpose by preparing everyone for the objections they will face when presenting the solution to management.

Beware of overusing the black mode. The goal is to flag potential failure points, not to generate alternative ideas or abandon the proposed solution altogether.

- **Green**

  Green represents creativity and forward thinking. When in green mode, a team wants to generate as many ideas as possible and not hold itself back from considering any possibility. Questions to ask in green mode include:

  - How can we improve on the idea?
  - How can we make the idea more practical or appealing?
  - How do we package the idea?

During the green mode discussion, the GreenJeans team suggests ways to overcome security concerns about the online service and how to differentiate the service from competitors.

If you're using six thinking modes to *generate* new ideas, instead of evaluating a few key ideas, start with the green mode.

• **Red**

The red mode gives everyone the opportunity to express opinions in a nonjudgmental forum. While in this mode, participants don't have to justify or prove their statements; it's the time to be subjective. "How do you feel?" is the key question. Alternatively, you can use the red discussion mode to vote on any idea variations that came up during the green mode session.

The GreenJeans Software team didn't know that several of its members were concerned and fearful that it really couldn't provide measurably more online value than competitors who had already been delivering online solutions for years—until it encouraged and cleared the road for red-mode thinking.

If the topic of discussion is controversial, start with the red mode to get everyone's emotions out in the open. In fact, until this happens, you may not get the focus you desire on other points of view.

• **Blue**

At the end of the exercise, everyone engages in the blue mode to outline next steps, assignments, and the like. The blue mode brings stability and predictability to the innovation team and idea development process; it fosters boundaries, time limits, and generally keeps the team on track and on schedule. In short, the blue mode (and the facilitator) ensures that the team progresses with a semblance of order, not chaos.

Resource

de Bono, E. *Six Thinking Hats*. Boston, MA: Little, Brown, 1999.

DEVELOP THE DESIGNS

Most organizations go about refining their products and services—making them better—without first questioning their legitimacy. But if you've gotten this far in the innovation process, then you've already legitimized your new solutions by (1) making sure they're well-defined and (2) making sure they've passed through a rigorous yet expansive ideation process.

This third phase of innovation transforms your great ideas from the white board into workable models. The questions become:

- What functions will it perform and how do I design it?
- How will I assess how good it is?
- What alternatives do I have?
- Can I make my solution invincible, and manage the risk of trying?

First you *formulate the design* by specifying the outcome-expectation-based functions your customers want in your new solution. Use the Functional Requirements technique to accomplish this. Then use any of these techniques to generate and further refine your initial design concepts: Axiomatic Design, Function Structure, Morphological Matrix, TILMAG, and Work Cell Design.

The next task is to *prioritize and select a design* by filtering through a number of concepts to the point where just one is pursued for further development. Two techniques are very helpful in this regard: Paired Comparison Analysis and Pugh Matrix. You can also use both of these techniques to test how well the output of an idea session stands up to customer outcome expectations upstream in the innovation process.

Once you know which solution you'll accept into your innovation portfolio, it's time to *validate and optimize the design*. For this, see these techniques: Process Capability, Design Scorecard, Design Failure Mode and Effects Analysis, Discrete Event Simulation, and Rapid Prototyping. Also, see Mistake Proofing and Robust Design, which can help make sure your new solution functions as intended regardless of uncontrollable events and circumstances.

Functional Requirements

Identify what customers want in your solution.

Functional requirements, and the degree to which they are satisfied, form the basis of customer satisfaction with your products and services. For example, people who drink diet soda expect it to have a certain taste and caloric content. If the soda fails in either regard, customers may move to a competing solution that better meets their expectations.

Just as outcome expectations (see Technique 3) provide solution-neutral *hiring criteria* to get a job done (see Technique 1), functional requirements provide solution-specific requirements against which designs are created. Therefore, functional requirements are a direct translation of outcome expectations with a specific solution in mind.

Designing the details of the solution begins with understanding and articulating functional requirements from the customer's point of view. The requirements provide limits on two types of functions addressed in the design—useful functions and harmful functions. As an example, the degree of brightness displayed by a candle is a useful function, whereas the amount of soot produced is a harmful function. So the candle design functional requirements will provide the targets and limits for amount of brightness and soot production.

To successfully establish the functional requirements, you'll need at least a modest understanding of how to gather voice-of-the-customer data via surveys, focus groups, and interviews.

Background

Some functional requirements are described in an objective, unambiguous, and measurable way. They must have an operational definition, a unit of measurement, and a desired target range. Examples include the weight of a product, service delivery lead times, product or service cost, and such product quality characteristics as durability, reliability, maintainability, and so on. Other functional requirements may be more subjective, ambiguous, and difficult to measure. Examples include ease of use, look and feel, ease of doing business, and timeliness.

Defining customer expectations as either outcome expectations (solution neutral) or functional requirements (solution dependent) allows us to avoid confusion around the many labels often applied to the voice-of-the-customer concept—customer needs, wants, requirements, standards, critical-to-quality (CTQ) factors, critical-to-satisfaction (CTS) factors, delighters, and so forth.

Similarly, customers are traditionally classified into confusing or misleading categories—internal customers, external customers, partners, patients, clients, patrons, guests, fans, and so on. In reality, all customers can be simply defined based on their role as an end user, an intermediary, or a fixer.

- *End users* buy (or hire) the solution to fulfill some JTBD.
- *Intermediaries* add value anywhere in a process along the chain of rudimentary inputs to complex outputs that are purchased by the end user. Intermediaries also transmit customer expectations to providers so they can improve the value of solutions. Examples include retail stores, car dealers, pharmacists, and travel agents.
- *Fixers* are individuals or organizations that improve the product or service during its life cycle through repair, modifications, corrections, additions, or deletions to better meet end-user expectations.

It's important to understand all three types of customers so you can consider the JTBD, outcome expectations, and functional requirements associated with each group when designing your solution. Once you've done this, you can determine how to best meet those expectations through the use of such techniques as Axiomatic Design (Technique 34), Function Structure (Technique 35), and TILMAG (Technique 37).

Steps

Scenario: To illustrate this technique, let's say we want to design or hire a VOIP (Voice Over Internet Protocol) service that allows people to make phone calls via the Internet. VOIP is a cheap alternative to the traditional land-based phone lines for home or office. Our goal is to extract the functional requirements of a VOIP system.

1. Review the JTBD, Outcome Expectations, and Chosen Solution for Design

At the outset, we review the job the customer is trying to get done, and we list the solution-neutral criteria (outcome expectations) she will use to hire the right solution. For our scenario, the JTBD is *conduct telecommunications for business needs*. Exhibit 33.1 shows a partial list of outcome expectations for this JTBD. We chose to "hire" VOIP from a list of several options because it better satisfies the key unmet needs, or outcome expectations.

2. Identify Customers

It's important to identify the customers for your solution by type, as each will have different functional requirements. As we mentioned earlier, customers fall into the three general categories of end users, intermediaries, and fixers.

Keep in mind that customer roles are dynamic—they are determined by the customer's relationship with the solution at a given moment. For instance, the end user in a restaurant is the person(s) having a meal. A waiter is an intermediary, unless that waiter comes in on his night off to enjoy dinner, in which case he becomes an end user. A restaurant critic having a meal is an end user but also a fixer, as his comments may influence the restaurant to provide a better product or service.

Think carefully about who the end users of your solution really are. For example, the end users for an airplane engine (target solution) are aviation manufacturing companies. The end users for an airplane (final solution) are airline companies. Passengers are actually end users of the transportation solution offered by the airline.

OE #	Outcome Expectations	Functional Requirements	Measurement Units	Target
1	Increase the likelihood that service is always available to make phone calls	VOIP System availability	% up time	>99.9999%
2	Minimize the effort it takes to place or receive a call	VOIP Call initiation effort	# of clicks or buttons to press for call initiation	less than or equal to digits in the phone number
3	Increase the likelihood that calls are clearly understood by the receiver and sender	Call clarity	standardized clarity test	>98%
4	Minimize the background noise generated during the call	Background noise level	% of call time with unacceptable noise level	<1%
5	Minimize the cost it takes to make a call	Cost per month for VOIP	dollars	50% of charges from local land-line provider
6	Increase the likelihood that calls can be originated from various locations with only access to computer, PDA, etc.	Access of VOIP service	Access from predefined devices (computer, PDA, and phone device)	100% access
7	Minimize the effort it takes to troubleshoot system-related problems when making calls	VOIP customer service	Customer satisfaction rating	>90%
8	Minimize the time it takes to resolve technical issues with the system failures	VOIP service hold time	Minutes	90% < 2 minutes
9	Minimize the time it takes to resolve technical issues with the system failures	VOIP service time to resolution	Minutes	90% < 15 minutes

EXHIBIT 33.1   Functional Requirements (Downloadable).

Copyright © 2012, BMGI. A blank version of this customized form is available for download at www.innovatorstoolkit .com.

3. Gather Expectations

Review each customer segment's JTBD and outcome expectations. Then, using our example, translate these outcome expectations into functional requirements that are specific to VOIP. Shown in Exhibit 33.1, these functional requirements focus on enhancing the useful functions and minimizing the harmful functions created by the VOIP system. You can create the functional requirements and validate them using customer surveys, focus groups, or interviews. (For more about translating outcome expectations into functional requirements, see Axiomatic Design, Technique 34.)

The specific approach will depend, in part, on the level of innovation in your solution. For instance, it would be difficult for people to fill out a survey on a completely new offering they've never seen, although a survey would be in order if you're simply adding new features to a well-known product. For the most part, focus groups work well because you can ask open-ended questions, and the group dynamic usually generates more discussion than individual interviews do.

Typically, functional requirements fall into five major categories: ease of use, timeliness, cost, options, and certainty, which refers to a series of such quality measures as reliability, maintainability, and so forth.

---

4. Classify Expectations by Type

Once you've gathered extracted functional requirements, establish a clear operational definition for each one, a target, and a way to measure it. If the functional requirements are subjective, a strongly correlated surrogate measure may be used. For example, *VOIP customer service* may be measured using a customer satisfaction rating.

For any solution, a performance expectation, such as *reliability*, would likely be tracked with a metric called *mean time between failures*. This metric, in turn, is included in one's Design Scorecard (Technique 43) for that solution.

---

5. Align Expectations between Customer Segments

After you have a thorough understanding of the functional requirements for each customer type, look for potential conflicts of interest and determine a way to minimize or resolve these issues. For instance, end users may desire a level of customization that makes it more difficult for fixers to service a product. In this case, the provider may choose to include fewer customization options to end users—to meet the fixer expectation of *easy to repair*.

Although it's critical to meet the expectations of end users, be careful not to alienate intermediaries or fixers along the way. The most successful organizations are able to align expectations between different customer segments so that conflicts are minimized.

---

6. Translate Expectations into Design Parameters

Use other design techniques and tools, such as Axiomatic Design (Technique 34), to convert your customer's expectations into a viable design starting with functional requirements.

In the language of Six Sigma, functional requirements are the ''Y-related'' *Key Performance Indicators (KPIs)* on which you'll focus your design and optimization efforts, and which you will track over time with your design scorecard and/or process behavior charts.

Axiomatic Design

Transform what customers want into the best products and services.

Axiomatic design is the process by which you translate your customers' *jobs to be done* and *outcome expectations* (JTBDs and OEs), into *functional requirements* (FRs), then *design parameters* (DPs), then *process variables* (PVs). It's especially helpful when working with complex systems that contain large numbers of FRs and, consequently, even larger numbers of DPs and PVs—sometimes numbering beyond the thousands. A jumbo jet or a powerful software application are examples of this.

The progressive axiomatic design activity ensures that the final solution is the best design, delivers what the customer needs, and can be reliably manufactured or delivered. While axiomatic design can be readily understood at a high level, applying it to complex systems (its purpose) requires an expert who has extensive education and experience with the technique.

In this chapter and book, we use the terms *jobs to be done* and *outcome expectations* in lieu of the classic Axiomatic Design term, *customer attributes*. Please keep this in mind if you are an experienced Axiomatic Design engineer or Axiomatic Design purist.

Background

Two axioms underlie axiomatic design—the independence axiom and the information axiom.

The *independence axiom* asserts that all FRs and their associated DPs remain independently attached; therefore, if you adjust a DP to satisfy an FR, you do this without affecting other FRs. Designs that don't satisfy the independence axiom are called *coupled*. Designs that do satisfy the independence axiom are called *uncoupled* or *decoupled*.

You always want to produce either uncoupled or decoupled designs because this keeps a design as modular and independent as possible. Therefore, if any one part of a system malfunctions, the unwanted consequences do not propagate throughout the entire system. Also, independent designs enable the segmentation of engineering work when dealing with very complex and extensive systems.

The *information axiom* is based on information theory, which essentially says that the best design is the one with the least information content—while also satisfying the independence axiom. Information content is defined in terms of probability: The more likely the design is to reduce the influence of variation from process parameter changes, different customer-usage conditions, and repeated use, the better it meets the information axiom.

A design that meets the information axiom is called a *robust design* (see Technique 42) because it maximizes the probability that it will meet its specifications (process variables or PVs) on an ongoing basis. For example, process variables like *tensile strength* or *data-entry errors* can function as intended along a spectrum from zero to absolute perfection; but in reality, it always functions somewhere in between the two extremes.

Axiomatic design is credited to Dr. Nam Pyo Suh, an emeritus professor of mechanical engineering at MIT.

In establishing designs that meet the independence and information axioms, the axiomatic design practitioner engages in a demanding and disciplined process of *zigzagging* between FRs, DPs, and PVs, as shown in Exhibit 34.1. In essence, this zigzagging is the process by which FRs are translated into their corresponding DPs and PVs—all the while maintaining as much independence as possible, and fulfilling the information axiom such that the design performs to its specifications as often as possible.

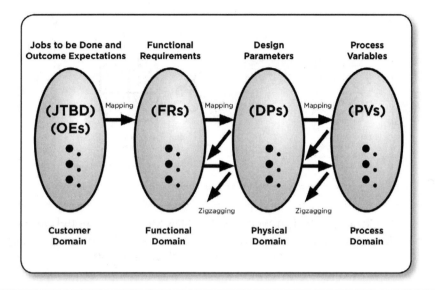

EXHIBIT 34.1   Axiomatic Design Domains.

Note: Classic Axiomatic Design uses the term *customer attributes* instead of the terms we use in this chapter and book, *jobs to be done* and *outcome expectations*.

Independence Axiom

We can illustrate the independence axiom by showing the relationship of two DPs and two FRs—knowing that for such a simple 2-by-2 design, one would not need axiomatic design. But since axiomatic design is so complex in practice, this is the best way to illustrate how it works at a high level. The examples that follow are highly stylized for illustration purposes; in reality, they would be more extensive and detailed.

1. Coupled Design

Looking at Exhibit 34.2, we see that both water flow (FR1) and temperature (FR2) are influenced by both the angle of the cold valve (DP1) and the angle of the hot valve (DP2). The design is therefore coupled. Taking a service example, both the quality of a new hire (FR1) and the speed of the hiring process (FR2) are influenced by the number of interviewers involved (DP1) and the method of scheduling interviews (DP2).

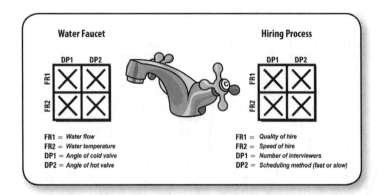

EXHIBIT 34.2 Coupled Design with 2 × 2 FR-DP Matrix. A coupled design is one in which all functional requirements cannot be achieved independently by adjusting design parameters without affecting other functional requirements.

2. Decoupled Design

A decoupled design is preferred over a coupled design. Looking at Exhibit 34.3, we see two simple FRs and DPs in a pulley-and-belt design for using the power generated from a car's crankshaft to run its air conditioner. The belt cannot slip sideways (FR1) and cannot slip forward or backward (FR2) as the system operates. In a decoupled design, both FR1 and FR2 are

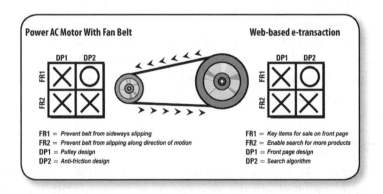

EXHIBIT 34.3 Decoupled Design with 2 × 2 FR-DP Matrix. A decoupled design is one in which all functional requirements can be achieved independently by adjusting design parameters. However, at least one design parameter affects two or more functional requirements.

influenced by the pulley design (DP1), but only FR2 is influenced by the antifriction design (DP2).

Also shown in Exhibit 34.3 is a web-based e-transaction where both FR1 and FR2 are influenced by DP1, but only FR2 is influenced by DP2. In other words, the home page design (DP1) determines what shows on the home page (FR1) and enables further searching (FR2); but the search algorithm (DP2) does not determine what is showing on the home page (FR1), and only enables the identification of additional products for sale (FR2).

3. Uncoupled Design

An uncoupled design is preferred over a decoupled or coupled design. Looking at Exhibit 34.4, we see two FRs and two DPs involved in a faucet design, where the flow rate valve (DP1) influences water flow (FR1), and the hot/cold mixing valve (D2) influences water temperature (FR2). The DP1/FR1 combination is totally uncoupled from the DP2/FR2 combination, thereby ensuring that each FR/DP combination can stand alone.

We can further illustrate an uncoupled design in the service world by looking at two DPs and two FRs related to purchasing a product online. In Exhibit 34.4, the shopping cart design (DP1) influences friendly checkout (FR1), and the secure payment transfer system (DP2) influences payment from the customer (FR2).

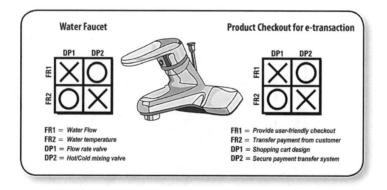

EXHIBIT 34.4   Uncoupled Design with 2 × 2 FR-DP Matrix. An uncoupled design is one in which each functional requirement is independently achieved by a corresponding unique design parameter.

Example—Information Axiom

The information axiom can be best explained with the help of Exhibit 34.5, which shows that the success probability of any design can be calculated by using the design range (usually tolerance) and the system range (described by process variation). The information content of the design is calculated by the area under common range (A_{CR}) and is given by the following equation: Information content $= I = \log_2 (1/A_{CR})$.

It's clear from the equation that if the $A_{CR} = 1$, or the design range is equal to the system range, then information content equals zero—indicating that the design is as good as it could be. If the information content is greater than zero, then risk of defect or malfunction is present and, therefore, the design may not be optimal or the best it could be.

This also means that any design is good as long as the system variation range is within the design range, irrespective of process variation. But if the system range is beyond the design range, then defects, errors, or malfunctions will occur. The extent to which the system range exceeds the design range is the extent to which you are exposed to potential failures.

Your first objective with axiomatic design is to make your design as independent as possible with reference to functional requirements. After this you would make it as robust as possible, as per the information axiom, using such techniques as Robust Design (Technique 42), Design Failure Mode and Effects Analysis (Technique 44), and Mistake Proofing (Technique 45).

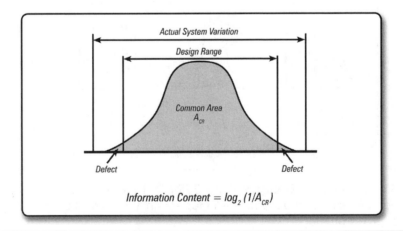

EXHIBIT 34.5   Information Axiom and Information Content.

Steps

1. Determine Job to be Done and Outcome Expectations

The JTBD and associated OEs can be defined in any number of ways (keeping in mind they are synonymous with customer attributes in classic axiomatic design). To remind, the JTBD is what the customer is trying to achieve, apart from any specific product, service, or solution. Then, when you have a specific solution in mind, OEs help you design that solution according to what customers expect, need, or desire.

2. Translate Outcome Expectations into Functional Requirements

This step entails moving from the language of customers into the language of the designer, or what the solution will do. While the customer might say, "I want it to look good," the designer might translate this into "I need it to be a transparent blue color." The customer wants to arrive safely on time on a cross-Atlantic flight (outcome expectation), so the designer needs 200,000 pounds of available thrust to get him and the other passengers there as they wish (functional requirement).

This step is also when the designer identifies any *design constraints* that need to be addressed. Such constraints (cost for instance) represent boundaries for acceptable design solutions—or realities you have to work around as you flow your functional requirements (FRs) into their corresponding design parameters (DPs) in the next step.

There are two kinds of constraints: *input* and *system*. Input constraints are imposed as part of the design specifications. System constraints are imposed by the system in which the design solution must function.

---

3. Translate Functional Requirements into Design Parameters

Next, the designer translates each FR into a corresponding set of DPs in the physical domain. These DPs are your critical material or service targets and specifications. For instance, if the FR is to make a part blue in color, then the DP for that FR might be to target 0/0/255 (blue) on the RGB color scale, with a tolerance of plus or minus five points on the scale.

4. Map Design Parameters to Process Variables

The final step of axiomatic design ensures that you map your design specifications to your process, so it can produce and deliver your new solution, time after time, without mistake. Using the same approach used in translating FRs into DPs, the designer translates each DP into a set of corresponding process variables (PVs). Therefore, if the DP is 0/0/255 on the RGB scale, plus or minus five points, then what are the variables in the process that make the part meet this specification? These are the related PVs.

Note that the process entailed in translating FRs into DPs and DPs into PVs is done hierarchically and iteratively—starting at a high level of detail, then decomposing into finer levels of detail (see Exhibit 34.1). This is the zigzagging aspect of axiomatic design, as FRs are decomposed into DPs, and as DPs are decomposed into PVs. At each level, design decisions are made for each domain, which is zigging. Then the design team backtracks to the functional domain and determines the next level down, reflecting all the design decisions across the domains at the level above. This is the zagging part.

While zigging and zagging, the designer ensures that each set of lower-order FRs, DPs, and PVs retains as much independence as possible and also fulfills the information axiom.

Resources

For more reading and knowledge, see:

El-Haik, B. *Axiomatic Quality: Integrating Axiomatic Design with Six Sigma, Reliability, and Quality Engineering*. Hoboken, NJ: Wiley Interscience, 2005.

Pyo Suh, N. *Axiomatic Design: Advances and Applications*. New York: Oxford University Press, 2001.

Function Structure

Identify how the solution functions in its whole and its parts.

Function structure breaks the intended overall design function into cohesive and naturally workable subfunctions that lend themselves well to error-free development. For example, you would use function structure when designing a refrigerator to move from the functional requirement (control freezer temperature at −18 degrees C) to the design parameter (turn compressor on or off when air temperature is higher or lower than the set temperature).

The function structure technique is employed when you need to create design concepts and are translating functional requirements into design parameters. But since function structure doesn't necessarily address the independence of requirements and parameters, it's most effective when applied in conjunction with Axiomatic Design (see Technique 34). Function structure is best applied with the help of a qualified engineer.

Steps

Scenario: To demonstrate function structure, we'll look at the design for an automatic hair-washing machine—a device that would take the place of the person who preps you for a haircut when you visit a salon.

1. Clarify the Design Problem

What is the overall intent of the design, or the function the design must perform? Write the function in the middle box of a function structure

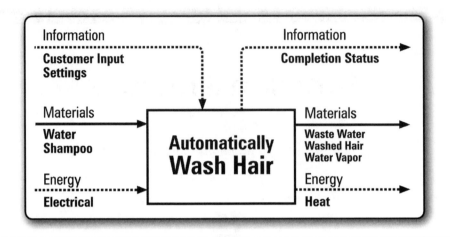

EXHIBIT 35.1 Key Function with Inputs and Outputs.

diagram (Exhibit 35.1). The intent of our example system is to *automatically wash hair*.

2. List the Inputs and Outputs for the Function

To the left of the function, list the inputs—what does the system need to perform its overall function? To the right, list the outputs—what will the system deliver (both intended and unintended)? List all inputs and outputs under the categories of *material, energy,* or *information.*

Exhibit 35.1 shows the inputs and outputs designated for the automatic hair-washing system.

3. Divide the Overall Function into Identifiable Subfunctions

Now ask, "What are the corresponding subfunctions needed to fulfill the main function?" List these subfunctions below the main function, connecting them in sequential order once you have listed them all (Exhibit 35.2). Keep in mind the following:

- Subfunctions are performed through some physical process or activity that is executed by a system or mechanism.

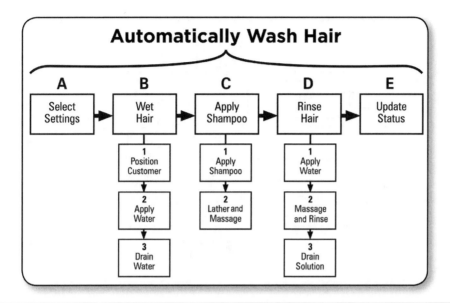

EXHIBIT 35.2   Function Structure.

- Subfunction statements should consist of a verb and a noun (for example, decrease pressure, register customer, rinse hair).
- You can keep dividing subfunctions until they cannot be subdivided further, but this isn't very practical. Only identify subfunctions to an appropriate level based on the type of design.
- Each subfunction should fulfill a customer need—either an Outcome Expectation (see Technique 3) or a Functional Requirement (see Technique 33).

4. Develop Possible Solutions for Each Subfunction

Once you've developed your function structure diagram to the appropriate level, the final step is to ideate possible solutions (design options) for each subfunction. You can combine or further subdivide the subfunctions as needed. Exhibit 35.3 shows the automatic hair-washing function broken down into subfunctions with the exchanges of material, energy, and information indicated. This can guide the ideation of solutions for each subfunction.

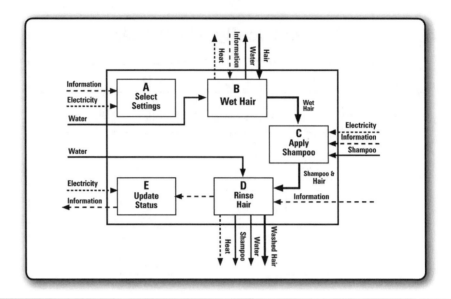

EXHIBIT 35.3   Complete Automatic Hair-Washing System.

When seeking subfunction solutions, use any of the more advanced ideation techniques in this book, as simple brainstorming can leave you void of innovative ideas. During this process, stay focused on solutions at the subfunction level. For example, ask:

- How can I select settings?
- How can I wet hair?
- How can I apply shampoo?
- How can I rinse hair?
- How can I update status?

For our automatic hair-washing subfunctions, a list of possible solutions or design options are shown in Exhibit 35.4.

If you're satisfied with the list of possible solutions, move on to Morphological Matrix (Technique 36) to see how the subfunction solutions can be combined to create an innovative design. If you're still struggling to surface innovative design options, try TILMAG (Technique 37) or HIT Matrix (Technique 18).

Subfunctions	Design Options
A (select settings)	Device control panel
B1 (position customer)	Reclining chair; massage table; lean forward; fitted hood
B2 (apply water)	Spray nozzle; water reservoir; fill hood with water
B3 (drain)	Sink drain; suction pump
C1 (spray shampoo)	Spray nozzle; soapy solution; deliver via bristles (see D2)
C2 (massage and lather)	Rotating bristles; jets; inflate inner hood lining
C3 (drain)	Same as B3
D1 (spray water)	Same as B2
D2 (massage and rinse)	Same as C2
D3 (drain)	Same as B3
E (update status)	Green flashing light; beeping sound

EXHIBIT 35.4   Possible Design Solutions.

Resource

For a full treatment of Function Structure, see:

Pahl, G., and W. Beitz. *Engineering Design: A Systematic Approach*. New York: Springer-Verlag, 1999.

Morphological Matrix

Generate solution concepts by combining design alternatives.

Morphological matrix combines design options at the subfunction level to help you come up with new solutions. For instance, if you are building a self-driving car, you have many ways to design the car's subfunctions (GPS navigation, voice recognition, external sensors, etc.). Morphological matrix enables you to determine all possible design solutions, including approaches that combine design options in ways you might not have thought of before.

You can use morphological matrix after you have identified your system's subfunctions with the Function Structure technique. Or, if you're following an axiomatic design, morphological matrix will help you translate functional requirements into design parameters. Although the technique itself is easy to use, the team must have significant expertise related to the system to understand its subfunctions and evaluate the design options.

The premise of the term *morphology* is that by understanding the underlying parts of a system (the system's subfunctions), you will better understand the entire system (the system's overall function). Thus, when you look at a system's morphology, you are essentially asking, "What parts make up the whole?"

Steps

Scenario: In Function Structure (Technique 35), we determined a list of design options for an automatic hair-washing machine. We can use morphological matrix to combine these options into possible solutions at the subfunction level.

1. Determine the System's Subfunctions

For simple designs, you can brainstorm a list of subfunctions. More complex systems require the use of Function Structure (Technique 35) or Axiomatic Design (Technique 34). For process-based innovations, a Process Map or Value Stream Map (Technique 51) will help you identify subfunctions, which may correspond to steps in the process.

Subfunctions should comprise the system as a whole, but should not be so granular as to overlap each other.

2. List the Design Options for Each Subfunction

Try to list at least two but no more than six design options for each subfunction; fewer than two options leaves no alternative routes through the matrix, and more than six makes it difficult to evaluate without the aid of a computer. Don't assess the options at this point; merely document them.

Unlike TILMAG (Technique 37), you can compare more than two design options simultaneously using morphological matrix, which makes it a more practical technique for complex systems.

3. Assess Feasibility of Design Options

Evaluate the design options for initial feasibility and eliminate any options that conflict with design constraints or the job to be done and outcome

Subfunctions	Option 1	Option 2	Option 3	Option 4
A (select settings)	Device control panel			
B1 (position customer)	Reclining chair	Massage table	~~Lean forward~~	Fitted hood
B2 (apply water)	Spray nozzle	~~Water reservoir~~	Fill hood with water	
C1 (spray shampoo)	Spray nozzle	Soapy solution	Deliver via bristles	
C2 (massage and lather)	Rotating bristles	Jets	Inflate inner hood lining	
D1 (spray water)	Spray nozzle	~~Water reservoir~~	Fill hood with water	
D2 (massage and rinse)	Rotating bristles	Jets	Inflate inner hood lining	
D3 (drain)	~~Suction pump~~	Sink drain		
E (update status)	Green flashing light	Beeping sound	~~Printout~~	

EXHIBIT 36.1 Morphological Matrix (Downloadable). After listing all design options in the matrix, take time to eliminate any that conflict with design constraints or customer requirements.

Copyright © 2012, BMGI. A blank version of this customized form is available for download at www.innovatorstoolkit .com.

expectations (Exhibit 36.1). Note that removing one option may make other options moot (such as the *suction pump* option in our example, which wasn't needed after the team removed the *water reservoir* option).

4. Generate Design Concepts

Combine the remaining options to derive design concepts (solutions for each subfunction). Choose one option from each row until all possible combinations have been documented (Exhibit 36.2). Depending on the complexity of the matrix, you may need to do this on a computer since the total number of combinations is likely to number in the hundreds, or even thousands. In our example, there are 648 possible design concepts, calculated by multiplying the number of options in each row ($1 \times 3 \times 2 \times 3 \times 3 \times 2 \times 3 \times 1 \times 2$).

5. Assess Feasibility of Design Concepts

The final step is to complete a preliminary evaluation of the design concepts that, as before, can be based on physical or cost constraints. Be careful not to eliminate ideas prematurely; if in doubt, leave them in. You can

	A (select settings)	B1 (position customer)	B2 (apply shampoo)	C1 (spray shampoo)	C2 (massage and lather)	D1 (spray water)	D2 (massage and rinse)	D3 (drain)	E (update status)
1	Device control panel	Reclining chair	Spray nozzle	Spray nozzle	Rotating bristles	Spray nozzle	Rotating bristles	Sink drain	Green flashing light
2	Device control panel	Massage table	Spray nozzle	Spray nozzle	Rotating bristles	Spray nozzle	Rotating bristles	Sink drain	Green flashing light
3	Device control panel	Fitted hood	Spray nozzle	Spray nozzle	Rotating bristles	Spray nozzle	Rotating bristles	Sink drain	Green flashing light
4	Device control panel	Reclining chair	Fill hood with water	Spray nozzle	Rotating bristles	Spray nozzle	Rotating bristles	Sink drain	Green flashing light
5	Device control panel	Massage table	Fill hood with water	Spray nozzle	Rotating bristles	Spray nozzle	Rotating bristles	Sink drain	Green flashing light
6	Device control panel	Fitted hood	Fill hood with water	Spray nozzle	Rotating bristles	Spray nozzle	Rotating bristles	Sink drain	Green flashing light
7	Device control panel	Reclining chair	Spray nozzle	Soapy solution	Rotating bristles	Spray nozzle	Rotating bristles	Sink drain	Green flashing light
8	Device control panel	Massage table	Spray nozzle	Soapy solution	Rotating bristles	Spray nozzle	Rotating bristles	Sink drain	Green flashing light
9	Device	Fitted hood	Spray	Spray	Rotating	Spray	Rotating	Sink	Green

EXHIBIT 36.2   Morphological Matrix Design Concepts (Downloadable). Here we see just a handful of the 648 possible design concepts for an automatic hair-washing machine that resulted from using a Morphological Matrix.

conduct further assessment using a structured evaluation technique such as the Pugh Matrix (Technique 40). In our example, we eliminated design concept numbers 4 and 5 because the fitted hood option will not work with a reclining chair or massage table.

Additional Example

In addition to complex designs, you can use morphological matrix to help you list and evaluate options for any type of process or service. In Exhibit 36.3, we see how one group used the technique to generate options for a fund-raising program sponsored by a local restaurant. The number of options in the matrix is nowhere near exhaustive, yet together they produce 500 different combinations (5 × 4 × 5 × 5). However, instead of combining all the design concepts in a list, the team chose one option from each row until they had enough viable solutions.

Subfunctions	Option 1	Option 2	Option 3	Option 4	Option 5
Determine sources of funding	Manny's Diner	Employees	Grants	Community	Other businesses
Identify participants	Employees	Employees and families	Local school athletes	Community groups	
Identify beneficiaries	Local schools	Homeless shelters	Programs for the physically challenged	Hospitals	Food banks
Determine types of activities	Bowling	Softball	Pledge walks/runs	Discount coupons for dinner at Manny's	Bake sale

EXHIBIT 36.3   Another Morphological Matrix Example (Downloadable).

Resources

For many helpful references, including information about morphological analysis from the technique's originator, Fritz Zwicky, see:

Swedish Morphological Society (www.swemorph.com).

For an interesting look at combining Morphological Matrix with axiomatic design concepts, see:

Weber, R., and S. Condoor. *Conceptual Design Using a Synergistically Compatible Morphological Matrix.* www.fie-conference.org/fie98/papers/1245.pdf.

TILMAG

Pair ideal solution elements to create new design concepts.

TILMAG uses pair-based analogical thinking to transform your innovation's main features into unique design concepts. For instance, if you paired the feature *renewable power* with *fast start-up*, you might think of a battery-free flashlight that you shake to turn on. The underlying principle used to make the flashlight work could also provide a solution for your innovation.

The principle behind TILMAG is that the human mind works best when comparing only two pieces of information at a time. Thus, TILMAG helps you create unique solutions without becoming overwhelmed by all the possibilities. However, the tool increases in complexity as the total number of features goes up. For this reason, it's best used at the subsystem level, or when you're comparing fewer than seven features.

If you use Function Structure (Technique 35) to identify your innovation's subfunctions, you can follow up with TILMAG to help you design a solution for each subfunction.

Background

The TILMAG method was developed by Dr. Helmut Schlicksupp, a German author and consultant known for researching and developing creativity techniques. TILMAG is a German acronym for what translates into English as "the transformation of ideal solution elements in an association matrix." It sounds like a mouthful, but it's actually quite simple:

- Ideal Solution Elements (ISEs) are the features or functions that your innovation must have to meet customer outcome expectations (for more information, see Outcome Expectations and Functional Requirements, Techniques 3 and 33 respectively).
- The association matrix helps you transform ISEs into new and innovative design concepts that meet the performance and perception expectations for your solution. It does this by pairing each ISE with every other ISE, which may bring to mind associations that were not evident before.

Steps

Scenario: Let's assume that your innovation is a laptop computer that police officers use in their cars. Using TILMAG, you can discover which features of the laptop will allow you to meet expectations and whether you can meet them in innovative enough ways to distinguish your laptop from the competition.

1. Develop Ideal Solution Elements

Translate your innovation's performance and perception expectations into ISEs: brief, concise phrases that describe a particular feature or function customers will expect your product or service to have. Note that ISEs should not be descriptions of the solution (e.g., long battery life), but instead should be conceptual (e.g., renewable power) so you have room for creativity. In other words, you should bias yourself upstream from functional requirements to outcome expectations.

In our example, the team determined that the laptop ISEs were *renewable power*, *fast start-up*, *large screen*, and *small size*. Of course, you may have other ISEs for a laptop used in a police car, including wireless connectivity and durable components. But since the complexity of the tool goes up as the number of ISEs increases, we'll limit our example to only four ISEs.

The TILMAG matrix needs at least three ISEs, and works best with four to six ISEs. With three ISEs, that's a relatively quick three cells to work. With six ISEs, the matrix grows to 15 working cells.

TILMAG	1 Renewable Power	2 Fast Start-up	3 Large Screen
4 Small Size	Self-winding watch Hybrid car battery Battery-free flashlight Electrochemical reaction	Portable radio	Fold-out map Roll-up mat Projector
3 Large Screen	Solar panel Microscope	Big screen TV Scenery backdrop	X
2 Fast Start-up	MP3 player	X	X

EXHIBIT 37.1   TILMAG Matrix (Downloadable).

Copyright © 2012, BMGI. A blank version of this customized form is available for download at www.innovatorstoolkit .com.

2. Add Ideal Solution Elements to TILMAG Matrix

Across the top of the TILMAG association matrix, list all the ISEs except for the last one. Down the left side, list the ISEs in *reverse* order leaving off the first one (Exhibit 37.1).

3. Eliminate Duplicate Pairings

Cross out the cells where the ISEs correspond to each other (you don't need to pair *large screen* with *large screen,* for example). Also, cross out the bottom right cell because this pairing already exists elsewhere in the matrix (Exhibit 37.1).

4. Pair ISEs

For each of the remaining cells, brainstorm and record associations that come to mind when you pair the ISEs. See what existing products, services, business models, or systems you can think of that have *both ISEs* as a feature or function. Try to identify at least one association for each pair. In some cells, you'll think of several associations. If nothing comes to mind, skip the pair and come back to it later.

5. Generate Design Concepts

Finally, translate the associations you brainstormed in step 4 into design concepts relative to your innovation. Discuss each association one at a time and determine if the association could be applied as a solution to your problem. For our example, we came up with several subsystem solutions for a police car laptop (Exhibit 37.2).

Association	ISEs	Defining Feature	Solution Idea
Self-winding watch	Small size, renewable power	Movement releases potential energy from internal spring	Same
Hybrid car battery	Small size, renewable power	Car battery recharged during braking	Laptop charged when car at rest
Battery-free flashlight	Small size, renewable power	Shake flashlight to turn it on	Laptop charged when car in motion
Electrochemical reaction	Small size, renewable power	Reaction produces energy	Laptop runs on electrochemically charged gel pack
Solar panel	Large screen, renewable power	Large panels produce energy	Install solar panels in car that charges laptop
Microscope	Large screen, renewable power	Runs on batteries, makes small items large	Use retinal projection technology
MP3 player	Fast start-up, renewable power	Operating system loads quickly	Use fastest loading operating system
Portable radio	Small size, fast start-up	Limited functionality (audio only)	Limit software on laptop to required programs
Big screen TV	Large screen, fast start-up	Image comes up quickly	Limit software that loads on startup
Scenery backdrop	Large screen, fast start-up	Fake background drops quickly	Emulate GUI operating system, and programs that load quickly
Fold-out map	Small size, large screen	Compact storage, yet large view	Screen that unfolds to larger view
Roll-up mat	Small size, large screen	Compact storage, yet large view	Keyboard that rolls up when not in use
Projector	Small size, large screen	Projector is small, yet projects onto a large screen	Project laptop display onto car windshield

EXHIBIT 37.2   TILMAG Design Concepts (Downloadable).

Work Cell Design

Configure the workspace for flow and optimization.

Work cell design organizes people, equipment, and processes into the most efficient combination of resources to maximize value creation while minimizing waste. This concept is leveraged by homebuilders, for example, when they design a kitchen. As a center of activity, the kitchen needs to be laid out in a way that supports the flow of making dinner, doing dishes, putting away groceries, and other activities.

Needless to say, if you have a new innovation—product, service, or business model—it pays for you to configure a work cell design before launching into full production or delivery. In doing so, you'll optimize your processes and reduce the time it takes to meet customer demand.

The Background and Steps in this chapter are a good start, but to take full advantage of work cell design, you need to understand more about the principles and practices of *Lean*—an approach that increases the speed, efficiency, and value of operations while reducing waste in both product and service environments (see Resources at the end of the Process Map/Value Stream Map, Technique 51).

Background

Traditionally, manufacturers sought to keep their machines running as much as possible to maximize productivity and decrease piece costs. These days, many manufacturers (and service providers) have realized the benefits of keeping parts, products, or service delivery flowing at a rate dictated by *customer demand*. This ensures that only the required amount of product or

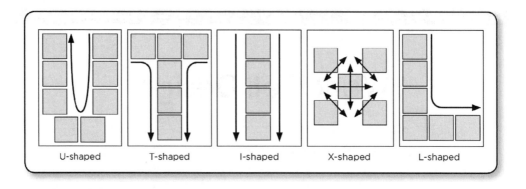

EXHIBIT 38.1   Common Work Cell Designs.

service is produced, as close as possible to the time it's actually needed. One component of achieving this objective is a properly designed work cell.

Exhibit 38.1 shows five common work cell designs that are effective in many manufacturing and service environments.

U-type workstations are typically used when you need the same operators to perform a number of different tasks. The U shape enables different tasks to be accomplished in close proximity, reducing the complexity of transportation and handling.

For example, a machine shop that produces handles for medical equipment might assemble various workstations in a U shape: a drill-station to create holes, a bending machine to make the handles curved, a de-burring machine to remove rough edges, a polishing machine to get the handles ready for priming and painting, and other workstations to apply the finish coatings.

When the work pace is slow based on *takt time* (the rate at which you must produce an order to keep up with demand), this design allows just one operator to quickly travel between equipment and keep work flowing. When takt time is reduced based on increasing customer demand, each workstation could be staffed with individual operators to maintain the pace required.

T-type workstations are often employed to accommodate just-in-time inventory management systems. The vertical part of the T represents the main assembly line, while the horizontal part of the T represents the just-in-time parts or subassemblies flowing into the main line. Often, the horizontal part of the T is modified depending on the complexity of the line.

For instance, a car manufacturer might set the work cell up to flow the chassis down the main line. Then, along the way, parts and subassemblies feed in from the left and the right in perpendicular fashion. Wheels are fed into the main line at just the right time. The same is true for seats, radios, dashboards, doors, windshields, and, of course, a huge variety of other parts and subassemblies.

While not always perfectly or even approximately mimicking a T shape, T-based thinking is applied when, say, designing passenger lines at airports. Premium or first-class customers are allowed to flow through much shorter lines when passing through security or boarding planes. Meanwhile, the main line is also flowing into the same transaction points.

I-type workstations are classic straight-line processes in which work flows from one end of the I to the other. They are used most often when parts are staged in advance (not arriving just in time), and one worker either walks down the line with the product or performs functions before releasing the product to the next worker on the line.

We don't recommend building an I-type workstation against a wall; doing so removes the possibility of doubling capacity by having work flow on both sides of the line, not just one. Some restaurants, for instance, build their salad bars against a wall or other barrier. This prevents them from doubling their service capacity moving the line away from the wall (a minimum investment).

X-type workstations are typically used when functional or cross-functional work teams need to openly and regularly communicate. Each gap in the X represents a person. Minimal partitions separate workers to keep the work orderly and to reinforce individual accountability—but the X configuration needs to be open enough to foster cross-communication and teamwork.

In a manufacturing office environment, you might co-locate dissimilar departments to enable a cross-functional effort like approving new products for release to the market. You might colocate a purchasing agent, design engineer, quality engineer, and manufacturing engineer—thereby making the process more efficient. In a single-function work cell, like a call center, an X might be used to enable one agent to help another when needed.

L-type workstations are fitting when you need to place two or more operations or operators near each other, reducing travel time, speeding communication, and instituting flexibility in meeting takt time. Just like the U-type workstation, the L type enables one worker to perform two different functions during slow demand cycles; during higher demand cycles, two workers can work adjacently to keep pace with orders and workloads.

L workstations work well in office environments where training is required. Experienced staff can be placed adjacent to new or inexperienced employees to demonstrate, answer questions immediately, and generally mentor. The cost advantage of an L design is the ability to reduce space requirements and share resources, such as a printer and fax machine.

Steps

Scenario: RayRay's House of Hair is a new chain of beauty salons that aims to reduce customer wait and servicing time. Let's see how RayRay's uses the Work Cell Design technique to optimize the flow of the haircutting process.

1. Gather Data

When designing a work cell, you need two key pieces of information—the customer demand rate and the time the process takes. With this data, you can determine *takt time*—the rate at which you must produce in order to keep up with demand.

- Customer demand can be represented in any increment that makes sense for your innovative offering. How many products do you sell in a day, a week, or a month? How many customers do you serve in a minute, an hour, or a day?
- Process time can be defined as either *lead time* (the total time the process takes from beginning to end, including wait time), or *cycle time* (the total time it takes to complete one process step).

In our example, RayRay's gathers this data by visiting other beauty salons to see how many customers come in during a given period. He does this several times, on different days of the week and during different times of the day, to determine customer demand rate. To determine process cycle time, RayRay's times several customers as they go through each step in the process (customer check-in, shampoo, haircut, and payment).

If your product or service is new, you may not have previous customer demand or time data. In this case, you can derive the data from a pilot study or prototype. Or, you can gather data from similar processes, or even from your competitors (if they'll let you).

2. Calculate Required Resources

Once you have the customer *demand rate* (DR) for your product or service, and the *cycle time* (CT), you can determine the *number of resources* (NR) needed to maintain takt time by using two simple formulas:

$$DR = 1/\text{takt} \qquad NR = (DR)(CT)$$

For example, RayRay's research shows that the *demand rate* for haircuts is one customer every 5 minutes (DR = 1/5, so the takt time is 5 minutes). The *cycle time* for a haircut (not including check-in, shampoo, or payment) is 15 minutes [NR = (1/5)(15) = 3]. So, RayRay's would need three resources, or stylists, to maintain takt time and keep up with customer demand.

If the process requires more than one person to maintain takt time, you can apply workload balancing to create an even distribution of work across the resources so that none are overburdened or underutilized. For more information about workload balancing, see *The Toyota Way Fieldbook,* by J. Liker and D. Meier, New York: McGraw-Hill, 2005.

3. Optimize Process Flow

Refer to your process or value stream map and identify the value-added and non-value-added steps. A value-added step is one for which the customer would pay. All other steps are non-value-added, even if they are essential to the process. Then:

- *Eliminate non-value-added steps.* For example, RayRay's determines that interrupting a haircut in progress so the stylist can check in a new customer is a non-value-added step. He eliminates this step by installing an automated kiosk where customers check themselves in for their appointments.

- *Minimize or eliminate excessive movement or transport of people or objects.* At RayRay's, customers pay for their haircuts when they check in, eliminating a trip to the cashier afterward.
- *Strive for one-piece flow.* To reduce wait time, parts, products, and customers should move through the process one at a time instead of in batches.

Depending on how complex your process is, you may need different process maps or value stream maps—one that provides a high-level view of the process, and any number of more detailed maps that document the subprocesses. In each case, you should attempt to eliminate or minimize non-value-added activities and wasted motion, and strive for one-piece flow.

---

4. Develop Standard Work

For each process step, develop *standard work*—a list of tasks required to complete that step, in order. This ensures an optimal work sequence and maintains consistency between employees who perform the same type of work. Train employees to follow the standard work documentation, and keep it in a place that can be conveniently referenced.

Note that optimizing the process flow and developing standard work may take several iterations. Repeat steps 3 and 4 as time allows, collecting data along the way, before moving on.

Don't confuse standard work with standard operating procedures (SOP). An SOP typically contains detailed and lengthy instructions for creating or assembling a product or delivering a service. Standard work identifies the best way for a person to complete a particular task and documents this information with pictures or very few words.

---

5. Arrange Workstations

Place workstations (desks or machines where work takes place) as close together as possible, in an arrangement that minimizes transportation and

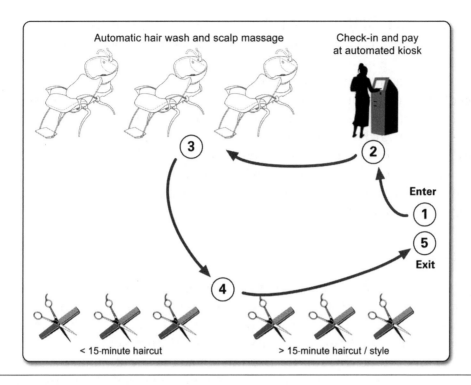

EXHIBIT 38.2   Work Cell Design Example.

motion and optimizes flow. Depending on the type of work performed, certain layouts will work better than others. Regardless of the design you choose, be careful not to sacrifice safety, cost, or quality for efficiency's sake.

In our example, the work cell design at RayRay's is carefully laid out to direct the customers along a designated path (Exhibit 38.2). After checking in and paying, clients proceed to a booth where their hair is washed and their scalps massaged by a specially designed machine. This allows the stylist, the critical resource, to remain dedicated to the haircutting and styling process.

6. Apply 5S

5S stands for Sort, Store, Shine, Standardize, and Sustain. Use this method to keep your workstations clean and to standardize item locations. At RayRay's, for instance, the stylists use certain items every day including scissors, a comb, clippers, styling gel, and so on. These frequent use items are placed in readily accessible locations at the haircutting workstations. Items used less frequently are kept in a centralized, but out of the way, location.

The difficult step to maintain in 5S is Sustain because people get busy and often return to previous habits. Therefore, RayRay's developed a *shadow board* to highlight any tools that are missing from their proper locations. The shadow board is essentially a checklist that all stylists must fill out when they leave their workstations—even if it's expected that they will be the ones using that same workstation when they return to work. This discipline allows RayRay's to avoid the need for inspection and maintain high levels of operational control at all times.

7. Test Design

When you're ready to put everything into place, conduct a test run of the work cell design and all the associated processes to make sure you can meet takt time and that everything goes as planned. Not only should the operation meet takt time and process time requirements, it should also portray an obvious rhythm. It's like the old adage about quality: You know it when you see it. So, too, you know a smooth and efficient operation when you see one (even if there are some isolated points of less than perfect flow).

Resource

For a thorough reference on work cell design, see:

Hyer, N., and U. Wemmerlov. *Reorganizing the Factory: Competing through Cellular Manufacturing*. Portland, OR: Productivity Press, 2002.

Paired Comparison Analysis

Rank design concepts against each other in pairs.

Paired comparison analysis relies on a simple matrix format to compare different and often divergent innovation ideas or design concepts, enabling you to choose the one that gives you the greatest chance of success. For instance, a carmaker might have five different design configurations for a new gas/electric hybrid; which design is the best one for the market?

Use paired comparison analysis when you need to compare either more upstream innovation ideas or more downstream design concepts. This technique is especially helpful when you don't have objective data regarding how different ideas could meet your customers' Outcome Expectations (see Technique 3), or when you're uncertain about how different design concepts could satisfy different Functional Requirements (see Technique 33).

Part of this technique's advantage is that it's easier to use than other comparative techniques such as the Pugh Matrix (Technique 40). Therefore, paired comparison analysis enables you to quickly but comprehensively assess the relative worth of all your options before committing to any specific one.

Steps

Scenario: Let's imagine an advertising agency that has the opportunity to land a multimillion-dollar client who wants to launch a new product (over-the-counter, common-cold medication). The client wants to know what the advertising theme will be and what other themes were considered. The ad agency uses paired comparison analysis to answer these questions.

1. Create a Clear Operational Definition

An operational definition is an unambiguous and understandable description of what your solution alternatives (ideas or design concepts) are trying to accomplish. In our example, the advertising agency's objective is to ensure the client *gains an extra 8 percent of market share* from the new cold-medication ad campaign. With this description documented, there is no ambiguity about why the agency is performing a paired comparison analysis—and different people can be involved, using and interpreting the analysis in a consistent manner without any confusion.

2. Generate or Discover Alternative Ideas

Classically, completing a paired comparison analysis calls for the use of brainstorming techniques to come up with great alternatives. We recommend using any or all of the ideation techniques in this book to move significantly beyond classic brainstorming. If simple brainstorming were sufficient, more teams would come up with more innovations more often than not. But this is not the case.

Write a clear description (operational definition) of each alternative idea, and assign a letter to each. You can also attach a descriptive title to the ideas. For example, possible advertising themes could include:

- *Dancing Ducks:* Take-off on AFLAC's talking duck, but uses a Nutcracker Suite or Swan Lake theme with ducks singing and dancing to lyrics describing the virtues of the product.
- *Breaking News:* News anchor delivering breaking news about how this new product alleviates the symptoms of the common cold so much better than competing products.
- *Expert Doctor:* Straight medical theme with actor posing as a doctor extolling the virtues of the product for treating colds for all members of the family. Provide comparative medical research findings.
- *Gospel Choir:* A gospel choir in a Sunday setting with uplifting and joyful music and lyrics describing how you will be saved from further suffering by using this product at the first sign of a cold.

You should not eliminate any alternatives at this point. Paired comparison analysis is a powerful tool for determining differences between alternatives, even if they seem very similar.

3. Create a Comparison Matrix

A comparison matrix (Exhibit 39.1) is used to rank the ability of competing ideas to provide a real solution. The matrix lists each idea under consideration as both a row and a column. For all ideas that are not comparing themselves, or are not redundant (gray shaded boxes in matrix), you must decide which of the two competing ideas is better based on your operational definition.

Comparisons should be made quickly—try not to take longer than 10 seconds on each decision. Write down the letter of the idea you chose as better in each white cell, then indicate how much better you think the idea is on a scale from 1 (minor difference) to 3 (major difference). If there is no difference between the ideas, choose any of the two compared letters and add a zero after it.

For example, let's compare the *Dancing Ducks* theme with the *Breaking News* theme. Given that the intrinsic worth of a new medicine can be more comically conveyed in the format of a news broadcast than by dancing ducks, we rank the *Breaking News* theme much higher.

		A Ducks	B News	C Doctor	D Choir
	Ideas	Ducks	News	Doctor	Choir
A	Ducks		B, 3	C, 1	D, 3
B	News			C, 1	D, 2
C	Doctor				D, 2
D	Choir				

EXHIBIT 39.1 Competing Advertising Themes.

4. Consolidate the Results

Add up the total of all the assessed values for each of the ideas. Convert these values into a percentage of the total score. For our advertising themes, the total score is 12 (derived by adding all the different values). The results are:

Dancing Ducks (A) = 0 (0 percent)

Breaking News (B) = 3 (25 percent)

Family Doctor (C) = 2 (16.7 percent)

Gospel Choir (D) = 7 (58.3 percent)

Based on these figures, the choir theme is the advertising idea seen as most likely to deliver on the market-share goal for the client's new product. Be careful, though—the Paired Comparison Analysis technique is used for determining which alternative is best based on only one criterion: the operational definition.

If you want a more rigorous method of comparing multiple design concepts against performance and perception expectations, use a Pugh Matrix (Technique 40).

Our advertising example compared a small number of ideas. In reality, many more ideas can be compared, provided that they are gauged on the same operational definition. Because comparisons are made quickly using this technique, many combinations can be assessed in a relatively short period.

Resource

If you are interested in the original, classic works on paired comparison analysis, see:

Thurstone, L. L. "A Law of Comparative Judgment." *Psychological Review* 34 (1927): 273–286.

Pugh Matrix

Evaluate all your design concepts to create the invincible solution.

A Pugh matrix assists in evaluating multiple ideas or design concepts against each other in relation to a baseline, or *datum*. For example, an innovation team might have many ideas about how to whiten teeth using new technologies. Then, based on this idea, the team might generate several specific design concepts for possible commercialization. The Pugh matrix can help refine these ideas and/or concepts, and even facilitate the creation of more invincible hybridized ideas or concepts.

Use the Pugh matrix when you need to evaluate ideas against a set of criteria related to solution-neutral Outcome Expectations (see Technique 3), or when you need to evaluate design concepts against solution-specific Functional Requirements (see Technique 33). The Pugh matrix is a form of risk management: rather than prioritizing based on gut feel, rule out alternatives and formulate superior ideas or design concepts in a more structured, objective, and revealing way.

The Pugh matrix and the concept of *controlled convergence* were invented by Dr. Stuart Pugh at the University of Strathclyde in Glasgow, Scotland. The basic idea behind the matrix is to discourage opinions and promote objectivity through the systematic elimination of inferior concepts and the elevation of superior concepts.

Steps

Scenario: RayRay's House of Hair has developed several competing design concepts for an automatic hair-washing function, possibly even with more features and benefits than provided by the traditional approach of having a human wash the customer's hair prior to cutting and styling.

1. Determine a Baseline (Datum)

The definition of your baseline depends very much on your innovation needs. When redesigning an existing product or process, if no specific alternatives have been defined, the status quo makes an ideal candidate. If you are investigating multiple different ideas or solutions, consider a middle-of-the-road example as a baseline. This will allow you to objectively compare all the options under consideration. In our hair salon example, we will consider the human hair-washing method as our baseline concept.

2. Select the Concepts to Be Evaluated

Consider all the alternative concepts for comparing to your baseline. These could be known alternatives, or new solution/design concepts you want to consider but have not investigated in detail. Remember that this is a group activity. Including a few way-out ideas often enhances group dynamics.

For automatic hair washing, RayRay's has five related but different automatic hair-washing design concepts for evaluation, as shown in Exhibit 40.1 Each is a variation on either a reclining chair, a straight chair, or a massage table system with such features as spray nozzles, bristles, massage jets, massage hood, and other options (music, foot massage, etc.).

3. Define Evaluation Criteria

Each alternative concept is compared to the baseline datum relative to several evaluation criteria: in this case, solution-level functional requirements. Each evaluation criterion becomes a row in the Pugh matrix. When using the Pugh matrix to evaluate initial innovation ideas relative to some job to be done, the list of evaluation criteria is synonymous with higher-level outcome expectations. (See the Outcome Expectations and Functional Requirements [Techniques 3 and 33, respectively] for more on how outcome

Expectations	0	1	2	3	4	5
Ease of use		−	−	−	−	−
Clean (no water or shampoo spill)		S	+	+	+	+
Comfortable		S	+	+	S	S
Speed		+	−	−	S	S
Efficacy		+	+	+	+	+
Reliable	DATUM	+	+	+	+	−
Clean (no water or shampoo spill)		S	+	+	+	+
Cost		+	+	+	+	+
Noise		S	S	S	+	S
Easy to maintain		S	S	S	S	−
Total −s (better than datum)		4	6	6	6	4
Total +s (worse than datum)		1	2	2	1	3
Total Ss (same as datum)		5	2	2	3	3
Comparison		3	4	4	5	1

Concept Summary
0 - Human washing method
1 - Reclining chair with spray nozzle & bristles
2 - Massage table with spray nozzle & massage jets
3 - Massage table with spray nozzle & fitted massage hood
4 - Straight chair with fitted massage hood & music
5 - Straight chair with fitted massage hood & foot massage

EXHIBIT 40.1   Pugh Matrix Example (Automatic Hair-Washing Solutions/Designs) (Downloadable).

expectations differ from functional requirements in the hierarchy and process of innovation.)

4. Use the Criteria to Compare Concepts

For our example, we are of course working with design concepts, which are sandwiched between outcome expectations and functional requirements in the hierarchy. The Pugh matrix is a very versatile tool that can compare nearly any set of alternatives against a datum.

Rank each design concept for each of the criteria against the baseline (Exhibit 40.1). If the concept is better than the baseline, assign it a plus; if it is worse, assign it a minus; if there is no discernable difference based on the criteria in question, assign it an S.

For each concept, add up the number of pluses, minuses, and Ss, and then record these at the bottom of the matrix. Compare the total number of pluses and minuses to help select the best concepts(s). The comparison row is the total number of pluses minus the total number of minuses for each design concept.

For our hypothetical example, the best design solution seems to be the straight chair with the fitted massage hood that also plays music. But the Pugh matrix isn't just a simple mathematical exercise; it's a qualitative technique that forces discussion and the development of new and alternative options to find the very best one.

Some people add an *importance* column to the Pugh matrix for the purpose of weighting certain evaluation criteria over others. But if this strategy is taken, be careful to remember that you still use this technique to spark discussion about how to create invincible ideas or solutions—not just select the one that has the highest rating or comparison score.

---

5. Scrutinize and Refine Concepts

In repeating rounds, develop new design concepts by (1) synthesizing the best features of different alternatives and (2) enhancing the strongest concepts by adding features from the unselected concepts to overcome weak areas. Doing this will result in the emergence of more and better innovative concepts, or hybrids, that can again be evaluated with the Pugh matrix.

For example, even though the straight chair with the fitted massage hood that plays music is the best option, is there a way to overcome any drawbacks of also adding other features and functions to the solution? Maybe the system with the foot massage (option 5) could be designed in a way that makes the multifunctional system just as reliable and easy to maintain as the simpler system (option 4). Design-for-reliability and design-for-maintainability principles could be applied in this regard.

Even though the massage table options seem inferior because they take more time, maybe some customers are willing to spend more of their time (and money) for this option. Maybe RayRay's could add still more features to this option to make it even more enjoyable and relaxing. Or maybe the simple straight chair with the fitted massage hood and music is the best choice to pursue.

Resource

For more details about the Pugh matrix and how to use it, see:

Pugh, S. *Total Design: Integrated Methods for Successful Product Engineering.* Wokingham, UK: Addison-Wesley, 1991.

Process Capability

Predict the performance of your new solution.

Process capability compares the actual performance of a product or service to its requirements or specifications under two major conditions. One is when you want to predict how well your newly designed product or service will perform prior to its release and full implementation. The other is after your product or service is in full operation and you want to measure how well it is meeting its performance specifications or expectations.

Because we're primarily concerned about innovation, we'll focus on its predictive use. For example, if you've designed a new insulin pump, it should be capable of administering a certain amount of the hormone at a certain rate into the patient's body. If you determine that the pump's ability to consistently perform is lacking, you can use the Process Capability technique to improve its design by optimizing the settings of the pump's input variables (radius of the piston, motor speed, etc.).

Because there are so many different ways to calculate process capability, it's common to use the wrong metric. This creates an erroneous impression of how well the process runs, and creates confusion when comparing the performance of different types of variables and processes (service, manufacturing, transactional). Therefore, this technique is best applied at first with the help of a statistical or Six Sigma expert.

Background

One way process capability can be measured is as a simple *yield*, or the percentage of times the process meets its requirements. The Six Sigma community created another metric, *sigma level*, to normalize capability readings for different types of processes. (How, for example, do you compare the capability of an invoicing process with the capability of a lightbulb manufacturing process?)

The sigma metric was also created to fine-tune performance measurement in a competitive business environment that requires perfection or near perfection. While a yield of 99.0 percent is equivalent to a 3.8 sigma level, a yield of 99.9 percent (just 0.9 higher) equates to a 4.6 sigma level. The goal of Six Sigma performance is to reach a sigma level of 6.0 or higher—equating to a yield of 99.99966 percent—or only 3.4 defects per one million opportunities for a defect.

The key is to make sure you determine the process capability for any new solution and, if it is lacking, improve its design—making it more robust to input variations through the principles of *parameter design*. Or, if this route isn't feasible, then you can take the less preferred but still effective route of tightening the tolerances of critical inputs (*tolerance design*), then improving your process capability while keeping your design as is. Rely on Robust Design (Technique 42) for executing both of these strategies.

Steps

Scenario: Let's suppose a bank is testing a new information kiosk that provides customers with rapid approvals on refinancing mortgages. The bank assembles a team, the Kiosk Configurators, to pilot the new system and determine its process capability—or how well it meets customer expectations.

1. Determine Specifications (Performance Criteria)

Process, product, and service specifications come from customer expectations, engineering calculations, or even from examining the process itself. Some specifications are very rigid (e.g., tolerances for parts in a turbine engine). Others are not as rigid (e.g., telephone hold time for customer service). In either case, specifications should be clear and unambiguous, employing a Measurement Systems Analysis (Technique 52) to verify that your measurements are valid and reliable over time—or unbiased with acceptable variation.

For our example, the Kiosk Configurators conducted a pilot during which the team measured customer reaction to the time elapsed between when a refinancing request is submitted and when the system displayed the refinancing terms. The team determined that 97 percent of customers are willing to wait up to two minutes before receiving information, 80 percent are willing to wait up to three minutes, and 50 percent will wait four minutes.

Based on this, the Kiosk Configurators determined that the kiosk should display the refinancing terms within two minutes (120 seconds) for all users. In essence, the team set an upper specification limit (USL) at 120 seconds. There is no lower specification limit (LSL) because an instantaneous response is still acceptable (although very unlikely).

2. Collect Appropriate Data

Process data is either quantitative or qualitative in nature. Quantitative data, or *variable* data, is measured along a continuous scale (i.e., 1 to 60 seconds). Qualitative data, or *attribute* data, is measured in categories, like pass/fail, yes/no, blue/green, and so on. Both types of data have value, but usually variable data is preferred over attribute data because it tells you more about the process.

The Kiosk Configurators were able to measure performance in seconds during their pilot using a timing device in the kiosk program. They captured 100 data points on a Saturday morning, relying on real customers. The data was considered *short-term* because it was collected under controlled circumstances in a short period of time when all equipment was working correctly. The results are displayed in the dot plot shown in Exhibit 41.1. The data is stable and typically below the USL of 120 seconds.

Specifications, process data, and capability metrics are directly related to design parameters and process variables (see Axiomatic Design, Technique 34). A specification is essentially a functional requirement or design parameter. Capability metrics are developed and process data is collected to ensure control over process variables, which in turn ensure the consistent fulfillment of functional requirements, design parameters, or specifications—depending on the language used. Many Six Sigma practitioners call process variables *key performance indicators* (KPIs).

---

3. Calculate Capability Metrics

The simplest capability metric you can calculate is the percentage yield. For example, using a pass-fail analysis, we can see in Exhibit 41.1 that 99 of the 100 pilot tests were below the 120-second upper specification. We could, therefore, report a yield of 99 percent. One issue with using pass-fail data is that we don't know how close the 99 successful tests were to the USL. Are we borderline or do we have a lot of wiggle room to accommodate any shifts or drifts in the process?

However, using the actual time measurements (Exhibit 41.2), we can identify where the *central tendency* of the data lies (as measured by the mean or median), how much variation is present in the data (range or standard deviation), and the shape of the data distribution (bell-shaped with most data in the center?). With these parameters, we can better describe the data and predict the impact of long-term shifts.

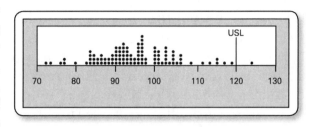

EXHIBIT 41.1   Time from Entry to Information Display, in Seconds.

Mean (average)	95.0 seconds
Median (middlemost)	94.5 seconds
Range (highest - lowest)	52 seconds (125 - 73)
Standard Deviation	10.0 seconds
Shape of Distribution	Normal (bell)
Stability	Appears Stable (short-term)

EXHIBIT 41.2   Descriptive Statistics—Kiosk Pilot Trials.

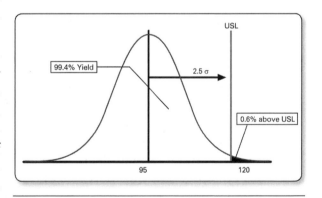

EXHIBIT 41.3   Response Time Capability $= 2.5\,\sigma$ (Short-Term).

A common capability metric for continuous data is the sigma level, or the number of standard deviation (σ) units that lie between the mean and the upper specification limit (USL). In our case, with a mean of 95, a USL of 120 and a standard deviation of 10, there are 2.5 standard deviations in between: $(120 - 95)/10 = 2.5$.

This would be described as a *2.5 sigma process*, depicted in Exhibit 41.3. Using the properties of the normal distribution, we would predict that 0.6 percent (derived from a standard table) of the total population of customers would experience response times in excess of 120 seconds.

Process capability is expressed in either the short-term or the long-term. Recall that the Kiosk Configurators determined capability by collecting data from one short period of time. Therefore, they can expect 0.6 percent of customers to have wait times longer than 120 seconds *in the short-term;* over the long-term, however, they can expect the process to shift and drift, thereby deteriorating process capability.

Specification limits can be one-sided or two-sided. For two-sided specifications, you combine the capability of the lower specification limit (LSL) and the upper specification limit (USL) to derive an overall sigma level. Extensions to unstable processes, two-sided specifications, and distributions that are not normally distributed require additional analysis.

---

4. Improve the Design or the Process

After you implement your innovation, or during a test or pilot, you may find your process capability lacking. Or, you may need to improve it over time as a response to competitive realities. Either way, you can improve process capability in one of two ways using Robust Design principles (see Technique 42). First, try improving the design (parameter design) so it can be more robust to input variation. Second, you can tighten the tolerances of critical parameters (tolerance design), followed by improving the associated process such that the design better meets Outcome Expectations and Functional Requirements (Techniques 3 and 33). Before either of these, however, make sure your process capability readings are correct and accurate using Measurement Systems Analysis (Technique 52).

For example, let's say the Kiosk Configurators want to significantly improve process capability due to new competitive pressures. They decide to redesign their solution, which is a transactional process comprised of various subprocesses, including but not limited to:

- Query for, obtain, and report the customer's credit score.
- Determine the dollar amount of the loan.
- Determine the interest rate of the loan.
- Query about and determine the loan down payment.

The Kiosk Configurators collect some data and discover that 80 percent of loan inquiries are delayed because of the time it takes to receive credit scores from bureaus. Therefore, for any loan below a certain loan amount, when the customer is also making at least a 25 percent down payment, the bank will provide a preliminary estimate of loan terms without utilizing the customer's credit score. This process parameter design enables customers to get a loan offer at the kiosk in 80 seconds on average, with an upper specification limit of 100 seconds. If such parameter changes do not improve the design to the extent wanted, we can employ a tighter tolerance on the cycle time for credit score reporting, and then improve the score-reporting process to make it faster.

Resources

Gygi, C., N. DeCarlo, and B. Williams. *Six Sigma for Dummies*. Hoboken, NJ: John Wiley & Sons, 2004.

Use the following software packages to quickly calculate a variety of capability metrics with additional analytic graphics:

JMP (SAS).

Minitab 16 (Minitab).

SigmaXL (SigmaXL).

SQCpack (PQ Systems).

Robust Design

Make your design insensitive to uncontrollable influences.

Robust design helps you reduce the sensitivity of your innovation to uncontrollable *noise* variables. For instance, an automotive designer might use robust design to develop a more fuel-efficient car engine that is less susceptible to the vagaries of customer driving habits and environmental conditions. Or a physician's office might design a patient-scheduling routine that is minimally impacted by variations in staffing or patients arriving late.

Throughout the life cycle of a product or service, variation can and will occur. Because variation negatively impacts performance, the resulting customer experience will also be negative when the product or service fails to live up to expectations. Robust design seeks to predict variation before it occurs, and then prevent or minimize it through design.

To undertake robust design, you'll definitely need help from an experienced engineer or statistician familiar with this approach to testing and analysis. You'll also need to know how to apply several other techniques in this book, including Functional Requirements (Technique 33), Axiomatic Design (Technique 34), Design Failure Mode and Effects Analysis (Technique 44), and Design of Experiments (Technique 53).

Noise variables are factors that negatively affect the performance of a product, service, or process, but which are difficult to control. Noise comes from three primary sources:

- Production variation (staffing, materials, supply, equipment, environment, skills, education, etc.).

- Customer use and abuse (improper use, varying expectations, high volume, high maintenance demands, etc.).

- Deterioration (drift in electronic parts, corrosion, employee fatigue, loss of effectiveness, etc.).

Steps

Scenario: As we proceed through the basic steps of robust design, we'll use the example of producing a skin patch that administers the correct dosage of medication to a patient over a specified time period. This can be a difficult job given that the drug's absorption rate depends on such uncontrollable factors as patient weight and skin thickness, correct application and usage of the patch, and variable environmental conditions that may affect the patch's efficacy.

1. Identify Customer Expectations

Robust design starts with conceptual *system design,* during which you define the ideal performance for your innovation, and make a list of measurable system features that are critical to the customer. You may have already done this using Functional Requirements (Technique 33). For our skin patch example, the ideal design will consistently dispense a dose of 1.0 mg/hr ± 0.2, regardless of patient fat content, skin condition, or other environmental factors.

A robust design is one in which the outputs are insensitive to input variation.

2. Develop Conceptual Design

Using the list of desirable and measurable features from step 1, create an initial design. For this high-level design, you can apply any number of techniques, including Axiomatic Design (Technique 34), Function Structure (Technique 35), Structured Abstraction (Technique 26), and Separation Principles (Technique 27). Our skin patch design consists of multiple layers of fabric webs at varying angles with a breathable, waterproof cover material and a hypoallergenic adhesive.

3. Identify Control Factors and Noise Variables

As you move to a more detailed design, make a list of control factors and noise variables that may cause variation in performance (Exhibit 42.1). Control factors include anything that you, the provider, can reasonably

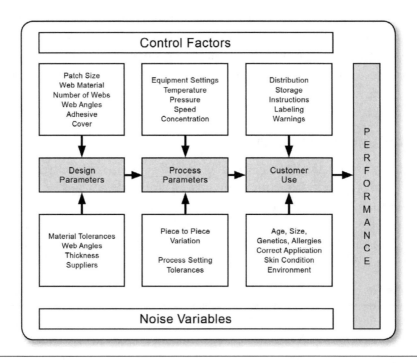

EXHIBIT 42.1 Sample Control Factors and Noise Variables. In this example, we see the factors that the skin patch manufacturer can control (top row), as well as noise variables (bottom row) that are beyond the manufacturer's control but have the potential to negatively affect product performance.

manage—product specifications, equipment settings, storage, and so on. Noise variables are factors that are beyond your control—material variations (within tolerances), customer use and abuse, environmental conditions, and the like.

4. Identify Potential Deterioration

Throughout the product or service life cycle, deterioration is likely to occur. Components wear out, materials become damaged or lose their effectiveness. In the service realm, human error and inconsistencies contribute to process variation and deterioration. To reduce the impact of these factors on performance, use Design Failure Mode and Effects Analysis (Technique 44) to flag areas that are susceptible to wear or failure, and then design your product or service to avoid or withstand deterioration as much as possible.

With regard to our skin patch, we need to address several deterioration factors, including how to best store the patch before use, and how to dispense consistent dosages over 12 to 36 hours as medication is depleted from the patch and absorbed into the skin.

5. Experiment and Determine Optimum Design

By this point, you've developed a conceptual design for your innovative product or service and have made a list of noise variables that could negatively impact performance. Now, entering the *parameter design* phase of robust design, you can use physical experiments and/or simulations to refine the design so that it is less affected by noise. For example:

- Use a Cause & Effect Matrix (Technique 57) to determine the relationship between the design's inputs and outputs. If you understand how each input affects the output, both individually and in combination, you can improve your design performance and reduce variability.
- Use Design of Experiments (DOE) (Technique 53) to test how varying control factors affect your design. You should also test control factors against noise variables to stress the design and ultimately reduce sensitivity to customer use and abuse, as well as deterioration.
- If physical experiments are not feasible or cost-effective, use a computer simulation such as Discrete Event Simulation (Technique 46) to determine which inputs result in the optimal output.

Through a DOE for our skin patch, we found an interaction between web thickness and web angles that will allow us to reduce the variation in hourly dosage (high thickness produces less web angle variation than lower thickness). We also found that the patch area has a curvilinear relationship with the dosage per hour. By working on the flatter part of the curve, we can widen the design tolerance to maintain the same performance over time.

Parameter design helps you determine optimal functional requirements for your innovation based on inputs, outputs, and the effect of noise variables.

---

6. Determine Detailed Design Tolerances

Now that you've minimized the impact of variation on your design, the last step in robust design is the *tolerance design* phase. Here you establish detailed tolerances or specifications that your design needs to operate within to meet expectations. For example, through our analysis of the skin patch design, we determined that expected variation, including noise, is approximately 0.033 mg/hr. This is more than acceptable if the required performance is 1.0 mg/hr $\pm$ 0.2.

Resource

For more information on the philosophy and method of robust design, see:

Fowlkes, W., and C. Creveling. *Engineering Methods for Robust Product Design: Using Taguchi Methods in Technology and Product Development*. Upper Saddle River, NJ: Prentice Hall, 1995.

Design Scorecards

Develop a dashboard to track your design and its underlying processes.

Functioning like the dashboard of a car, design scorecards provide critical feedback data on three levels: system performance, component performance, and process performance. For example, consider the design of a new washing machine that uses no detergent but works on the principle of ultrasonic waves and electrolysis. We can use design scorecards to record the progress of the design process, enabling necessary modifications to maximize the probability of implementation success.

For innovation, the key benefit of design scorecards is their ability to predict the final quality of a design and recognize gaps so it can be improved *before* it's implemented. Is there a risk that your design will go wrong? How will you know if and when it does? As well, you'll have to track your new innovation *after* it's implemented, making sure its performance record is visible to stakeholders so they can prevent malfunctions, if possible, or at least react quickly to fix problems if they do occur.

Naturally, the more valid and robust your design scorecards, the more likely you are to notice and fix production problems or service issues before they lead to serious customer dissatisfaction. In this preventive regard, use design scorecards in conjunction with techniques such as Design Failure Mode and Effects Analysis (Technique 44), Measurement Systems Analysis (Technique 52), and Robust Design (Technique 42)—with the help of a qualified engineer if working with more complex systems.

273

Design Scorecards have many uses, but primarily they identify which parameters or *indicators* contribute most to an optimized design. This helps your innovation team decide where to focus efforts early in the design cycle.

Background

You should be concerned with three design scorecard levels, as follows:

- *Performance scorecard:* Predicts how the overall design will perform against its outcome expectations and functional requirements. Once implemented, this is a summary comparison of actual-to-planned performance of the innovation.
- *Component scorecard:* Predicts the performance of key components that affect the overall performance scorecard elements. Once implemented, this summarizes the extent to which component quality levels fulfill design intent and expectations.
- *Process scorecard:* Predicts the overall quality level of key processes that produce the product or deliver the service. Once implemented, this summarizes the extent to which key processes and subprocesses meet overall performance targets.

While the purpose of design scorecards is to *prevent* problems, defects, and errors through superior design, they also enable better problem *detection* after a new solution (design) is implemented. If you are in detect-and-fix mode, any number of process-optimization techniques may help, such as Process Behavior Charts (Technique 55), Cause & Effect Diagram (Technique 56), Mistake Proofing (Technique 45), and Design of Experiments (Technique 53).

Steps

Scenario: An automaker is configuring a disc brake subsystem for its 100-mile-per-gallon light vehicle. Before, during, and after the design process, we can predict and evaluate the quality of the design with the help of design scorecards.

1. Identify the Critical Parameters for the Performance Scorecard

Identify all the relevant customer expectations associated with your planned system or subsystem (see Outcome Expectations, Technique 3). In addition, locate any functional requirements that are not specifically addressed by your planned design (see Functional Requirements, Technique 33).

Functional requirements are measured in different ways, subject to the nature of the solution involved. For each expectation, clearly identify: (1) the type of variable (discrete, continuous), and (2) the measurement unit (percentage, currency, feet, hertz, decibel, pass/fail, etc.).

In our example braking system, we use a number of descriptive statistics at the performance, component, and process levels. For example, at the performance-scorecard level (Exhibit 43.1), to gauge the performance of our new braking system, we measure the following variables, or *performance indicators:*

Performance Indicator	Unit	Variable Type
Stopping distance	Ft	Continuous
Low vibration	Hz	Continuous
Noise level	dB	Continuous
Appearance	Pass/Fail	Discrete

Continuous indicators are tracked by looking at their mean and standard deviation over a series of tests and observations. For example, the noise level associated with our braking system was measured at a mean value of 34 dB with a standard deviation of 1.5.

Discrete indicators are tracked by looking at their success rate. For the appearance indicator in our example, we are interested in the number of *passes*, considering the total number of observations or survey responses.

If you're implementing a business model innovation, then you might have such performance indicators as *profit, earnings, volume, customer loyalty, market share, revenue,* and so on.

	Requirement	Units	Continuous?	Continuous Data						Attribute Data			
				Target	μ	σ	USL	LSL	ST or LT	opp/unit	DPU	DPMO	Zst
1	Stopping Distance	Ft	Yes		50	2	55		LT			0.0	>6
2	Low Vibration	Hz	Yes		16	3.5	30		ST			0.0	>6
3	Noise Level	dB	Yes		34	1.5	35		LT			0.0	>6
4	Appearance	pass/fail	No							1	0.00001	10.0	5.76
										Total Opps			4
										Product DPU			0.00001
										Product DPMO			2.5
										Product RTY			100.00%
										Product Zst			>6

Product Description: Light Vehicle Air Brakes

System Subsystem: Front Brake System

Finished Prod./Final Assembly: C6 Sedan

Date: 3/1/2013

EXHIBIT 43.1 Overall Performance Scorecard (Downloadable).

Copyright © 2012, BMGI. A blank version of this customized form is available for download at www.innovatorstoolkit.com.

Some Performance Metrics and Terms

Requirement—Performance specification

Units—Items produced

GRR—Gage Repeatability & Reproducibility (Gage R&R)

Continuous—Type of data (scale)

Attribute—Type of data (categories)

Target—Desired performance level

μ—Average or mean

σ—Standard deviation

USL—Upper specification limit

LSL—Lower specification limit

ST or LT—Short-term, long-term

Opportunity—Chance for a defect or error to occur

DPU—Defects per unit

DPMO—Defects per million opportunities

Zst—Short-term capability

Product RTY—Rolled throughput yield

---

2. Determine Target and Specification Limits for Performance Parameters

These limits are obtained from customer input, regulatory requirements, or design functional requirements. Upper specification limit (USL) refers to the maximum allowable value for the parameter, whereas lower specification limit (LSL) indicates the minimum allowable value.

Typically three scenarios apply to specification limits: (1) more is better, (2) less is better, or (3) achieve a specific target. More-is-better type requirements will have only an LSL; less-is-better type will have only a USL; and achieve-a-target types will have an LSL and a USL.

In our example (Exhibit 43.1), let's consider *stopping distance.* Customer input and legislation require that the distance be *55 feet or less*. In reality, a stopping distance less than the specification is preferred, so an upper specification limit of 55 feet is used. Because any shorter stopping distance would be acceptable, specifying a lower specification limit (LSL) is not necessary.

Discrete indicators, such as *appearance,* will typically have a target value of *none* or 0: We would always want our test to pass. For example, customers might be asked if the appearance of a product pleases them or not. They can answer *yes* (pass) or *no* (fail) on a questionnaire.

3. Predict the Performance Indicators

In this step, we predict the values of each of the performance indicators (parameters). This is achieved through the use of transfer functions in the form of $y = f(x)$. The transfer function is obtained from scientific principles, design of experiments, or other known empirical relationships.

For example, we can predict the deflection performance of a spring by utilizing the transfer function, $F = K \times X$, where F is the spring force, K is the spring constant, and X is the deflection. By measuring the mean and standard deviation of K and F, and using the transfer function, we can predict the mean and standard deviation of X. This, in turn, can be converted to a sigma level or defect level.

The predicted values are later compared against actual measured performance values collected during prototyping, piloting, and design implementation.

When assembling your scorecard for your new design, keep in mind how data will be collected and reported for your performance indicators. Actual, observed indicator values may be sourced from specific test runs, data collected from usage in the field, customer satisfaction records, call center logs, and so on.

---

4. Build the Overall and Individual Component Scorecards

Identify the critical components that significantly influence the performance of the overall system. Major components of our disc brake system are *caliper, brake pad, rotor, piston,* and *hub,* as shown in Exhibits 43.2 and 43.3.

Once the components are identified, predict their performance by identifying their critical inputs. For example, the performance of the caliper component is affected by *surface area, parallelism, volume, clamp load, deflection,* and *appearance* of the caliper (Exhibit 43.4). By measuring the performance of these individual items, we can predict the performance of the caliper.

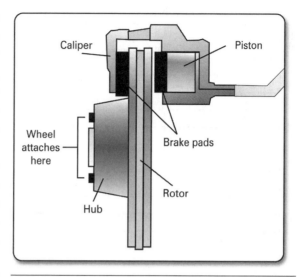

EXHIBIT 43.2   Disc Brake System.

Build a scorecard for each critical component using historical Process Capability data (see Technique 41), Design of Experiments (Technique 53), and simulations. You can then use this data to predict the overall performance of each of the components.

By evaluating alternative components to optimize or improve designs, the component scorecard facilitates dialog between designers and suppliers.

5. Build the Overall and Individual Process Scorecards

Identify the critical manufacturing and/or service delivery processes (and subprocesses) that significantly influence the performance of the overall system and its critical components. For the disc brake system, some of the manufacturing and assembly processes include *caliper welding, caliper mounting,* and *rotor mounting* (Exhibit 43.5). Recognize that we've itemized these few processes as an illustration; in reality, there are dozens and even hundreds of processes associated with complicated designs.

	Part	# Requirements	Part Count	Total Opps	Part DPU	Part DPMO	Part RTY	Part Zst
1	Caliper	6	4	24	0.00080	33.33	99.92%	5.49
2	Brake Pad	4	4	20	1.41699	70849.54	24.24	2.97
3	Rotor	5	4	20	4.01690	200845.05	1.80%	2.34
4	Piston	4	4	20	0.04580	2280.05	95.54%	4.34
5	Hub	3	4	16	0.00007	4.38	99.99%	5.95
6								
7								
8								
9								
10								
	OVERALL	22	20	100	5.4804	54803.629	0.42%	3.10

Finished Prod./Final Assembly:	C6 Sedan
System Subsystem:	Front Brake System
Prepared by:	A.B. Smith
Date:	3/1/2013

EXHIBIT 43.3   Overall Component Scorecard (Downloadable).

Once the critical processes are identified, you can predict their performance by identifying the parameters that affect them. Again, we identify only two parameters that affect the caliper-welding process: *strength* and *surface* appearance (Exhibit 43.6). By measuring the performance of these parameters, we can predict the performance of the caliper-welding process.

Build a scorecard for each critical process using data from capability studies (see Process Capability, Technique 41), past experience, manufacturing data, and estimates from similar processes. You can then use this data to predict the overall performance of each of the critical processes and subprocesses.

At a glance, the process scorecard uncovers weak processes and improvement opportunities.

	Requirement	Units	GRR	Continuous?	Continuous Data							Attribute Data			
					Target	μ	σ	USL	LSL	ST or LT	Opp/unit	DPU	DPMO	Zst
1	Surface Area			Yes		15	2	20	10	LT			0.0	>6
2	Parallelism			Yes		25	5	30	20	LT			0.0	>6
3	Volume			Yes		35	2	40	30	LT			0.0	>6
4	Clamp Load			Yes		45	2.22	50	40	LT			0.0	>6
5	Deflection			Yes		55	1.444	60	50	LT			0.0	>6
6	Appearance			No							1	0.0002	200.0	5.04

Total Opps	24
Product DPU	0.00080
Product DPMO	33.3
Product RTY	99.92
Product Zst	5.49

Part:	Caliper
Part Count:	4
Supplier:	AJB
System Subsystem:	Light Vehicle Air Brakes
Finished Prod./Final Assembly:	C6 Sedan
Prepared By:	A.B. Smith
Date:	3/1/2013

EXHIBIT 43.4 Component Scorecard (Downloadable).

	Process Step	# Requirements	Total Opps	Process DPU	Process DPMO	Process RTY	Process Zst
1	Caliper Welding	2	57	0.0001	1.7544	99.99%	>6
2	Caliper Mounting	2	9	1.07091	118991	34.27%	2.68
3	Rotor Mounting	3	8	2.54288	317860	7.86%	1.97
4							
5							
6							
7							
8							
9							
10							
	OVERALL	7	74	3.6139	48836	2.69%	3.16

Finished Prod./Final Assembly:	AMF Sedan
System Subsystem:	Front Brake
Prepared by:	A.B. Smith
Date:	3/1/2013

EXHIBIT 43.5   Overall Process Scorecard (Downloadable).

6. Interpret the Scorecard

You interpret the completed design scorecards after you implement your new solution and have enough data for a specified period of time. As you interpret your scorecards, consider the following:

- Do your chosen measurements enable you to accurately, precisely, and reliably evaluate the indicators? (See Measurement Systems Analysis, Technique 52.)

- Are there any design corrections that can be made to improve performance? (See Robust Design, Technique 42, and Process Capability, Technique 41.)

	Requirement	Units	GRR	Continuous?	Target	μ	σ	USL	LSL	ST or LT	# applications	DPU	DPMO	Zst
						Continuous Data					All Data	Attribute		
1	Strength	kPa		Yes		10000	1000		9000		13		0.0	>6
2	Surface Appearance	pass/fail		No							44	0.0001	2.3	>6

	Total Opps	57
	Process DPU	0.00010
	Process DPMO	1.8
	Process RTY	99.99%
	Process Zst	>6

Process:	Welding of Slide Caliper
System Subsystem:	Automotive Air Brake
Finished Prod./Final Assembly:	C6 Sedan
Prepared By:	A.B. Smith
Date:	3/1/2013

EXHIBIT 43.6 Process Scorecard (Downloadable).

- Are performance, component, and process indicators linked in a direct and complete cause-and-effect way? (See Axiomatic Design, Technique 34).

- Are there any unanticipated business considerations (such as cost and timing)? (See Innovation Financial Management, Technique 13).

- Are there any unanticipated marketplace considerations, such as new competitive threats or changing customer expectations? (Go to Scenario Planning, Technique 6, for help).

- Are any of your indicators too volatile? (See Control Plan, Technique 58.)

Design Failure Mode and Effects Analysis

Anticipate what can go wrong with your solution before it does.

Design failure mode and effects analysis (DFMEA) is used to anticipate possible failures or problems with your new solutions *before they occur*, and to have a plan for what to do in response. Carmakers, for instance, anticipate what could go wrong and prevent it when they install mechanisms that don't allow a driver to shift from *park* into *drive* unless the person's foot is depressing the brake.

Use DFMEA during your preliminary, initial, and detail design reviews to uncover any potential *failure modes*. Then your first priority is to prevent these modes by improving the design itself (see Mistake Proofing, Technique 45). If you can't fully mistake-proof your solution (as in the foot-on-brake example), your next priority is to detect a failure mode before it occurs and prompt the user to take action. The oil warning light in a vehicle is an example of this approach.

With DFMEA, you attempt to predict future risks and mitigate or head them off in advance. Predicting what could fail, and what you will do about it, could keep you out of firefighting mode and enable you to avoid unnecessary and costly delays in getting your new solution to market. For more complex solutions, you may need the help of an expert to apply this technique.

A *design* FMEA focuses on the interface of a new product, service, or solution with customers. A *process* FMEA focuses on the behind-the-scenes steps that produce the product or enable the service provided. However, both FMEAs share a common format, approach, and interpretation.

Steps

Scenario: Suppose a company that currently manufactures disposable razors and shaving lubricants is developing a new product that combines both shaving and lubricating functions in one. The new design is for a disposable razor that houses shaving gel in a hollow handle. The gel is automatically dispensed through a porous pad just below the blades. Since the product is disposable, the amount of gel in the handle should be matched to the life of the blades.

In constructing a design FMEA, the language differs in a few key spots from a process FMEA. For example, in a process FMEA, the first column usually lists the process step under analysis. The first column of the design FMEA, however, is a list of product or service components and the functions they're supposed to perform.

1. Complete Administrative Information

Using a DFMEA worksheet (Exhibit 44.1), complete the product/service name, the name of the team leader who prepared the DFMEA, and when it was initiated.

2. Identify Items and Functions

In the first column of the DFMEA worksheet, list all the components that could contribute to a failure mode and the intended function for each one. For example, one component of our shaving system is the blade, and its

Product/Service Name:	Mark 7 Razor				Prepared by:		Page ___ of ___			
Responsible:	Mary Jones, project leader				FMEA Date (Orig) _____ (Rev) _____					

Item and Function	Potential Failure Mode	Potential Effects of Failure	SEV	Potential Cause(s) or Failure Mechanism(s)	OCC	Current Design Controls	DET	RPN	Recommended Action(s)	Responsibility and Completion Date
Name of Item being analyzed and its functions required to meet design intent.	In what ways might the component/ subsystem/ system potentially fail to meet the design intent?	What is the effect of each failure mode on the function as perceived by the customer? (internal or external)	How severe is the effect to the customer?	How can the failure occur? Describe in terms of what can be corrected or controlled. Try to identify the causes that directly impact the failure mode.	How often does the cause or failure mode occur?	What are the existing prevention, design verification, or other activities that will (1) prevent the cause of the failure mode or reduce its rate of occurrence, (2) detect the cause and lead to corrective actions, or (3) detect the failure mode once failure has occurred.	How well can you prevent/detect cause or failure mode?	SEV x OCC x DET	What are the actions for reducing the occurrence, or improving detection, or for identifying the root cause if it is unknown? **Should have actions only on high RPNs or easy fixes.**	Who is responsible for the recommended action?
Blades – cut hair	Too dull	Hair not cut close enough, discomfort	7	Not sharpened properly in manufacturing	3	Statistical tolerancing of edge angle, capability verified	3	63	None	N/A
			7	Worn out prematurely	3	Specification of optimum steel grade (440C) for blade and supplier quality management plan	3	63	None	N/A
			7	Corroded	3	Specification of optimum steel grade (440C) for blade and supplier quality management plan	3	63	None	N/A
	Wrong angle	Hair not cut close enough, discomfort, injury	7	Deformed blade spacers	5	Statistical tolerancing of spacer dimensions, but difficult to hold tolerance with current material	7	245	Investigation of alternative spacer materials	Joe Martin, Materials department, Dec. 1, 2013
Porous gel pad – apply gel, control gel flow	Low or no flow of gel	Inadequate lubrication, discomfort, injury	10	Clogged	3	Gel formulation to ensure adequate solubility	5	150	Ensure gel specifications are adequate and achievable	Mary Jones, project leader, and Scott Perkins, Cream & Gel Products Manuf. Mgr, Oct. 15, 2013
			10	Pore size too small	7	Spec limits for pore size from pad supplier, but impact of variation not well understood currently	7	490	DOE or other study to determine effect of pore size and other potentially interacting variables	Fred Fritz, Design Engineering, Nov. 30, 2013
	Excessive gel flow	Gel runs out too soon	5	Pore size too large	7	Spec limits for pore size from pad supplier, but impact of variation not well understood currently	7	245	DOE or other study to determine effect of pore size and other potentially interacting variables	Fred Fritz, Design Engineering, Nov. 30, 2013

EXHIBIT 44.1   Design FMEA (Downloadable).

desired function is to *cut hair*. The gel component is designed to *provide lubrication*. The porous pad *applies gel* and *controls flow of gel*. The hollow handle *provides grip* and *holds gel*. And so on. For this example, we'll limit ourselves to the blades and porous pad.

3. Identify Potential Failure Modes, Failure Effects, and Potential Causes

Now ask, "What can go wrong with this component?" The answer is your *failure mode*. Then ask, "If this does go wrong, how will it affect customers?" This is your *failure effect*. Finally, brainstorm the possible reasons for your failure mode. These are your *potential causes*. Keep in mind that one item or function can have multiple potential failure modes, and each failure mode can have multiple potential causes.

In the razor example, the blades item has two potential failure modes shown—*too dull* and *wrong angle*, both with the same effects of shaving discomfort and an unclose shave. Potential causes of these failure modes are poorly sharpened edges, wear, corrosion, and deformed plastic spaces that position the blades.

4. Determine Severity and Rate of Occurrence

The severity (SEV) of a failure effect and the rate of occurrence (OCC) of a potential cause are rated on a 1 to 10 scale, according to Exhibits 44.2 and 44.3.

		Rating
Extreme	Affects product safety. Catastrophic consequence on customer.	10
High	Product inoperable, with loss of primary function, customer highly dissatisfied.	7
Moderate	Product inoperable with moderate consequences on customer.	5
Low	All systems functional. Minor defects noticed by some customers.	3
None	No effect. No defects or defects too minor to be noticed by customer.	1

EXHIBIT 44.2   Severity of Effect (Downloadable).

In our example, severity scores range from a moderate 5 to the highest severity of 10, because the customer could get injured by some failures. Occurrence ratings range from 3 to 7, predicting that some causes would occur very infrequently, while others could become a chronic issue.

	Likelihood of Occurence	Rating
Very High	Failure is almost inevitable.	10
High	Repeated failures.	7
Moderate	Occasional failures.	5
Low	Relatively few failures.	3
Remote	Failure is unlikely.	1

EXHIBIT 44.3   Likelihood of Occurrence (Downloadable).

Copyright © 2012, BMGI. A blank version of this customized form is available for download at www.innovatorstoolkit.com.

If you need a more granular or finely tuned approach for your severity and occurrence ratings, see *Potential Failure Mode and Effects Analysis* (2001), available from the Automotive Industry Action Group at www.aiag.org.

---

5. Establish Current Design Controls

Establishing design controls entails examining current design features, component specifications, and necessary information to ensure that the potential cause can be avoided, or at least detected if it occurs. These controls then become inputs into making a Control Plan (Technique 58). Controls in the razor example include specifications for incoming parts or materials, material selection, and an understanding of the impact of component variation on performance.

Another area where a design FMEA differs from a process FMEA is in the *controls* and *detection* sections. In a process FMEA, controls are production controls; in a design FMEA, controls are design controls.

---

6. Determine the Detection Rating for Each Design Control

How likely is it that the control in place will either detect the failure mode or its cause, or prevent the failure mode or its cause from happening? Rate this on a scale from 1 to 10 using the guidelines in Exhibit 44.4.

For our razor, some controls are deemed reasonably effective (3), while others suffer from known materials issues or lack of solid information (7).

		Rating
None	Design control will not and/or cannot detect/prevent a potential cause/mechanism and subsequent failure mode.	10
Low	Design control has a low chance of detecting/preventing a potential cause/mechanism and subsequent failure mode.	7
Moderate	Design control may detect/prevent the existence of a potential cause/mechanism and subsequent failure mode.	5
High	Design control has a high probability of detecting/preventing the existence of a potential cause/mechanism and subsequent failure mode.	3
Very High	Design control will almost certainly detect/prevent the existence of a potential cause/mechanism and subsequent failure mode.	1

EXHIBIT 44.4   Likelihood that Control Will Detect or Prevent Failure (Downloadable).

Copyright © 2012, BMGI. A blank version of this customized form is available for download at www.innovatorstoolkit .com.

7. Determine Risk Priority Number for Each Failure Mode

The Risk Priority Number (RPN) is the pivotal column and set of numbers on the DFMEA worksheet. To calculate the RPN for each failure mode, multiply the scores for *severity, occurrence,* and *detection.* The higher the number, the higher the priority should be for design revisions or corrective actions. You can see in our example which failure modes have a higher priority of occurring and, therefore, are candidates for immediate corrective action.

However, even if the RPN is low, but we have a severity rating of 10, that failure mode must be addressed because the effect would be catastrophic (like an air-travel accident or death related to surgery).

A key difference between a process FMEA and a design FMEA is in a corrective action's impact on failure effect severity. With a process FMEA, it's usually not possible to change the severity of a given failure effect, as improvements are usually limited to reducing its occurrence or enhancing its detection. This is not the case with a design FMEA, where design changes *can* reduce the severity of a particular failure mode.

8. Implement Corrective Actions for High-Risk Priority Numbers

The next portion of the DFMEA consists of a section for tracking corrective actions, responsible parties, and the results of those actions. When corrections have been made, the severity, occurrence, and detection values are

Recommended Action(s)	Responsibility and Completion Date	Action Results				
		Actions Taken	SEV	OCC	DET	RPN
What are the actions for reducing the occurrence, or improving detection, or for identifying the root cause if it is unknown? **Should have actions only on high RPNs or easy fixes.**	Who is responsible for the recommended action?	List the completed actions that are included in the recalculated RPN. Include the implementation date for any changes.	What is the new severity?	What is the new failure rate?	Are the detection limits improved?	Recompute RPN after actions are complete
None	N/A	N/A	N/A	N/A	N/A	N/A
None	N/A	N/A	N/A	N/A	N/A	N/A
None	N/A	N/A	N/A	N/A	N/A	N/A
Investigation of alternative spacer materials	Joe Martin, Materials Dept., Dec.1, 2013	Complete. Nylon selected to replace polystyrene on Nov. 15. Manufacturing capability confirmed to required tolerance on Nov. 25.	5	3	3	45
Ensure gel specifications are adequate and achievable	Mary Jones, project leader, and Scott Perkins, Cream & Gel Products Manufacturing Manager, Oct.15, 2013	Specification requirements confirmed. Gel production study still underway to confirm capability.	10	TBD	TBD	TBD
DOE or other study to determine effect of pore size and other potentially interacting variables	Fred Fritz, Design Engineering, Nov. 30, 2013	Study completed, determined USL and LSL for pore size on Oct.20, met with pad suppliers Oct.30 and confirmed capability to produce.	10	3	3	90
DOE or other study to determine effect of pore size and other potentially interacting variables	Fred Fritz, Design Engineering, Nov. 30, 2013	Study completed, determined USL and LSL for pore size on Oct.20, met with pad suppliers Oct.30 and confirmed capability to produce.	5	3	3	45

EXHIBIT 44.5   Design FMEA (*continued*) (Downloadable).

revisited to help judge success. Our example shows several corrective actions taken (and one underway), and their effects on their respective failure mode RPNs (Exhibit 44.5).

Note the actions taken to prevent the wrong angle of blades. Implementing a material change for the blade spacers ameliorates this problem, because the new material has much better dimensional stability, and variation in blade angle will be much smaller. This changes the severity of the potential problem from one of possible injury to only discomfort.

When driving design changes from a DFMEA, here are some common themes:

- *If high severity is the problem,* first attempt to eliminate the failure mode altogether. If this is impractical, aim for reducing the severity of the effect. Some potential activities include changing materials, increasing strength, reducing stresses, incorporating redundancies or backups, and other design changes aimed at making the performance less sensitive to unforeseen variation. See Robust Design (Technique 42) for help.

- *If high occurrence is the problem,* first attempt to eliminate the potential cause altogether. If this can't be done, work toward making the cause less likely to occur. Again, such actions as material changes, redundancies, and spreading out stresses or loads are often successful. See Mistake Proofing (Technique 45) for help.

- *If high detection ratings are the problem,* the corrections should be aimed at making the design failures easier to perceive, or to fill in the gaps of required information. Actions like additional testing, changes in testing procedures, or other studies are the ticket. (Consider using Process Capability, Technique 41, and Design Scorecards, Technique 43, for help in this regard).

Resource

An excellent reference for both design and process FMEAs is:

Automotive Industry Action Group. *Potential Failure Mode and Effects Analysis*. 2001. www.aiag.org.

Mistake Proofing

Install measures to prevent human and system error.

Mistake proofing uses a device or procedure to reduce or eliminate the possibility for an error to occur. For example, every vehicle in Canada is fitted with a device that senses dusk and automatically turns the headlights on, a simple act that has reduced accidents.

In the realm of innovation, mistake proofing helps you combat the possibility that your product or service doesn't function properly due to unforeseen events, equipment failure, and other factors. Mistake proofing also makes it easier for employees to perform their work correctly and ensures immediate recognition and repair when a mistake is made.

Mistake proofing can be as straightforward as a checklist or warning label, or as complex as a computerized system that regulates a nuclear power plant. Regardless of the situation, you should strive to apply the maximum level of mistake proofing that is both affordable and feasible for your innovation.

The Mistake Proofing technique can be leveraged early in the innovation process to help you scope your opportunity and generate ideas. For instance, a new feature in some automobiles makes the car brake automatically if it senses that you're about to hit the vehicle in front of you. The mistake-proofing strategy of *preventing accidents* was leveraged early on when the job to be done was identified.

Mistake Proofing Principles

Before we look at the steps involved in mistake proofing a process or product, here are 19 principles anyone can use (either separately or in combination) to avoid costly or unsafe defects or errors:

1. **Layout and arrangement.** *Layout* refers to the relative position of an item, and *arrangement* refers to putting an item in a designated place. An example of this is a package delivery company that places a template over its boxes, leaving a window where shipping labels are attached.

2. **Positive stop.** Systems that don't allow users to get hurt or damage products—such as a safety hood that must be closed on a tire-balancing machine before it starts to spin at high speeds. Or dishwashers, washers, dryers, and microwaves that stop when their door is opened.

3. **Parcel out.** Dispensers that ensure only the correct amount is provided, such as a french-fry scooper. This tool ensures that bags of fries are slightly overflowing without too much generosity.

4. **Space separation.** Systems that control physical space, such as chains that configure waiting lines. Or turnstiles that prevent customers from entering through exits, leaving through the entrances, or otherwise moving against the flow.

5. **Confirmation of existence.** Technology that knows when a condition exists and reacts, such as a home alarm system that sounds when a door or window is breached. Or software that detects the type of data in a column and limits the format for subsequent entries in that column.

6. **Alternative use of resources.** Use texture, mass, or other properties unique to an item—like using gravity to ensure the last drop of product is used (ketchup, shampoo, toothpaste) by turning traditional containers upside down.

7. **Visual management.** Using visual cues to control actions, such as a hotel that wraps paper strips around clean towels, thereby separating them from those that need to be replaced. Or making highly visible

marks on inventory pallets to indicate when new supplies should be ordered.

8. **Go/No go.** A device that detects the presence or magnitude of a characteristic and provides a *go/no-go* or *pass/fail* assessment. Many airports have go/no-go gauges that are the same size and shape of overhead compartments to prevent people from carrying on bags that are too large.

9. **Time separation.** Preventing mistakes by separating contradictory or opposing feature requirements in time—as in a traffic light. Many stoplights are timed with a three-second delay to allow previous cars to exit the intersection before cross traffic is permitted to enter.

10. **Conditional stop.** You can't take your car out of the parking gear until the key is in the unlock position and the brakes are activated. The safety beam light sensor on a garage door senses an object and reverses operation of the door.

11. **Eliminate, replace, or alternate.** If the task that is creating the error or defect is eliminated, replaced, or substituted, then the error or defect will disappear too—as in fingerprints to verify identity.

12. **Kitting.** An example of kitting is do-it-yourself furniture; buyers are given the appropriate number of screws, parts, and even tools to assemble the furniture.

13. **5S (sort, store, shine, standardize, sustain).** Clutter and waste are removed by applying the principles of 5S to an area. Grocery stores do this when they purge of old inventory and arrange by first-in–first-out. Labels and bins prevent products from becoming disorganized.

14. **Kanban.** Arranging items, information, and people according to a particular sequence, pattern, or method—such as a car dealership that places color-coded numbered markers on cars as they arrive at the service facility. Take-a-number systems help prevent serving customers out of turn.

15. **Templates.** In manufacturing, templates align the orientation of brackets and rivets. Another example is paper templates that ensure correct location of the jamb, door, and handles of door locks.

16. **Checklists.** Checklists ensure that similar and repetitive tasks are verified. A typical example is the review of a bill of material to ensure all components are provided to the department or customers.

17. **Highlight.** Make something obvious so it stands out. A large bank requires tellers to verify the eye color of each customer, encouraging eye-to-eye contact. Web pages that highlight needed information on a form are another example.

18. **Information transfer.** The efficacious communication of critical information, such as road signs, color-coded office files, and an alarm that sounds when it's time for a nurse to refill an IV bag.

19. **Trend prediction.** The observation of history to predict the future, maybe using a Process Behavior Chart (Technique 55) that anticipates errors by measuring observed variation versus expected variation.

The presence of certain characteristics can make your mistake-proofing solution as robust as possible. Once electrical plugs weren't mistake proofed, so people could mix up the positive and negative poles—creating risk for the user, the device, and the electrical system. Now each prong has a different width, which meets the following conditions:

- Always present: The mistake-proof device is present every time a user wants to plug it into the outlet.

- Infallible: There isn't one single time in which the user can connect the poles incorrectly.

- Immediate action: If the user attempts to connect the device in the wrong way, the solution will detect it and force the user to correct it.

- Ergonomic: The solution doesn't add any level of complexity or discomfort to the user.

- Does not add extra steps: The mistake-proofed solution requires the same effort to use.

Steps

Scenario: Producers of home security systems must take care to mistake-proof their offerings. After all, if the system is confusing to use or fails to perform as designed, it could lead to a costly or even a dangerous situation. In this example, we'll look at a few areas that, if neglected, could lead to potential errors in a home alarm system.

No matter how well you design your new product or service, and its associated processes, there will still be opportunities to make mistakes. Each mistake, in turn, costs time and money to fix, and you risk losing customers as a result.

---

1. Identify Potential Mistakes

Review your innovation and its associated processes to determine where mistakes are likely to cause a defect or error:

- Use Design Failure Mode and Effects Analysis (Technique 44) to determine what is likely to go wrong with your innovation, as well as the extent of the damage you can expect if it does.
- Use a Process Map or Value Stream Map (Technique 51) in conjunction with a process FMEA to discover potential mistakes related to how you produce or deliver your innovation.
- Also look for technical or physical contradictions that could cause defects or errors. See Structured Abstraction (Technique 26) and Separation Principles (Technique 27) for more information about contradictions.

For our home-alarm example, potential mistakes fall into two categories: *false positives*, where the alarm goes off when it's not supposed to, and *failures*, where the alarm fails to trigger when a security breach occurs (Exhibit 45.1).

False Positive	Failure
Motion sensitivity too high	Motion sensor hindered
Power surge	Power failure
Incorrect code	Not armed (human failure)
No code entered	Not armed (device failure)
Premature notification	Notification failure

EXHIBIT 45.1 Potential Mistakes for Home Alarm System.

10 Situations That Lead to Mistakes

1. Tool or equipment error.
2. Measurement error.
3. Misunderstanding or lack of training.
4. Poor procedures and control plans.
5. Forgetfulness or distraction.
6. Incorrect or missing parts/supplies.
7. Set-up errors.
8. Unclear specifications or expectations.
9. Ignoring the rules or willful sabotage.
10. Low safety standards.

2. Prioritize Potential Mistakes

Prioritize the list of potential failure points to determine which ones are most worth your time and effort to prevent. One way to do this is by using a Design Failure Mode and Effects Analysis (Technique 44) to calculate a Risk Priority Number (RPN), and then address issues with high RPNs, as well as those with higher severity ratings.

In an ideal world we'd make perfect products and provide flawless service, but that's not reality. You'll have to choose which imperfections you'll try to prevent, and which ones you can let go. For instance, we could approach our alarm system example by focusing on the failure-type mistakes first, since the consequences of an error in this realm are more severe than for the false positives.

Mistake proofing was originated by Dr. Shigeo Shingo, a Japanese industrial engineer well-versed in manufacturing best practices. Dr. Shingo coined the term *poka* (errors) *yokeru* (to avoid), or what we now call *poka-yoke.*

3. Determine Root Cause

Use a Cause & Effect Diagram (Technique 56) to determine the root cause for each potential error. This is a critical step in mistake proofing that is often missed because too many people confuse errors with *defects*. For example, *motion sensor failure* is a defect; *motion sensor zone set incorrectly* is an error. You can only truly solve a problem at the error level, so make sure you understand the difference.

Safety and risk considerations are often at the center of mistake proofing. Imagine the risk associated with unveiling new investment software or with implementing a new surgical procedure. Both the financial and health care industries have a host of mistake-proofing measures in place to avoid costly errors and litigation.

---

4. Choose a Mistake-Proofing Strategy

For each root cause, identify an appropriate mistake-proofing strategy. You can devise a strategy using other techniques in this book, such as Value Quotient (Technique 4), to understand your offering's ideal state and any number of ideation techniques to generate ideas for moving closer to this ideal. The exact approach, however, will depend on the specific mistake you're trying to prevent.

For example, we could prevent a homeowner from forgetting to activate the front-door security alarm by automatically arming the system. Of course, this would introduce problems when the homeowner wanted to enter or leave. Perhaps this problem could be solved by installing a fingerprint-sensitive doorknob that allows authorized individuals to enter and leave at will without setting off the alarm. Even so, you would still have to consider how to mistake proof this solution.

Don't confuse *correction* with *prevention*, which is the ultimate goal of mistake proofing. Many people assume, for instance, that a battery backup is a mistake-proofing strategy for combating power failures. However, a battery only corrects or minimizes the damage caused by losing power; it doesn't *prevent* power loss in the first place. Thus, while it may be the best option available to you at the time, it's not as good as a power source that never fails.

---

5. Test the Mistake-Proofing Solution

The final step is to actually create and test your mistake-proofing solution. You can do this before you move on, or as part of a Prototyping or Piloting process (Techniques 48 and 49, respectively).

It is not one poka-yoke device, but the application of hundreds of these very simple fail-safing mechanisms that, day after day, has brought the quality miracle to industries around the world. Each one is relatively simple—something you easily could do on your own. But it is the totality, the hundreds of devices, that is almost frightening to behold.

—Dr. Shigeo Shingo

Discrete Event Simulation

Visualize and test your innovation through computer modeling.

Discrete event simulation (DES) is a computer-based modeling approach that enables you to simulate processes with substantially less cost, time, and risk than full-blown models. If you have an innovation in mind—such as a way for travelers to get through airport security more quickly—you could use DES to try out your ideas without physically changing the security layout or shuffling travelers through an unfamiliar system.

You should use DES when your innovation is particularly process dependent, with many variables that could affect the flow of customers or products. It does require a significant amount of time to build a detailed and accurate model, especially for more complex processes. But don't shy away from making the effort to learn this powerful technique—you can always enlist the help of a DES expert.

Not all systems can be modeled with *discrete* event simulation. Some events are *continuous*, such as the rate of evaporation. These occurrences can be modeled, but they require a different approach. For more information, see *Theory of Modeling and Simulation: Integrating Discrete Event and Continuous Complex Dynamic Systems,* second edition, by B. Zeigler, H. Praehofer, and T. G. Kim, New York: Academic Press, 2000.

Steps

Scenario: Imagine that you're building the tallest skyscraper in the world and you need to know how many elevators to include. The plans call for a building 850 meters high, with 170 floors housing a mix of residential and commercial areas. To meet these demands, your team estimates that 100 elevators will be required. The hope is that this number can be reduced by simulating traffic patterns using DES.

1. Choose Software

DES requires the use of a modeling software application. Depending on the one you choose, you may need some experience with software logic to program the model with all the details related to your process. Recommended simulation software packages include: AutoMod, SigmaFlow, ProcessModel, Arena, and iGrafx. While some have higher-end features and incorporate complex logic rules (like AutoMod), others allow you to get started with DES for a minimal investment (SigmaFlow, iGrafx); these more affordable applications provide most basic users with everything they need to conduct valuable simulations.

Discrete event simulation is performed often in the banking and call center industries—or any industry that processes resources through a system at unpredictable flow rates with a large variation in volume.

---

2. Develop Process Flow

The success of the simulation depends on your ability to describe the process in sufficient enough detail to produce realistic results. You can derive this information from a Process Map or Value Stream Map (Technique 51). Be sure to include key subprocesses, decision points, and queues (waiting lines).

Discrete event simulation is based on queuing theory, which is the mathematical study of waiting in lines or queues.

---

3. Assign Process Attributes

For each process step, enter the associated attributes—characteristics or factors that have the potential to affect the process flow or outcome. The specific attributes you use will depend on your process. To determine the number of elevators for our skyscraper example, we'll use the following process attributes:

- *Queue capacity:* An estimated number of passengers for each floor, varied by time of day and day of the week.
- *Cycle time:* The time it takes to complete a specific process step, such as loading the elevator with passengers.
- *Arrival rate per floor:* Varies by time of day and floor function (a food court at lunchtime will see more arrival traffic than one of the residential floors).
- *Resource capacity:* The number of elevators and the specific floors serviced by each elevator.

Costs and value-add designations can be assigned for each process step. This enables you to summarize the overall cost and value-added time of the process during the simulation.

---

4. Determine Resources and Attributes

Enter the resources and associated attributes. Resources are people or equipment on which the process relies. If the resources are people, attributes might include work schedules, percentage availability, and specific roles or tasks. In our skyscraper example, the resources are the elevators, which have the following attributes:

- *Capacity:* The maximum number of people each elevator can accommodate and the weight limit for each elevator.
- *Transportation time:* The elevator speed as a function of direction (up or down) and as a function of distance between stops.
- *Measurement statistics:* Attributes that are not assigned a value up front, but are incremented throughout the simulation to keep track of events like elevator utilization, availability, downtime, and so on.

To simulate reality, all models must run through random scenarios many times. These random distributions are accomplished by a computer algorithm known as the *Monte Carlo method,* which tells the computer what random scenario to generate next.

---

5. Determine Process Entities and Attributes

Enter the process entities and associated attributes. Entities are the objects that move through the process—people, parts, raw materials, and so on. The entity attributes interact with the process and resource attributes and result in random outcomes during the simulation. For our skyscraper simulation, the entities are the elevator passengers. The attributes we've identified include:

- Elevator call time (the specific time an entity pushes the call button).
- Wait time for the elevator to arrive.
- Entity weight.
- Entity pairing/grouping, (Is the passenger alone, or with others?)
- Departure floor.
- Departure time.
- Arrival floor.
- Arrival time.

Each process has a finite amount of capacity. If this becomes full, new entities are blocked from entering or proceeding through the process. Understanding how to optimize the capacity for a particular process is one of the benefits of discrete event simulation.

---

6. Run Trial Simulations

The first few times you run the simulation, you'll be validating the model. Choose how long you want the simulation to run, and pause it any time to examine how well the model is working. Allow for a warm-up period to fill the pipeline and reach steady-state.

During these early runs, look for deficiencies in logic or process settings that are not realistic. For instance, you might have built an infinite waiting line for the elevator (this is not actually realistic, although sometimes it feels like forever before an elevator finally arrives). Or, the elevator may be processing calls in sequence instead of following a logic algorithm or rule set that, for instance, tells the elevator to stop for a passenger on floor 55 on the way down to floor 50, even though the button for floor 55 was pressed after the one for floor 50.

It may take several iterations before you get the model just right, especially if you're new to this technique. *Don't give up!* Once you get the hang of it, you'll find that discrete event simulation can be an invaluable approach.

---

7. Run Actual Simulations

When you have a valid model in place, run as many simulations as needed, varying both the process and entity attributes to see how they affect the model. Some software allows you to watch the process in action during the simulation, although this will slow it down. Or, you can let it run and track the resulting data both during and after the simulation. Either way, the longer you run the simulation, the larger the sample size will be and the closer to reality your results will come.

During the skyscraper simulation, we changed a few of the elevators to a double-deck style, with two elevators linked one on top of the other. We also sped up the single-deck elevators. These changes reduced the number of elevators to 56, a significant reduction over the initial estimate (Exhibit 46.1).

You can use Design of Experiments (Technique 53) to help you determine specific attribute combinations you should test during the simulation. Design of experiments allows you to identify interactions caused by changing two or more variables simultaneously.

---

8. Verify Results

After the simulation, you should further validate your findings using Prototyping (Technique 48) or Piloting (Technique 49).

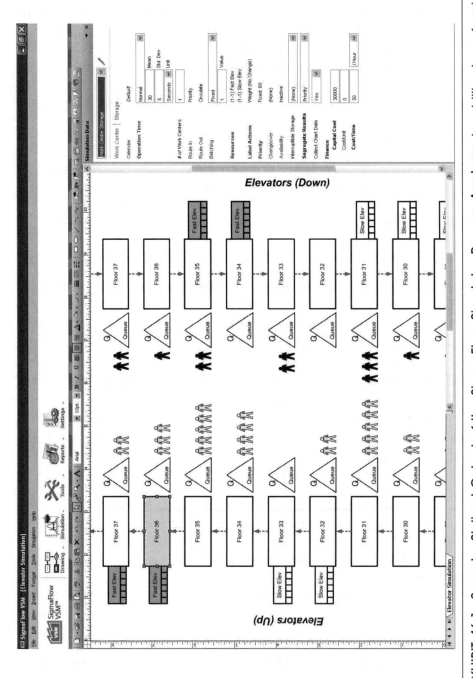

EXHIBIT 46.1   Sample, Stylized Output of the SigmaFlow Simulator Process Analyzer. In addition to performing discrete event simulations, this product also performs value stream mapping, improvement scorecarding, and other analytics.

The advantages of discrete event simulation are speed, flexibility, and cost. However, poor modeling or failure to verify your findings in the real world can lead to processes that are unexpectedly impacted by small fluctuations in demand or resources.

Resources

For more information about DES, see:

Banks, J., J. Carson, B. Nelson, and D. Nicol. *Discrete Event System Simulation,* 4th ed. Upper Saddle River, NJ: Prentice Hall, 2004.

SigmaFlow's Simulator Process Analyzer software (www.sigmaflow.com).

Rapid Prototyping

Make a fast 3D model of your solution to explore its viability.

Rapid prototyping is a design and communication technique that quickly (in less than a few days) creates a three-dimensional model of a new innovation or product design. When NASCAR race teams have to make fast design changes, they use rapid prototyping to identify potential production pitfalls. The University of Tennessee Anthropological Research facility uses rapid prototyping to recreate skeletal remains for forensic reconstruction.

The value of rapid prototyping comes in when you need to dramatically reduce the time and expense involved in making a model of your innovation so it can be assessed and optimized by designers and manufacturing engineers before it goes into production. Rapid prototypes are also used by marketing and sales professionals to test and anticipate customer reactions.

Gaining from this technique requires skill with *computer aided design* (CAD) software, as well as the availability of a rapid prototyping machine (Exhibit 47.1). Therefore, you may need the help of someone who is versed and knowledgeable in this arena and its associated technologies.

Rapid prototyping is about creating a better, faster, less expensive and more precise mousetrap—one that is built from the bottom (or concept) up to the finished product, ready for manufacture. The faster and more accurately you make your prototype, the faster you can get it to market and sell it.

EXHIBIT 47.1   3D Systems' Viper Pro SLA. System builds accurate and durable parts quickly through an additive manufacturing process.

Background

There are three main ways to create a rapid prototype. *Formative* techniques use machines to make raw materials into the desired shape. *Subtractive* processes start with a large solid, and then remove material to make the shape desired. *Additive* processes rely on layering material over and over until the part or product reaches its final position and shape.

While there are many choices and options for engaging in rapid prototyping, we'll cover the basic steps involved in *stereolithography*—an additive technique by which plastic models are built thin layer upon thin layer, resulting in a three-dimensional prototype created by a machine with very little human involvement.

Some Advantages of Rapid Prototyping

- Don't have to machine, mold, or cast a prototype.
- Shortens prototype construction time and improves product design.
- Uncovers expensive mistakes *before* producing millions.
- Requires fewer steps than traditional part creation.
- Doesn't require human input, except some data entry.

In addition to stereolithography, other rapid prototyping techniques include: free-form fabrication, auto fabrication, digital fabrication, used deposition modeling, 3D printing, selective laser sintering, powder-binder printing, layer-based manufacturing, and solid imaging.

Steps

Scenario: Let's say a company is developing a new product that can play all handheld game brands and associated games on one simple device—stretching our minds to assume the owners of this new product have hurdled all the associated patent, legal, and technology barriers. The company assembles the Cool Case team to design a case for the new universal game platform—the outer shell that houses its components.

To begin, the Cool Case team has a few dimensions in mind: height, width, depth, lightweight, big screen, the needed control buttons, and so on. Note that any team ready for prototyping has already determined the expectations of the customer, as well as the functional requirements of the product and many or most of its design parameters (see Outcome Expectations (Technique 3), Functional Requirements (Technique 33), and Axiomatic Design (Technique 34) for more.

At the outset of rapid prototyping, ask yourself how soon you need the prototype. Also ask how finished it needs to be. Is a fairly raw form sufficient, or does it have to be polished and smooth for a presentation? These questions guide the level of detail you need and the process involved in building your prototype.

1. Input Computer-Aided Design Data

Using computer-aided design (CAD) for rapid prototyping involves entering dimension-related data into the system, which then creates an electronic model based on that data. The key at this step is to ensure you have the correct data according to your design specifications, and that your data doesn't violate any rules of geometry that are embedded in CAD. If these rules aren't followed, files will be defective and possibly unusable—so, needless to say, CAD and geometry skills are very helpful at this stage.

The Cool Case team enters all its dimension data—the height, width, and length of the handheld case; all the inner and outer diameters of each hole where the playing buttons will protrude; the angle of the spherically shaped case; and several other design parameters. Having done this, assuming no geometry rules are violated, CAD will generate a three-dimensional image of the prototype on the screen. Of course, with CAD, you can turn and rotate the screen image to perform a visual inspection of its integrity.

2. Export Data into Stereolithography Files

The stereolithography (STL) process requires that you export your CAD file into an *STL file*. In turn, this file directs the stereolithography machine to build your prototype. If you aren't using stereolithography, you will have to convert your CAD data into another type of file format, depending on the process used.

3. Select Material and Specify Process

Different rapid prototyping machines use different materials within a limited range. Some examples of materials are: thermoplastic resins, polycarbonate, wax, powdered materials, plastics, and metals. Depending on the materials chosen and type of machine involved, you'll also have to perform other set-up steps that shouldn't require much time.

Generally speaking, the stereolithography process works by building the prototype, layer by layer, using a laser beam that solidifies each slice of the model until it is complete. As the model is created, multiple horizontal slices are stacked on top of each other until the model is complete. Most stereolithography machines take specifications for layer thickness within the range of 0.0005 to 0.02 inches.

The thicker your stereolithography layers are, the less accurate your prototype will be, and the less time it will take to build. Thinner layers create a smoother, more accurate model, but it takes a longer time to complete the process.

Also at this stage, you want to determine how many prototypes you want to build at one time—or during one run cycle of the stereolithography machine. Basically you are limited by the size of your prototype and the area in which the stereolithography machine has to work. If the area is 36 in. × 36 in. × 36 in., that designates your working areas.

We should mention, too, that you can build different parts or prototypes during the same machine run. Such variety can be programmed into the machine, and the operator can set the machine up for such varied output. As long as your job doesn't exceed the working space limits and STL file-size limits, you can run as many parts with as many designs as you want.

4. Create Rapid Prototype

This is when all of your initial data, prep work, and STL files merge to create your rapid prototype. The human involvement is over, and the rapid prototyping machine builds the prototype in layers—a process that can take from 10 minutes to several hours or more. Exhibit 47.1 is a stereolithography machine made by 3D Systems Corporation.

The Cool Case team decides to build 14 plastic prototypes of the game case—enough for the upcoming core design team meeting (eight people)—plus four more that are needed at another location for a customer focus group session, plus two for the chief designer on the project.

5. Clean and Finish the Prototype

Depending on which method of rapid prototyping is chosen, all prototypes require some type of cleaning. Some parts might need to be taken off their frames, and others might require dusting. Some parts require curing in an oven. Parts must then be finished by rubbing off jagged or rough edges.

Resource

Grimm, T. *User's Guide to Rapid Prototyping*. Dearborn, MI: Society of Manufacturing Engineers, 2004.

DEMONSTRATE
THE INNOVATION

Even great designs or solutions can be thwarted by poor implementation. Most organizations know this, but they still struggle to position their solutions for the activities involved in commercialization. Can your processes make your new product or service easily and cost-effectively? Can you deliver your new product or service to customers consistently with no errors? Will your new business model actually work in the real world?

This final phase of innovation's front edge is when you create, test, and prove the feasibility of your new solution. First, you *build a working model* of your new solution using Prototyping or Piloting techniques. Just because a design is sound on paper, or sound as a preliminary model, doesn't mean it will perform as expected under all working circumstances at all times. Information gathered from the working model is used to improve or optimize your solution.

When your working model proves ready, it's time to preliminarily *map the processes* involved in making and delivering it—a task for which you can use the SIPOC Map and Process Map/Value Stream Map techniques.

After processes are documented, it is advisable to see what can be done at this stage to ensure the processes will be as fast, efficient, and flawless as possible—even before you engage in the exploitation and commercialization aspects of innovation (referring back to the two-sided model we presented in the introduction).

This means you *optimize the processes* that you'll later deploy for making and/or delivering your new solution. Several techniques will help you do this, but you should start with Measurement Systems Analysis, because it ensures the validity of any data you use in optimization studies (as per the Design of Experiments and Conjoint Analysis techniques). With an optimized innovation ready to further develop from a commercialization standpoint, it's time to *anticipate and rectify production and delivery problems before they occur*. For this, use Process Behavior Charts and Control Plans. Also use the Cause & Effect Diagram and Cause & Effect Matrix to diagnose, solve, or at least mitigate any anticipated implementation problems.

Prototyping

Make a fully functioning model of your new product to test and perfect it.

Prototyping is building an initial physical, functioning model of your innovation. As such, it helps you verify the design of the supersystem—say, a bicycle—as well as the interoperability of the subsystems—the drive train, gears, brakes, tires, and so on. A prototype also tests the robustness of your design and its sensitivity to uncontrollable factors. Additionally, prototyping helps you verify that the required resources and processes are available to support full-scale production or delivery of your innovation.

Prototyping is typically leveraged by product or component manufacturers who need to prove a new design concept, or when the design is particularly complex or expensive to produce. By working out any issues before the design goes into full production, prototyping helps prevent rework and the costs associated with tweaking functions when the product doesn't work in the real world the way it was designed on paper.

If you've never done prototyping before, you can benefit by working with someone who has. For the most part, though, expertise on the product's specific design requirements is the main prerequisite.

Rapid Prototyping (see Technique 47) is often used as a precursor to prototyping. A rapid prototype is usually made of plastic and is not meant to be structurally sound. A prototype, on the other hand, should resemble the finished product in materials and functionality as much as possible.

Steps

Scenario: Imagine an airplane that mimics the silent flight characteristics of owls to reduce aircraft noise. The design features a retractable, brush-like fringe on the plane's wings that breaks up airflow to lessen sound waves. The feasibility of this design could be verified by building a series of prototypes.

Geoffrey Lilley, a professor emeritus at the University of Southampton in England, has pioneered research related to the silent flight of owls and the potential applications in aeronautics. It seems the fringe on an owl's trailing feathers enables significant noise reduction during flight. In addition, a coating of down-like feathers on the owl's wings and legs absorbs sound. Similar features may someday be incorporated into airplanes to dampen sound.

---

1. Design Prototype Evaluation

Prototyping is an iterative process—you'll likely need to build more than one full-scale, working model in order to thoroughly evaluate your design. Thus, when designing a prototype, you'll need to determine the purpose of the prototype evaluation, as well as what changes to the product design will be needed to meet this objective. You'll also need to determine how you will measure the design's performance relative to the specific evaluation; often, this is done by adding instruments to the prototype that measure the design's response to test variables.

For example, our first retractable fringe prototype could measure the device's functionality, as well as our ability to build the device itself. Our second prototype could be a modified wing assembly with the fringe device attached, which would determine if the fringe device works well with other subsystems in the wing (e.g., flaps, spoilers, ailerons). Our third prototype could be a set of modified wings on an airplane. At this level, we would measure the fringe's effect on noise and the amount of drag it adds during flight. We would also determine if the new design affects other systems, such as the landing gear or control system.

Along the way, we would test for *noise* sensitivity—how the design reacts to changing environmental conditions or customer use/abuse. We may use one of the prototypes as a proof of concept to secure funding. We may also demonstrate it to customers.

Some innovations are so new that customers don't *get it* until they see it. The microwave oven and the sliding door on minivans were such inventions; both used prototypes to bring the idea home.

2. Build a Prototype

Once you've determined what you need to evaluate with a particular prototype, build the prototype using production equipment and staff as much as possible. This enables you to validate several key items:

- *Manufacturing and assembly processes:* Do you have the right materials, equipment, and tools to produce the new design? Is the design easy to assemble and repair? What is the defect rate?
- *Human capital readiness:* Are employees properly trained and staffed to meet the requirements of the new design? Does the design introduce any safety concerns?
- *Production tooling issues:* Do you need any special tools to assemble or manufacture the design? Does assembly require any *jigs* or *fixtures* (functional aids) that make assembly possible?

Prototypes often progress from a high-level design to more detailed iterations to allow the team to work out issues with production tooling, fixtures, and processes.

3. Evaluate the Prototype Using a Function Audit

After the prototype is built, the next step is to evaluate your design using a *function audit*. A function audit (Exhibit 48.1) is similar to going to the doctor for a stress test; only in this case, the product is the patient, and you're the physician measuring the design's response to both controllable and uncontrollable factors. To do this, you'll need to determine the following:

- The subsystems you want to test (based on your particular objectives for the prototype).

Function Audit

Product: X947-400QSV231 Aircraft Wing Assembly   Date: 10/8/2013

Subsystem Trailing Edge Retractable Fringe 32-P2V1				
Supersystem Function	**Measure**	**Target**	**Tolerance**	**Measured Value**
Lift	Pounds of lift force during level flight	600,000	-0.3%	-0.1%
Noise level	Decibels	80	$+2.0\%$	75
Drag	Pounds of drag force during level flight	60,000	$+1.0\%$	-0.1%
More . . .	. . .	. . .	. . .	. . .
Subsystem Interface Function	**Measure**	**Target**	**Tolerance**	**Measured Value**
Activate trailing edge fringe	Pound force	1.75	$+0.2$ -0.2	1.76
Retract trailing edge fringe	Pound force	1.7	$+0.2$ -0.2	1.7
More . . .	. . .	. . .	. . .	. . .
Subsystem Leading Edge Slat 24-Q1V4				
Supersystem Function	**Measure**	**Target**	**Tolerance**	**Measured Value**

EXHIBIT 48.1   Function Audit (Downloadable). This is a partial *function audit* for the wing fringe prototype.

- The functions each subsystem provides, both to the supersystem and to other subsystems.
- The target and specification desired for each function, and how you will measure compliance. Typically, measurements are done by specially designed measurement devices that are integrated into the prototype design at critical interfaces.

4. Evaluate the Prototype for Robustness

In addition to evaluating functionality, both at the subsystem and super-system levels, a prototype should help you test the design for robustness. In other words, how well does the product perform under varying conditions, such as changing environmental conditions or customer use and abuse? If you leveraged Robust Design principles (see Technique 42) during the design process, and if you have been thorough in your prototype testing thus far, you should encounter few issues at this stage.

In our example, we would make sure to test the wing fringe concept at varying altitudes, in high and low humidity/temperatures, and in various weather conditions (snow, rain, wind, etc.).

5. Consider Additional Evaluations

In many cases, you'll need to evaluate the prototype for availability, main-tainability, environmental impact, and reliability. For example, if we wanted to know how well our wing fringe design functions over a long period of time (reliability), we could use a Highly Accelerated Life Testing (HALT) device to activate and retract the wing fringe continuously until it fails. Another option would be Highly Accelerated Stress Screening (HASS) testing, which subjects the prototype to worse conditions than the product is likely to undergo—for example, exposing the fringe to extremely high temperatures, compression, or tensile stress (to simulate wind).

6. Repeat the Prototype Process

It's unlikely that you'll test everything with a single prototype. Therefore, be sure that your schedule and budget allow for repeating steps 1 through 5, based on varying objectives. Also, remember that your innovation may still need to undergo a pilot or finished product testing, both of which are more focused on real-world system performance.

Piloting

Implement your solution on a limited basis to work out any problems.

Piloting is the practice of guiding your innovative offering through real, yet controlled conditions to test performance, safety, quality, durability, and marketability. Restaurant chains, for example, sometimes make a new food or beverage available in a test market before expanding the item to all locations. Banks run pilots before offering new services or opening new branches.

Prior to full-scale production or delivery, a pilot demonstrates to stakeholders and customers how your innovation addresses both provider and customer expectations. In addition, feedback at this stage helps you hone your offering, increasing its Value Quotient (see Technique 4) and bringing you closer to achieving the ideal innovation.

Prototyping is typically the precursor to a *product pilot,* while Discrete Event Simulation (Technique 46) can be conducted before or instead of a *service pilot.*

Steps

Scenario: A highly renowned culinary school wants to appeal to future chefs who might not be able to afford going to school full-time for two years. It develops a hybrid course that features online instruction for the first and third semesters, with hands-on semesters at the school in between. Prior to launch, the school runs a pilot to work out the kinks in their *V-Chef* course, and to gather initial customer feedback.

1. Plan the Pilot

Using a *pilot charter* like the one shown in Exhibit 49.1, develop and document the objectives, metrics, scheduling, and cost estimates for the pilot. Time spent here will help you achieve your objectives rather than having to compensate for poor planning during the pilot run. Your planning session should answer the following questions:

- What are the objectives of the pilot? What features or functions of the innovation need to be validated?
- How will you measure product or service performance? What metrics will you monitor?
- Who are the customers for this product/service, and how will you involve them in the pilot?
- How much will the pilot cost, and how does that compare to the cost of launching an innovation that flops?
- Is there data available from a previous pilot that would be helpful for this pilot?
- Are there any piloting mistakes your organization made in the past? If so, how can you avoid the same pitfalls during this pilot?

Referring to our V-Chef example, the objective is to *assess the online course* and its ability to successfully convey culinary concepts to the students. The team will track two key metrics: *course completion rate* and *level of skill at graduation*. As an incentive to participate, pilot students will be offered a substantial discount on the course.

Before designing the pilot, make sure your team agrees on what constitutes a successful (and an unsuccessful) pilot.

---

2. Design the Pilot

Determine and document all the logistical and technical details that are needed to make the pilot a reality. For example:

- What should the pilot environment look like? What is the setup?
- Where will the pilot be held?

Team Name: VCP

Charter Date: 20-Apr-12

Pilot Name: Virtual Chef (V-Chef) Course

Pilot Leader: J. Moynette

Pilot Start Date: 01-June-12

Executive Sponsor: A. Fields

Product/Service Description:

Hybrid Culinary Course (1st, 3rd semesters online; 2nd, 4th semesters on-site)

| Previous Pilot? | Y | (N) | Where: |
| Is there data available | Y | (N) | Data Source: |

Pilot Study Objectives:

Assess the online course and its ability to successfully convey culinary concepts to students.

Metrics:	Baseline	Target
Course completion rate	92%	85%
Percentage of passing grades on first semester exam	84%	80%

Financial Impact:

Cost of Pilot Study: See attachment   Cost of Field Failure: See attachment

Logistics:

Location of Pilot: online (various); main campus

Duration of Pilot: 6 months

Resources:	Role / Responsibility:
J. Moynette	Pilot Team Leader / Instructor
V. Nanard	Instructor
R. Raoun	Instructor
TBD	Online course hosting / tech support
TBD	Students

| Roles - skills gap analysis complete? | Due Date: 1-May-12 | Date Completed: |
| Training completed? | Due Date: 31-May-12 | Date Completed: |

Approvals:

_____   _____
Pilot Team Leader   Executive Sponsor

_____   _____
Date   Date

EXHIBIT 49.1   Pilot Charter (Downloadable).

- How long should the pilot run?
- Will you need multiple pilots? With the same or different participants?
- Where will you find participants? How will you request their assistance? How will they be compensated?
- How will you collect data? How will you quantify participant responses?
- In the event something goes wrong, what is the backup plan? If changes are needed during the pilot, how will they be implemented?

The V-Chef team must work out several issues, including how to locate qualified students and how technical support will be provided during the pilot. In addition, the team realizes that one of the metrics it chose (*level of skill at graduation*) will make the pilot extremely long (an entire two-year program). So, it opts to replace this metric with one that can be measured earlier (*percentage of passing grades on first semester exams*).

Of course, you expect some things to go wrong during the pilot—otherwise you wouldn't need a pilot. But you should have a backup for critical resources who, were they unavailable, would keep you from running the pilot as planned.

---

3. Designate Resources

Identify and schedule resources—people who will run and monitor the pilot, plus customers or other participants. Resources also include physical equipment, rooms, and other enabling tools. When reviewing your resource list, consider the following:

- What is the role of each participant, both employees and customers?
- Are the selected personnel equipped to perform their respective roles? If not, what training is needed to close the gap?
- Which performance metric will be tracked by which resource?
- Have you established a clear communication strategy for participants and other stakeholders?
- Have you addressed all remaining questions, especially safety issues?

The resources involved in the V-Chef example include the pilot team, the technical support team, the students, and an infrastructure for the online course.

The U.S. government recently piloted the *Registered Traveler* program with 10,000 frequent travelers. In exchange for filling out detailed background checks, participants receive a card that allows them to go through expedited airport security checkpoints.

4. Run the Pilot

Running the pilot brings all your planning and preparation together. During the live pilot, people are actively involved, and data is collected and communicated as needed. Be sure to consider the following:

- Have enough people on hand to answer questions.
- Monitor your data collection points periodically to ensure everything is working as planned.
- Make sure that participants know their feedback is valued—even if it's not what you expected or you don't like what they have to say.
- If the pilot lasts more than one day, keep communication lines open with participants, resources, and stakeholders.

During the V-Chef pilot, all technical issues are reviewed by the team on a weekly basis, and adjustments are made as necessary. At the end of the first semester, the pilot students complete an online exam designed to test their knowledge. Only students with a passing grade are invited to attend the second semester. In addition, all students complete a questionnaire and an interview regarding their experience with the online portion of the course.

5. Analyze the Results

After the pilot, take time to correlate and analyze the data you collected. Depending on the complexity of the pilot data, you may need to conduct statistical analysis to determine what changes, if any, need to be made to the product or service. Discuss the results with the team and determine:

- What aspects of the product or service do you need to modify for it to better meet customer expectations?

- What additional opportunities for improving the offering did you uncover?
- Did the pilot achieve its objectives, or do you need to run another pilot?

The V-Chef pilot demonstrates that the hybrid course is a viable option for the school. However, the amount of technical support required for the online course far exceeds the team's expectations. Since many of the issues are platform-related, the school decides to delay commercial launch of the hybrid course until it can find a more reliable vendor.

After making changes to your offering, schedule another pilot to make sure the changes work as planned and don't introduce any unacceptable side effects.

SIPOC Map

Identify the key inputs and outputs of your process.

SIPOC (Supplier, Input, Process, Output, Customer) is a high-level map of a process that helps springboard the transition of a developed solution into production or delivery. For example, one pharmaceutical design team made a SIPOC map to demonstrate the process involved in developing a new drug for reducing the risk of diabetes. Another healthcare provider leveraged a SIPOC map when introducing an integrated hardware/software system for allowing patients access to their medical records over the Internet.

Use a SIPOC map when you need a shared understanding of how you plan to produce and deliver your innovation to customers. This is your first order of definition, to be followed by more detail using a Process Map or Value Stream Map (Technique 51).

Steps

Scenario: With the nation on the verge of an obesity crisis at all age levels, market research concludes that there would be serious demand for a drug that integrates with diabetic diets and associated exercise programs. A pharmaceutical design team developed a promising chemical compound to meet this need, and used a SIPOC map to design a *new drug development process* that would ensure a smooth path for bringing the drug to market.

1. Create a High-Level Map of the Process

The P in SIPOC designates the *process*—the set of activities or tasks that transform inputs into outputs. To begin, identify the first and last tasks in the process, where it starts and stops. Specifying these steps helps to scope the project and clarify boundaries between the organization and its suppliers and customers. Next, identify the sequential steps between the first and last steps. Specify an action and an object in each box.

Be sure to define the process in general terms, listing just the high-level steps. For our example, these steps are:

---

1. Conduct preclinical testing.
2. File an investigation for a new drug with the Food and Drug Administration (FDA).
3. Complete clinical trials (Phases I, II, III).
4. File a new drug application (NDA) with the FDA.
5. Secure FDA approval for NDA.

It's extremely important to keep the development of the SIPOC map *high-level*. If team members want to talk in depth about a particular step, the facilitator should focus on the big picture instead.

Sometimes, it can be helpful to do a fun or simple SIPOC example first (such as ordering and delivering a pizza) to warm the team up and demonstrate the level of discussion required to complete the SIPOC map.

---

2. Identify the Outputs of the Process

The O in SIPOC designates the final *output*, or the final product, service, or information provided to the customer. For our example, the pharmaceutical team identified the following outputs associated with its new drug development process:

- New drug.
- New drug information.

- An approved NDA.
- New drug specifications.

There may be more than one output to a process, and sometimes outputs have secondary value for internal customers or regulators. Having a common and consistent definition of outputs allows everyone to set their sights on what the process produces and for whom—again, at a macro level.

As you build your SIPOC map, you can use the *cheat sheet* shown in Exhibit 50.1 to guide your answers.

---

3. Identify the Customers of the Outputs

The C in SIPOC designates the *customer*, or the person, group, or process receiving the output(s). The pharmaceutical team documented these relationships as direct links:

- New drug → Patients
- New drug information → Physicians
- Approved NDA → FDA
- New drug specifications → Manufacturing group

SIPOC	Questions	Quick Tips
Supplier	Who is the supplier?	Consider person, department, or organization.
Input	What are the inputs into the process?	Consider materials, equipment, procedures, people, and policies.
Process	What are the actions necessary for each step in the process?	Include an action (verb) and object (noun) for each step.
Output	What is the final product, service, or solution provided to the customer?	Identify the specific item that is provided to a specific customer.
Customer	What is the person, group, or process that will be using or benefitting from this output?	Link a specific output to a specific customer.

EXHIBIT 50.1   SIPOC Map Cheat Sheet.

While the pharmaceutical team identified one customer per output, there can be multiple customers and outputs in a SIPOC map. For example, when a pizza is delivered, the customer gets both the product and the bill—two different outputs for the same customer. But sometimes, different outputs go to different customers. A car dealer repairs your car, which is under warranty. The repaired car goes back to you, the customer, and the invoice goes to the car manufacturer, which is also a customer.

4. Identify the Inputs Required by the Process

The I in SIPOC designates the key *inputs*—materials, information, or products that are essential to the process. The inputs for our pharmaceutical process are:

- Chemical compounds.
- Diabetes knowledge.
- Drug research data.
- Trial patients.
- FDA regulations.

Inputs may take on different roles in the process. Some act as key ingredients and are consumed in the transformation; in the drug-development process, chemical compounds are such ingredients. Other inputs are used to enable the operation of the process; in our example, we might designate *physicians* and *policies* as such inputs, but we didn't list them on our example SIPOC map (Exhibit 50.2).

5. Identify the Suppliers of the Inputs to the Process

The S in SIPOC designates the *suppliers*, or the individual, group, or department that provides the input(s). There is a direct link between a specific supplier and the specific input, such as in our example:

- Chemical lab → Chemical compounds
- Medical community → Diabetes knowledge
- R&D team → Drug research data

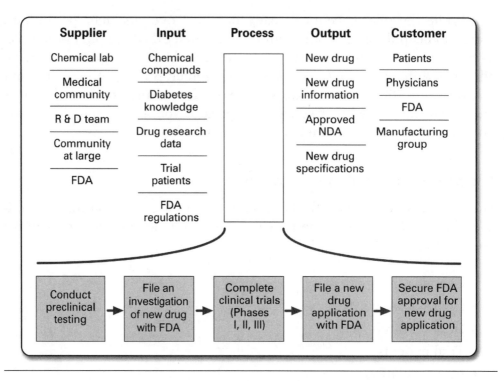

EXHIBIT 50.2 SIPOC Map (New Drug Development Process) (Downloadable).

Copyright © 2012, BMGI. A blank version of this customized form is available for download at www.innovatorstoolkit .com.

- Community at large → Trial patients
- FDA → FDA regulations

Exhibit 50.2 shows a completed **SIPOC** map for the new drug development process.

Process Map/Value Stream Map

Flesh out the details of your process.

Process maps are basic flowcharts that depict the progression of steps, decisions, and handoffs involved in transitioning a new product or service from paper (its design) into production/delivery to customers. Value stream maps do this too, but they add a level of sophistication related to time and the identification of value-added versus non-value-added activity (waste identification).

For instance, designing inflatable movie screens that can float in pools is one thing, but making them is another. It's the same with transactional processes like those in banking and insurance: There's no substitute for a robust, well-documented, and efficient process that all can see and follow.

Process and value stream maps can be used in one of two ways: to document the as-is process the way it currently runs, or to document the future state of the process if it hasn't been developed, tested, and implemented. Obviously, in the context of innovation, these maps are used to develop the future state. While you can apply them without the help of an expert or facilitator, it's best to enlist one, especially when building value stream maps.

Using a process or value stream map to document how work will be accomplished—how process inputs are transformed into process outputs—creates necessary consensus and positions the organization needs to implement an innovation as planned, with quality and reliability. No mishaps, defects, or costly mistakes.

Background

Everything an organization does for customers—with suppliers and behind the scenes—should be done according to an established, measurable process. When it comes to innovation, this process shows how you *will* produce your new product or deliver your new service. What work needs to be done? How will it be accomplished? Who will be responsible for each of the process steps, and in what sequence will all the detailed tasks be performed?

Typically, when building future-state maps, you have an existing process that's well-documented—so the job is to improve or innovate what you already do. But you may not have any process at all to make or deliver your new innovation, so you have to start from scratch. Or you might have an existing process that you can adjust to accommodate your innovation.

There are numerous ways to draw process maps and value stream maps, and numerous symbols used for depicting various activities and actions. But it is best to develop your own approach that works for you and your organization, and not get too hung up on whether you are using the *correct* method and symbols.

To make value stream mapping as smooth as possible, have your team prep itself by reading up on the basic principles of *Lean*—an approach that increases the speed, efficiency, and value of operations while reducing waste in both product and service environments.

First articulated in *The Machine That Changed the World* (New York: Harper Perennial, 1999), authors James Womack and Daniel Jones distilled Lean into five principles in their follow-up work, *Lean Thinking:*

1. Specify the *value* desired by the customer.
2. Identify the *value stream* for each product, service, or solution—and eliminate, consolidate, or streamline all steps that are wasteful or include waste (non-value-added activity).
3. Make the product *flow* continuously through only value-added steps.
4. Introduce *pull* between all steps to enable continuous flow.
5. *Strive for perfection* so the number of steps, time, and information required to operate the process continually drops, while quality levels are maintained or improved.

Steps—Future-State Process Map

Scenario: Imagine a corporation has developed a new product called a *gutter slapper,* a device that moves from end to end inside a gutter sweeping away leaves and debris. To produce this device, you must control the flow of information and material through a process—as seamlessly, efficiently, and flawlessly as possible.

A good future-state mapping team is comprised of several key people, including a good facilitator or team leader, the person who is in charge of the process (process owner), those who will actually perform the work later, and any others as needed—such as scientists, engineers, subject-matter experts, suppliers, regulators, or customers.

---

1. Define the Map Boundaries

The first step in building a process map is to identify the scope of the map—its starting and ending point. As you do this, keep in mind that you can't eat an elephant in one bite, so begin with a manageable portion. For the gutter slapper, we begin at *order entry* and end at *invoicing.*

If you've already developed a SIPOC Map (Technique 50), this will give you the starting and ending points for your process—and the main steps in between. You can always go back and add or subtract scope to your process map after you determine more about what will be involved in bringing your innovation to market.

Give yourself plenty of space to draw your process map, using a long stretch of wall. Many facilitators line the wall with a 36-inch roll of butcher-block paper or brown paper.

---

2. Map the Future-State Process

To map a process, keep asking: *What will happen next? Who will perform this step or action?* Write this information on note cards or Post-it notes and tape it to the working surface on the wall.

As you go along, create *swim lanes* as necessary. These depict all the steps performed by certain individuals, teams, or departments, and they show when handoffs are made from one person or group to another.

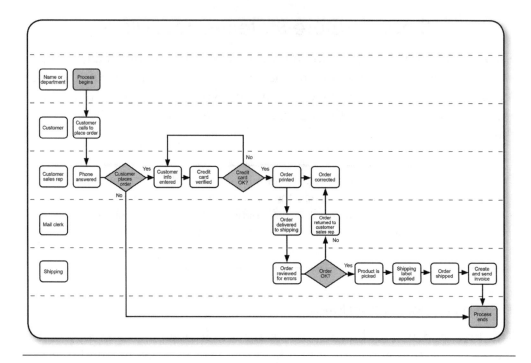

EXHIBIT 51.1   Order-to-Invoice Process.

There are several standard symbols used when mapping a process, all of which are available in software applications such as Microsoft Visio and iGrafx. Note that we only show you two of the most important symbols in our example—a box that depicts a step in the process that always flows into the next step, and a diamond shape, which depicts a yes/no question.

After an eight-hour session, the gutter slapper team decides how its future order-entry process should look (Exhibit 51.1).

3. Finalize the Future-State Process Map

As a final step, add any information to your map that might further illuminate the process. Some people add the element of time across the top of the map to show how long steps take. You can also attach documents or forms to certain steps; doing so provides details that aid in the further development, testing, implementation, measurement, and monitoring of the process.

In addition, you may want to identify areas where you anticipate possible problems, such as bottlenecks, service errors, poor productivity, defects, shift imbalances, changeover snags, and excessive handoffs. Doing this gives you a basis for making anticipated process improvements and ensures that your innovation has the best chance of success as you bring it to market.

Steps—Future-State Value Stream Map

The steps involved in value stream mapping are much the same as they are for process mapping. But since value stream mapping is more complex, you may want to have a Lean consultant present, or at least read up on value stream mapping.

With any new innovation that doesn't simply plug into an existing process, the intent is to design a superior process from the outset. And a superior process is one in which value-added time is maximized while non-value-added time is minimized. The definition of value-added time is that for which customers are willing to pay because it directly relates to what they are buying.

For example, the step of *reviewing order for errors* is an internal activity that doesn't directly concern the customer. While the customer doesn't want any errors related to his order, he's not thrilled about paying for this activity because he'd rather the company not commit any errors in the first place. On the other hand, the customer is willing to pay for the *ship order* step. Therefore, checking for errors is non-value-added, while shipping a product to a customer is value-added.

We'll give you the steps for completing a future-state value stream map, using part of the order-to-invoice process as an example (Exhibit 51.2). The steps and figure are reprinted with permission from *The Complete Idiot's Guide to Lean Six Sigma*, by Breakthrough Management Group (New York: Alpha, 2007):

1. Place each of the planned process steps in order from first to last in the center of the document.
2. Place the substeps under the major steps in a vertical stack.
3. Label each process step with who will do it.
4. Indicate any rework loops by drawing lines back to any place in the process where work must return based on inspection or any other decision criteria.

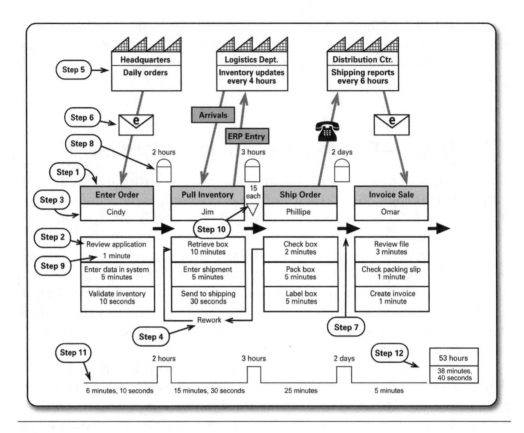

EXHIBIT 51.2　Value Stream Map.

Source: Breakthrough Management Group, *The Complete Idiot's Guide to Lean Six Sigma.* New York: Alpha, 2007. Reprinted with permission.

5. Identify any supplier or recipient of information or material from the process, and draw a separate icon to represent each one.

6. Draw a line in the direction of the material or process flow from or to the outside entity with an arrow. Use icons to help clarify in what format the information is moving (e.g., use an envelope to indicate it is mailed, and an envelope with an *E* in the middle to indicate it's e-mail).

7. Insert arrow in between each major step indicating process flow (left to right, generally).

8. Insert any anticipated queues in between the steps and use the queue symbol.

9. Collect basic data around how long it will take to complete the major steps or substeps. Fill in any times or piece-count information in the relevant steps (e.g., 10 orders/hour). Write the estimated process cycle times on the bottom of the baseline chart. (Cycle time is how long a step spends on one unit, not including how long the unit is in a queue waiting for work to be performed.)

10. Measure any inventory wait expected at any step. Insert the inventory icon with the estimated average piece count above it. (Piece count is the number of separate items to be shipped.)

11. Forecast the wait times for any of the steps and insert on the baseline chart.

12. Calculate the total queue times and the total time for the process, and display this in a time line at the bottom of the chart. This distinctive time line is found on all value stream maps, and at a glance, it shows how much of the total elapsed time (lead time) is value-added.

Resources

Good reading for value stream mapping is:

Rother, M., J. Shook, J. Womack, and D. Jones. *Learning to See: Value Stream Mapping to Add Value and Eliminate MUDA*. Cambridge, MA: Lean Enterprise Institute, 1999.

For a general background in Lean, see:

Womack, J., and D. Jones. *Lean Thinking*. New York: Free Press, 2003.

Womack, J., and D. Jones. *The Machine That Changed the World*. New York: Harper Perennial, 1991.

For a summary and description of value stream map symbols, visit:

Strategos (www.strategosinc.com/vsm_symbols.htm).

Several software applications aid in the creation of process maps and value stream maps. Three we recommend are:

iGrafx.

Microsoft Visio.

SigmaFlow.

Measurement Systems Analysis

Make sure you know your measurements are valid.

Measurement systems analysis (MSA) assesses your ability to accurately and precisely measure your innovative solution. For instance, if you're designing a device that detects the presence of airborne biohazards, you need to be sure that the device performs accurately and consistently over time. An MSA would help you identify and reduce variation both in the manufacturing process and in the device itself.

Even when it's not a life-or-death situation, variation leads to customer dissatisfaction and the inability to reliably fulfill Functional Requirements (see Technique 33). As you near the completion of your innovative solution design, you can use MSA to identify and correct measurement system error, resulting in a higher quality, more reliable design. To be successful with MSA, you will need some experience with statistics.

Background

Measurement systems analysis starts with translating customer and process requirements into metrics (measurable outcomes). These metrics can be based on subjective qualitative data (taste, appearance, etc.), or objective quantitative data (e.g., seconds, number of defects). The type of data determines the type of MSA:

- An *Attribute MSA* evaluates qualitative data for accuracy (the percentage of agreement with a known standard) and precision (how often the people or systems taking measurements agree with themselves and each other).

- A *Variable MSA* evaluates quantitative data for accuracy, precision, and stability (the consistency of the measurement system over time).

Accuracy compares measurements to a known standard. Quantitative measurements frequently have an international standard that is considered the truth. Qualitative measurements, however, require a strong operational definition of the standard based on customer expectations.

Precision tracks the amount of variation when the same item is measured multiple times. It's typically measured relative to *repeatability* (same person, differing results) and *reproducibility* (multiple people, different results).

Steps—Attribute MSA

Scenario: Motivated Helpers International (MHI) is a start-up company that wants to break into the virtual personal assistant market. As such, MHI needs to hire many new employees, all with similar skills. Applicant resumes must be reviewed quickly by several different appraisers to determine if a face-to-face interview is in order.

An Attribute MSA determines: (a) if MHI's appraisers are consistent when reviewing the same resume more than once, (b) how each appraiser's reviews compare to the others, and (c) if the appraisers agree with the standards that MHI's human resources department has established for new employees.

1. Review Current Measurement Systems

At the outset of every MSA, make sure you understand the current measurement system. Answering these key questions can help:

- How and where is measurement data initially collected?
- Who conducts the measurement or observation? Who are the appraisers?
- What is the root source of the data (e.g., customer complaints, inspectors, derived from other metrics)?

- Is the measurement altered through calculations, filters, or sampling?
- Can you verify the correctness of the measurement calculations?

An attribute MSA is not limited to binary (pass/fail) decisions. The same method can be used to evaluate responses that have multiple categories (such as emergency room triage codes or help desk severity levels).

---

2. Establish Operational Definitions

Develop an *operational definition* that provides a clear and standard explanation of each metric and how it should be measured. Be sure to include:

- What is the standard for acceptance? Is it well-defined?
- Are there written and visual procedures for measuring/observing?
- How are appraisers trained?
- Do all appraisers have access to the same evaluation tools?
- Do appraisers take any shortcuts during the measurement process?

No two things are alike, but even if they were, we would still get different values when we measured them.

—Donald J. Wheeler, *Evaluating the Measurement Process,* Knoxville, TN: SPC Press, 1990.

---

3. Select Samples

Choose a number of samples that will serve as the *baseline* for appraisals. Samples should reflect a wide spectrum of expected results, with about half meeting the operational definitions established for the metric and half falling short. The degree to which the samples meet or fail the standard should also vary.

Sample size depends on the acceptable margin of error. For an attribute MSA, a typical sample size is 30 with a margin of error near ± 10 percent at 90 percent agreement.

4. Select Trained Appraisers

Select at least three appraisers (people who will measure or evaluate) who are trained in the proper evaluation of samples based on the operational definitions.

5. Conduct the Measurement Study

Provide the appraisers with the MSA samples and record their evaluation results. After some time has passed, conduct a second evaluation session in a different order than the first. Appraisers should not be aware that they are evaluating the same samples.

For the MHI study, three appraisers were given 20 sample resumes as part of a larger group. A week later, the 20 samples (with only the applicant names changed), were mixed into another group. The appraisal results were recorded in a standard Attribute MSA worksheet (Exhibit 52.1).

6. Summarize MSA Results

After both evaluation sessions, compare the appraisals as follows:

- *Repeatability (within appraiser agreement):* Does each appraiser agree with himself between the evaluation sessions? If one person measuring the same item with the same device gets widely varying results, repeatability is poor and the fundamental measurement system is flawed.
- *Reproducibility (between appraiser agreement):* Do appraisers agree with each other? If repeatability is good but results vary between appraisers, then reproducibility is a problem with the measurement system.
- *Agreement with standard:* Does each appraiser agree with the standard?

Product/Unit Name:	Resume Review - Motivated Helpers International
Date of Study:	January 18, 2013
Performed By:	Lisa Hireu
Rejects	True standard based on job requirements; 8 samples are marginal

Good Resume (Interview): [Accept]   Bad Resume (Don't Interview): [Reject]

Resume	True Standard	Appraiser A		Appraiser B		Appraiser C	
		Trial #1	Trial #2	Trial #1	Trial #2	Trial #1	Trial #2
1	Accept	Reject	Reject	Accept	Accept	Accept	Accept
2	Reject	Reject	Reject	Reject	Reject	Reject	Reject
3	Reject	Reject	Reject	Accept	Accept	Reject	Reject
4	Accept	Reject	Accept	Accept	Accept	Accept	Accept
5	Accept	Accept	Accept	Accept	Accept	Accept	Accept
6	Accept	Reject	Accept	Accept	Accept	Accept	Accept
7	Reject	Accept	Reject	Accept	Accept	Reject	Reject
8	Reject	Reject	Reject	Reject	Reject	Reject	Reject
9	Accept	Accept	Reject	Accept	Accept	Accept	Accept
10	Accept	Reject	Reject	Reject	Reject	Reject	Reject
11	Reject	Reject	Reject	Reject	Reject	Reject	Reject
12	Reject	Reject	Reject	Reject	Reject	Reject	Reject
13	Accept	Reject	Reject	Accept	Accept	Accept	Accept
14	Reject	Reject	Reject	Accept	Accept	Reject	Reject
15	Accept	Reject	Reject	Accept	Accept	Accept	Accept
16	Reject	Reject	Reject	Reject	Accept	Reject	Reject
17	Accept	Accept	Accept	Accept	Accept	Accept	Accept
18	Accept	Accept	Accept	Accept	Accept	Accept	Accept
19	Accept	Reject	Reject	Accept	Accept	Accept	Accept
20	Reject	Reject	Reject	Accept	Accept	Reject	Reject

EXHIBIT 52.1   Attribute MSA Worksheet (Downloadable).

Copyright © 2012, BMGI. A blank version of this customized form is available for download at www.innovatorstoolkit .com.

The evaluation results for MHI's study are shown in Exhibit 52.2.

When we summarize all appraisers versus the standard, we see that all appraisers agreed with each other *and* the standard only seven times out of 20 (35 percent). This is far below the minimum recommended 90 percent

Within Appraiser Agreement:	# Inspected	# Matched	Percentage
A	20	16	80.00%
B	20	19	95.00%
C	20	20	100.00%

Between Appraiser Agreement:	# Inspected	# Matched	Percentage
	20	8	40.00%

Each Appraiser vs. Standard Agreement:	# Inspected	# Matched	Percentage
A	20	11	55.00%
B	20	14	70.00%
C	20	19	95.00%

Summary

All Appraisers vs. Standard Agreement:	# Inspected	# Matched	Percentage
	20	7	35.00%

EXHIBIT 52.2   Attribute MSA Results (Downloadable).

agreement rate for an attribute measurement system (the bar would be set even higher for processes with more severe consequences).

Some appraisers may have a bias relative to the standard (they tend to fail when the standard is pass, or pass when the standard is fail). A careful review of the MSA results will bring this bias to light.

7. Improve as Needed

If your measurement system is flawed, the MSA study will lead you to specific actions to improve consistency and operational definitions, and reduce appraiser bias.

The consequences of poor measurement systems include:

- Misunderstanding customer requirements.
- Rejecting products that a customer would deem acceptable.
- Shipping products that are unacceptable to the customer.
- Not identifying changes in performance in your processes.
- Mistakenly believing that an improvement has been made when, in reality, none has occurred.
- Making data-driven decisions based on inaccurate data.

Steps—Variable MSA

Scenario: The Getcher Fish Company wants to offer a small handheld turbidimeter that measures the amount of suspended solids in water. This new product will help sports fishermen detect high fish activity (indicated by low turbidity). A variable MSA measures the accuracy and stability of the turbidimeter.

1. Review Current Measurement System

As with an attribute MSA, you need to have a good understanding of the process or product requirements, and how compliance is measured (see Attribute MSA step 1).

2. Establish Operational Definitions

The fundamental requirement for a variable MSA is that the data can be measured on a continuous quantitative scale. As such, a standard operational definition for the performance metrics may already exist. If not, develop a clear definition suitable for your purposes.

For example, Getcher Fish's turbidimeter is aimed at the sport fishing market, so it does not have to be as accurate as similar instruments used for environmental measurements. At a level of 10 NTUs (nephelometric turbidity units), the measurement variation can be within ±2.5 NTUs and still be acceptable.

3. Select Samples

Many variable MSA studies are run on test instruments in a lab setting to measure physical characteristics of a device. As a result, the sample size can be limited. For the turbidimeter, we'll test one known standard sample 20 times over a 20-day period.

4. Conduct the Measurement Study

If you're running a simple variable MSA in a lab setting, the procedure is fairly straightforward. Most importantly, ensure that all tests are done by appraisers who have been trained to correctly and consistently measure and document the process or product output.

Software packages, such as Minitab or SigmaXL, make MSAs easier by reducing tedious calculations to a few keystrokes.

---

5. Summarize MSA Results

After completing the measurements, review the results for:

- *Accuracy:* The average difference (bias) between the results and the known or agreed upon standard.
- *Stability:* Any trend patterns or significant shifts in the output.
- *Repeatability:* Random variation in the measurement results.

With regard to our turbidimeter, the variable MSA determined that the device exhibits a tolerable amount of variation (only 0.25 NTUs above the reference value of 10 NTUs). However, the study did not measure *reproducibility* (variation that may result when the device is used by different fishermen). For this, we would need to run an MSA study that measures both the repeatability and reproducibility of the device by testing 10 samples, three times each, with three appraisers.

Resource

For more on analyzing MSA results, see:

Automotive Industry Action Group. *Measurement Systems Analysis*. Southfield, MI: AIAG Publications, 2002. www.aiag.org.

Design of Experiments

Analyze input and output variables to identify the critical few.

Design of experiments (DOE) is a complex but powerful method of validating your innovative solution during the design process or prior to entering full production. For example, we could run a DOE to identify the optimal settings for a new ultralight, high-mileage vehicle. The DOE would tell us how varying factors (such as tire pressure, fuel octane rating, speed, and road conditions) affect gas mileage.

DOE is an alternative to best-guess or one-factor-at-a-time experiments, which are time- and resource-intensive and may not produce the optimal solution in the end. By using DOE to test more than one factor at a time, you'll end up with better, more reproducible solutions in less time, and you'll expend fewer resources. However, the approach does require rigorous statistical analysis and should only be used with support from statisticians or others who have been trained in DOE.

Steps

Scenario: Suppose you're designing a small robot that picks up metallic objects (screws, staples, metal shavings, etc.)—and one of the key components for the robot is an electromagnet. DOE can help you determine the electromagnet configuration that will best meet your design criteria.

1. Determine Response Variables

Responses are the *outputs* that you will study during the experiment. Identify the key responses you want to measure, but keep in mind that as the number of responses goes up, so does the experiment complexity. In our example, *electromagnetic force* is the primary response; we need to hit a target force of 20 units while keeping costs low.

DOE is a team-oriented event that benefits from a variety of backgrounds (design, operations, statistics, etc.).

---

2. Identify Factors

Factors are the *inputs* you will vary during the experiment to determine the effect on the response. Use a Cause & Effect Matrix (Technique 57) to help you identify all possible factors that contribute to the responses you listed in step 1. Then, narrow down the list based on cost and time constraints. Typically, two to seven factors work best.

For our example, we could identify 50-plus factors that affect electromagnet design, but those most relevant to our chosen response are *battery type, circuit design,* and *wire length.* We also want to investigate interactions between these factors. Does one circuit perform significantly better with a particular battery, and the other circuit perform better with the other battery? If so, this would be an interaction between the circuit and battery type.

3. Determine Factor Levels

Levels are the specific settings that determine at what point you will take your measurements, and how far apart each measurement will be. Levels can be categorical (on/off, up/down, type A/B/C, etc.) or quantitative (length, weight, pounds per square inch, etc.). Experimenting with too many levels will create a large number of trials. Experimenting with too few levels might cause

Factors			Interactions			
A	B	C	AB	AC	BC	ABC
−	−	−	+	+	+	−
+	−	−	−	−	+	+
−	+	−	−	+	−	+
+	+	−	+	−	−	−
−	−	+	+	−	−	+
+	−	+	−	+	−	−
−	+	+	−	−	+	−
+	+	+	+	+	+	+

EXHIBIT 53.1 Sample Design Array.

you to miss an important peak on a curve. For the electromagnet DOE, we chose two levels for each factor (Exhibit 53.1).

4. Select Experiment Design

The experiment design specifies which factors you will combine during the experiment and in what combination. One of the most commonly used designs is called *full factorial*, which simply tries all possible combinations of factors and levels. Although a full factorial is not as efficient as other designs, it provides reliable information on effects and interactions. To conduct our electromagnetic trials, we chose a full factorial design of three factors at two levels each, which calls for eight trial combinations ($2 \times 2 \times 2$).

Screening designs test only a fraction of the possible combinations in return for less knowledge about interactions. For example, a DOE with 11 factors at two levels each would require 2^{11}, or 2,048 combinations. A highly efficient screening design could reduce the 2,048 possible combinations to only 12.

---

5. Determine Sample Size

The sample size is the number of trials you need to run to detect significant differences between factors and levels. Detecting smaller differences requires larger sample sizes. For the electromagnet experiment, we want to detect differences in force effects of five or more units, so three replications (24 trials) should provide a sufficient sample size.

Sample size calculations are frequently accomplished by statistical software, but might also be limited by the amount of resources available to run the experiment.

---

6. Assign Factors to Design Array

Statisticians have created a battery of standard design arrays to ensure integrity in experimenting. These arrays allow quick setup through many software packages. Additional on-demand, computer-generated designs are also available for special needs. For our electromagnet, we can use a standard eight-run array (Exhibit 53.2). Converting the minus and plus coded values gives us the combinations to run (Exhibit 53.1).

Circuit Type	Battery Type	Wire Length
Series (−1)	General Purpose (−1)	2 Feet (−1)
Parallel (+1)	General Purpose (−1)	2 Feet (−1)
Series (−1)	Alkaline (+1)	2 Feet (−1)
Parallel (+1)	Alkaline (+1)	2 Feet (−1)
Series (−1)	General Purpose (−1)	4 Feet (+1)
Parallel (+1)	General Purpose (−1)	4 Feet (+1)
Series (−1)	Alkaline (+1)	4 Feet (+1)
Parallel (+1)	Alkaline (+1)	4 Feet (+1)

EXHIBIT 53.2 Electromagnet DOE Design.

7. Determine Experiment Sequence

The sequence in which you will run trials is important because you don't want uncontrolled factors to change in the same pattern as one or more of the factors in your trial. This would create a false analysis of the data. To help prevent such confounding, you can randomize the order of the trials by rolling dice, pulling numbers out of a hat, or using computer-generated random sequences.

8. Prepare Data Collection Method

Before running the experiment, make a data collection sheet for each trial with the run order and factors, as well as a place to record results and comments (Exhibit 53.3).

Standard	Run Order			Factors			Force			Observations
Order	B1—1st Shift	B2—2nd Shift	B3—3rd Shift	Circuit Type	Battery Type	Wire Length	B1	B2	B3	Assembly
1	3	15	17	Series	General Purpose	2	6	4	5	Difficult – bent clip B1
2	8	10	20	Parallel	General Purpose	2	18	14	16	Easier than series
3	1	13	18	Series	Alkaline	2	6	5	7	Difficult – about 30 seconds
4	4	14	23	Parallel	Alkaline	2	12	13	17	Easy – 12 seconds
5	2	9	22	Series	General Purpose	4	7	6	8	Difficult – need new clip B3
6	5	16	24	Parallel	General Purpose	4	24	25	23	Difficult – about 15 seconds
7	6	11	19	Series	Alkaline	4	11	12	10	B3 – Wire length – 2" short – Easy
8	7	12	21	Parallel	Alkaline	4	24	19	26	B2 – New lot of Alkaline batteries

EXHIBIT 53.3 Data Collection Sheet—Electromagnetic DOE. In this DOE, eight experiments (*Standard Order* column) were repeated by three shifts (*Run Order* column), resulting in 24 total trials.

9. Run the Experiment

Finally, the moment arrives. Make sure each trial is closely observed by one or more team members. Sometimes observations are more important than the data. In our example, the assembly of the electromagnets proves to be easier with parallel circuits than with series circuits. This is a key observation to note.

10. Analyze Results

Circuit Type	Average Force
(+1) Parallel	19.25
(−1) Series	7.25
Difference (Effect)	12.00

Battery Type	Average Force
(+1) Alkaline	13.50
(−1) General Purpose	13.00
Difference (Effect)	0.50

Wire Length	Average Force
(+1) 4 Feet	16.25
(−1) 2 Feet	10.25
Difference (Effect)	6.00

EXHIBIT 53.4   Factor Effects Analysis.

CL Interaction Calculation		
Interaction Level	Circuit Type x Wire Length (CL)	Average Force
+1 (−1 x −1)	Series (−1) x 2 Feet (−1)	5.5
+1 (+1 x +1)	Parallel (+1) x 4 Feet (+1)	23.5
−1 (−1 x +1)	Series (−1) x 4 Feet (+1)	9
−1 (+1 x −1)	Parallel (+1) x 2 Feet (−1)	15
CL Interaction		
+1 Average		14.5
−1 Average		12
	Difference (Interaction Effect)	2.5

EXHIBIT 53.5   Interaction Effect Analysis.

When analyzing DOE data, you're looking to quantify the effect each factor has on the response(s), as well as any interaction effects caused by a combination of factors. For a $2 \times 2 \times 2$ example, the effects can easily be calculated by averaging the data at the +1 levels, and subtracting the averages of the −1 levels. This calculation works for both averages and interactions according to the coded table.

Exhibit 53.4 shows the analysis from our electromagnet DOE. The four Parallel Circuit (+1) combinations averaged 19.25 force units. The four Series Circuit (−1) combinations averaged 7.25 force units.

Thus, the effect of Circuit Type is $19.25 - 7.25 = 12$ force units. Using the same type of math, the effect of battery type is 0.5 force units and the effect of wire length is 6 force units. Thus, the circuit type factor produced the greatest effect, with the wire length factor producing a moderate effect.

In addition, Exhibit 53.5 shows that there is a circuit

type/wire length *interaction effect* of 2.5 force units. Further analysis conducted with the help of a statistical software program would show that circuit type, wire length, and the interaction between them are the three most statistically significant factors.

Several software programs are available to help you design and track DOEs, including Minitab, SigmaXL, Design Expert, and JMP.

---

11. Verify Results

Verification is a necessary step in DOE. Not only do you need to verify your best combinations, you also want to demonstrate that you can manipulate factors to produce a specific response. This is particularly true if the best combination of factors was *predicted* but not actually run during the experiment. You can verify the DOE results by running individual trials to confirm the best combinations. Or, you can run a small experiment using only a few of the significant factors to demonstrate your ability to change the response.

Resource

To take your understanding of DOE to the next level, read:

Montgomery, D. *Design and Analysis of Experiments*. 6th ed. Hoboken, NJ: John Wiley & Sons, 2004.

Conjoint Analysis

Compare solution attributes to cull out customer preferences.

Conjoint analysis is a simplified experimental technique for determining the best combination of attributes to include in a product or service design—based on the trade-offs customers are willing to make. For example, you could have a new laptop computer that gives more benefits and costs less than what competitors offer. But before you release it you might want to find out what customers prefer in terms of the product's attributes, and what price they are willing to pay for them.

Conjoint analysis is used when you need to optimize a design prior to releasing it for production or delivery to customers. But it can also be used further upstream when making initial design trade-offs prior to producing a prototype or pilot. The biggest challenge is to generate viable attribute options that the customer can realistically evaluate, using the help of an expert for more sophisticated analyses.

Originating in mathematical psychology, conjoint analysis was developed by marketing professor Paul Green at the Wharton School of the University of Pennsylvania.

Steps

Scenario: An adventure equipment company is considering different alternatives for a down jacket with a built-in global positioning system (GPS) to avoid storing maps and fumbling with them when your fingers get cold. Called the *PosJacket*, the new product could have any number of combined attributes. What trade-offs are customers willing to make? What is the best combination of attributes for the PosJacket product?

1. Formulate an Attribute List

Attributes are the features (design parameters based on functional requirements based on outcome expectations based on the job to be done) associated with your product. Each attribute can assume different levels, representing different options. Our PosJacket has the following set of features and levels:

- GPS system: Completely removable, semi-removable, or integrated (not removable).
- Price: $350, $450, $750.
- Weight: 8 pounds, 5 pounds, 3 pounds.

With this list of attributes, there are $3 \times 3 \times 3 = 27$ possible jacket combinations. Product levels are assumed to be mutually exclusive; therefore, a design concept may only assume one of the levels for each attribute.

Levels should have a concrete/unambiguous meaning. For example, better to say $750 than *very expensive*. Better to say *8 pounds* than *5 to 10 pounds*. The first descriptions leave meaning up to individual interpretation, while the second descriptions do not. In the language of this book, we can consider this to be synonymous with the difference between outcome expectations (more vague) and functional requirements or design parameters (more concrete).

---

2. Define Concept Products or Solutions

We don't have to ask our focus group to evaluate each possible product attribute permutation. By referring to published design tables, or with the aid of software programs, you can find an efficient subset of the total possible combinations of product concepts. For our study, one efficient *design plan* yielded the PosJacket attribute combinations shown in Exhibit 54.1.

	GPS System			Price			Weight		
	Removable	Semi	Integrated	$350	$450	$750	8 pounds	5 pounds	3 pounds
Jacket #1			X			X		X	
Jacket #2		X				X			X
Jacket #3	X				X				X
Jacket #4		X		X			X		
Jacket #5			X		X		X		
Jacket #6			X	X					X
Jacket #7	X			X				X	
Jacket #8		X			X			X	
Jacket #9	X					X	X		

EXHIBIT 54.1   Conjoint Analysis Matrix (Downloadable).

Note that not all possible combinations are represented, but only those that fit the specific design plan. Each row in the table represents a product concept we'll ask our focus group to evaluate. Each *x* corresponds to a level each jacket prototype represents. For example, Jacket #1 has an integrated GPS, costs $750, and weighs 5 pounds.

Of course, only those combinations that are realistic will make it to the prototyping stage. For instance, a removable GPS jacket weighing 3 pounds for a price of $350 will not be profitable; therefore, this option is not offered.

The design plan in our example has clever *independence* properties:

- Each level appears exactly once with every other level. For example, 3 pounds appears an equal number of times (once) at each of the levels of GPS system and price. Such a design reflects complete independence of attributes and is termed *orthogonal*.

- An orthogonal design makes it possible to estimate the independent effect of each attribute with a relatively high degree of precision. For example, it would be difficult to distinguish separate effects if the 3-pound weight always appeared at the lowest price. Would the preference for such a concept be due to desiring low weight or low price?

3. Collect Data

Convene a focus group and ask respondents to express the trade-offs they're willing to make by rating, sorting, or choosing among hypothetical concepts and their associated attribute levels. To evaluate the PosJacket, we ask participants to evaluate each of the nine possible three-way combinations according to the design plan. Respondents rate on a 0-to-10 point scale, with 0 meaning a completely undesirable offering and 10 meaning an extremely desirable offering. One respondent's feedback is shown in Exhibit 54.2.

Jacket #1	Jacket #2	Jacket #3
Integrated GPS $750 price 5 lbs weight Score: 3	Semi GPS $750 price 3 lbs weight Score: 8	Removable GPS $450 price 3 lbs weight Score: 9
Jacket #4	**Jacket #5**	**Jacket #6**
Semi GPS $350 price 8 lbs weight Score: 2	Integrated GPS $450 price 8 lbs weight Score: 2	Integrated GPS $350 price 3 lbs weight Score: 10
Jacket #7	**Jacket #8**	**Jacket #9**
Removable GPS $350 price 5 lbs weight Score: 6	Semi GPS $450 price 5 lbs weight Score: 5	Removable GPS $750 price 8 lbs weight Score: 1

EXHIBIT 54.2 Conjoint Analysis Ratings (Downloadable).

Copyright © 2012, BMGI. A blank version of this customized form is available for download at www.innovatorstoolkit.com.

4. Calculate Utilities

Preference values, called *utilities,* are calculated from the feedback of each respondent. Utilities represent the trade-offs made while selecting between different attribute levels. Because each attribute level appeared exactly once with every other level in the study, there is a simple way to estimate attribute level utilities. (Of course, conjoint studies in the real world are rarely so straightforward.) We've constructed this example so that the utility estimation may be done with simple arithmetic.

For our illustration, the utility score for each attribute level is simply the average score for jackets that are included at this level. In our example, three PosJackets—#4, #6, and #7—were priced at $350. The average respondent

		Level	Utility
Attribute	**GPS**	Removable	5.33
		Semi	5.00
		Integrated	5.00
	Price	$350	6.00
		$450	5.33
		$750	4.00
	Weight	8 pounds	1.67
		5 pounds	4.67
		3 pounds	9.00

EXHIBIT 54.3 Conjoint Analysis Utility Score (Downloadable).

Copyright © 2012, BMGI. A blank version of this customized form is available for download at www.innovatorstoolkit.com.

score awarded to these was 6. Using the same approach, we can calculate utilities for each attribute level (Exhibit 54.3).

To project which product a respondent would choose, add up the level utilities for each product concept. The product concept with the highest sum of utility values may be regarded as the chosen preference. So looking at Exhibit 54.3, we see that the *integrated* (5.00), *$350* (6.00), *3-pound* (9.00) jacket is the preferred choice.

Recall that the PosJacket team determined that combining the *removable* attribute, which received a rating of 5.33 from this respondent, could not be produced profitably; therefore, we move down the chain to the *integrated* GPS option, a better choice over the *semi* option even though it was given the same rating of 5.00 (due to thinking through system simplicity/complexity and other factors, like the risk of losing or damaging the GPS device while in the wilderness).

5. Calculate Importance Scores

Where utilities characterize choices between product levels, *importance scores* signify the relative worth or impact of each attribute on product choice. They are derived by calculating the difference between the best and worst utility scores for each attribute for each respondent, and then averaging the results for all respondents. This defines the impact each attribute has on choice (according to the levels included in the study). The raw differences can be converted to percentages. Obviously, the weight attribute has the greatest influence on product choice for the PosJacket example:

$$
\begin{array}{lll}
\text{GPS System:} & 5.33 - 5.00 = 0.33 & 3\% \\
\text{Price:} & 6.00 - 4.00 = 2.00 & 21\% \\
\text{Weight:} & 9.00 - 1.67 = 7.33 & 76\% \\
& 9.67 & 100\%
\end{array}
$$

To elegantly present the results of a conjoint analysis, the values derived from respondents can be converted to a market simulator (*what-if* tool). Some software programs worthy of investigation are SAS, SPSS, and Sawtooth.

Utility values and importance scores can mean quite a lot to the trained eye, but could be challenging for others not familiar with the details. Conjoint analysis recognizes that people make trade-offs, and that different people make different trade-offs. If you know what those trade-offs are, you have a powerful tool to predict consumer behavior.

Resource

Try this supplemental paper if you need more on conjoint analysis:

Krieger, A., P. Green, and Y. Wind. *Adventures in Conjoint Analysis: A Practitioner's Guide to Trade-Off Modeling and Applications*. 2004.

Process Behavior Charts

Monitor process performance to keep the new solution in control.

Process behavior charts are used to monitor the performance of a process, product, service, or solution at the output (Y) and input (X) levels, answering the simple question: Is my process running as expected? For example, the mortgage loan approval process has several inputs that eventually result in the output of an approved loan. Process behavior charts can be used to monitor these input and output variables as a mechanism for helping manage loan turnaround times.

Use process behavior charts to monitor the performance of your new innovation as it goes into production or commercialization after its design—or even during a pilot. By doing this, you create the visibility that is necessary to ensure your new innovation is successfully positioned to make the transition from the drawing board into the real world.

We only cover the most basic chart types here, so it would be necessary to have help from a process expert or statistician if your needs are more sophisticated. As well, you may need or benefit from process behavior chart software if not performing your own calculations.

Process behavior charts are often called *control charts,* but this convention implies that a control function is performed; on the contrary, process behavior charts only perform a monitoring function. The control function is performed by virtue of a good Control Plan (Technique 58).

Steps

Scenario: SkiBlades use ski-boot technology to lace up in-line (single line of wheels) roller skates. Just pull on a super thin-but-strong cord and your SkiBlades tighten around your foot. When fully tight, you release your pull and the excess thin cord retracts back into a small coil, while your boot remains very tight around your foot. Making these blades consistently requires keeping a number of production variables under control.

The general sequence for constructing process behavior charts is the same for all types of data, but there is some variation depending upon whether *attribute data* (data you can count) or *variable data* (data on a scale) is involved. We'll show you the steps and some details for each type of process behavior chart.

1. Attribute Data

During pilot production of SkiBlades, some became defective when the pull-cord broke away from the boot. After some early improvements, the pull-cord problem stabilized at just a few defects per day. But to enable continued monitoring, the production team develops a *C-chart*.

2. Gather and Plot the Data

- Determine the frequency of data collection (daily, for our example).
- Record the defect counts.
- Plot the defect data on a time series chart (i.e., number of boots scrapped per day as a result of broken pulls).

3. Calculate Control Limits

- Calculate the process average (the average defect count) and add this to the chart.
- Calculate the upper and lower control limits (UCL and LCL); these are the *statistical signals* that will show when the process is not running in its usual mode.

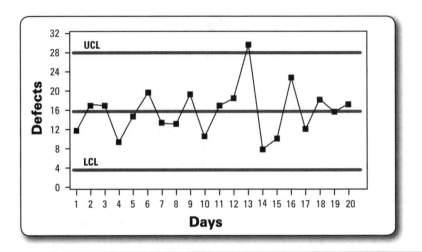

EXHIBIT 55.1   C-Chart for Defects.

Many statistical programs (such as Minitab, SigmaXL, and JMP) auto-matically calculate control limits for the various types of process behavior charts. If you're curious or want to perform your own calculations, see the resources listed at the end of this technique.

The C-chart in Exhibit 55.1 shows time series data in defects per day, the average number of defects, and the upper and lower control limits for the process. Note that day 13 is above the UCL, indicating a day with an unusually high defect rate.

When a process is in control, the control limits show the ordinary amount of variation, called *common cause variation*. When measurements fall outside of the limits, the variation is extraordinary, called *special cause variation*.

---

4. Interpret the Chart According to Established Rules

Here you are looking for *rule violations*, which are process behavior chart readings that indicate the process is out of control and needs help.

Exhibit 55.1 shows a *rule one* violation: There is a large shift in the process that should be investigated immediately. On day 13, the chart shows a much higher than normal defect rate, outside the UCL.

A *rule two* violation is when the process operates above or below its average performance for an extended period of time, specifically for nine or more consecutive measurement cycles. When this happens, investigating the causes could lead to permanent process improvement and defect reduction, even when the process has shifted in a favorable manner.

Even if the shift is favorable, the process needs attention so it becomes more stable and predictable.

A *rule three* violation is when the process drifts in one direction or the other for a duration of at least six measurement cycles. So if SkiBlade defects go up or down consistently for six days, then it's time to investigate the causes and fix the process.

5. Variable Data

Many processes have characteristics that are measured on a variable scale rather than counted on a discrete scale. There is much more information in variable data than in count data, so charts made from these yield more signals or information than their attribute counterparts.

One of the most common types of process behavior charts for variable data is the X-bar/R chart, or average and range chart. While the overall procedure for constructing this chart is the same as for the C-chart, a few additional calculations are necessary due to the nature of variable data.

The SkiBlades defect rate was mostly steady, with one exception on day 13. A team of process experts then discovered a correlation between fluctuations in the temperature of the resin curing oven and the defective pulls that broke away from the boots. At the team's recommendation, the temperature controller was replaced with a more modern unit, and the oven temperature was recorded and monitored using an X-bar/R process behavior chart.

6. Gather and Plot the Data

- Determine the frequency of data collection and the size of the subgroup. A subgroup is defined as a few measurements gathered from the same logical grouping (i.e., data from the same machine on same shift in short period of time).

- For the oven temperature data, five measurements were taken each day for 20 days, and this constituted the subgroups.
- Record the raw variable data.
- Compute the average and range of each subgroup. Plot the subgroup averages and ranges.

7. Calculate the Control Limits

- Calculate the process average (the average X-bar) and the average range, and add them to the charts.
- Calculate the upper and lower control limits (UCL and LCL) for the average chart and the range chart; these are the statistical signals that will show when the process is not running in its usual mode. Add the control limits to the charts (Exhibit 55.2).

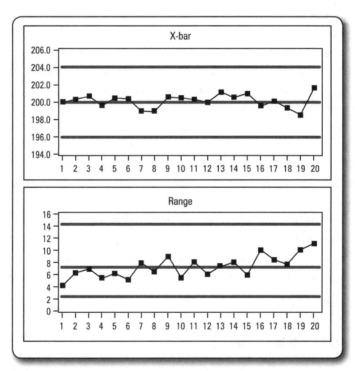

EXHIBIT 55.2   X-bar and R Chart.

Use such statistical software as Minitab, SigmaXL, and JMP to calculate control limits for X-bar/R charts. If you're curious or want to perform your own variable process behavior chart calculations, see Resources at the end of this technique.

Variable behavior charts are also interpreted according to the rules shown for the C-charts, but, due to the richness of information inherent in variable data, there are additional rules for detecting more subtle changes.

Exhibit 55.2 shows that the curing temperature process is now running in control and, if the team is right, there should be a reduction in boot-pull defects. (Recall that the SkiBlades team replaced the curing oven's temperature controller with a more modern unit.)

Since the X-bar/R Charts for the oven cure data show that the curing process is now in control, there should be a corresponding shift downward in the defect rate. This improvement in the defect rate can be illustrated by combining defect data from before and after the process change into the same C-chart.

8. Interpret the Chart According to Established Rules

Two additional process behavior chart rules come into play when dealing with variable data. For these rules, the area between the process mean and the control limits is divided into thirds, that is, 1σ, 2σ, and 3σ zones, as shown in Exhibit 55.3. (σ stands for *standard deviation*, the variance or spread of a given data set).

A *rule four* violation occurs when two of any three data points reside more than two standard deviations from the process mean. This indicates that the process has unnecessarily shifted higher or lower, and the out-of-control state should be addressed.

A *rule five* violation occurs when the process has shifted higher or lower to a smaller degree than a rule four pattern. The fourth point of any five points residing in more than one standard deviation beyond the mean indicates that the process shifted—obviously sometime before the first point fell beyond the one standard deviation zone.

When out-of-control conditions are identified, you can use any number of other techniques in this book to help you figure out what happened

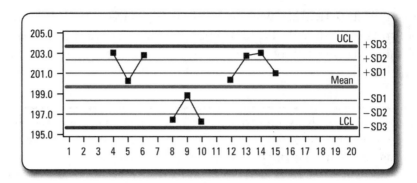

EXHIBIT 55.3   X-bar Chart Depicting Rule 4.

and how to prevent it from happening again. Some of these include Cause & Effect Diagram (Technique 56), Design of Experiments (Technique 53), Conjoint Analysis (Technique 54), and Measurement Systems Analysis (Technique 52).

Resources

For more information and process behavior chart calculations, see:

> Wheeler, D. J., and D. S. Chambers. *Understanding Statistical Process Control.* Knoxville, TN: SPC Press, 1992.

The National Institute of Standards and Technology (NIST) has a good online resource for process behavior charts called the *Engineering Statistics Handbook*.

Cause & Effect Diagram

Investigate the root causes of performance problems.

A cause & effect (C&E) diagram enables you to brainstorm and categorize the variables that might be causing poor performance in your new process, product, service, or solution. Say you produce a high-tech oven that monitors the internal temperature of whatever you're cooking and tells you when the food is ready. If the oven occasionally misses the mark, you need to know whether the problem is with the temperature gauge, the humidity sensor, the notification system, or the food itself. A C&E diagram helps you determine the root cause of the problem (output) by systematically identifying all the potential causes (inputs).

If your innovation isn't performing as expected or specified, or if you want to anticipate what could go wrong with your design before going into production, you can use a C&E diagram. Just make sure that your team is knowledgeable about the system or process in question, and that they're open to getting to the root cause of any issues.

Process Capability (Technique 41) is the metric by which you know if you are having any performance issues or defect problems to solve. Once you use process capability to determine this, you then use a cause & effect diagram to start analyzing the problem.

367

Steps

Scenario: Let's say you have a new service that rents DVD movies to customers through the mail. Recently, you've detected a decrease in customer satisfaction and retention. Using a C&E diagram, you can systematically identify all the potential causes that may be contributing to low customer satisfaction.

1. State the Effect

Draw a horizontal arrow from left to right. Next to the arrow's point, write the *effect* (the problem you're looking to solve).

The cause & effect diagram is also called a *fishbone diagram* because of its resemblance to a boned fish. Fishbone diagrams were first demonstrated in the 1940s by Dr. Kaoru Ishikawa, a Japanese engineer. He wanted a simple, graphical way to show the relationships between the inputs and outputs of a process.

---

2. Choose Cause Categories

Draw diagonal lines that connect to the horizontal arrow in the middle (Exhibit 56.1). These represent *cause* categories. You can use the traditional categories following or make up your own. Another common category set is *Policies*, *Place*, *People*, and *Procedure*.

3. Identify Inputs

For each of the main categories, use a Process Map or Value Stream Map (Technique 51) to help you brainstorm all the causes, or inputs, that may be contributing to the problem. You can go category by category, or brainstorm freely and list the cause under the appropriate category. Write each input on its own line that extends from the category line (Exhibit 56.2). Continue until you have listed all the potential causes.

For instance, our DVD-by-mail customers could be dissatisfied because delivery takes too long. Or maybe the order process is too cumbersome. Both of these factors would be listed under the Method category.

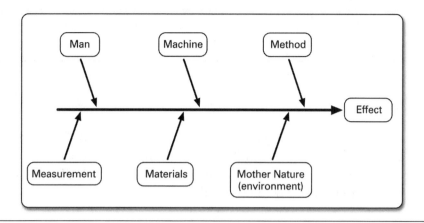

EXHIBIT 56.1 Common Cause & Effect Diagram Categories (Downloadable).

Copyright © 2012, BMGI. A blank version of this customized form is available for download at www.innovatorstoolkit .com.

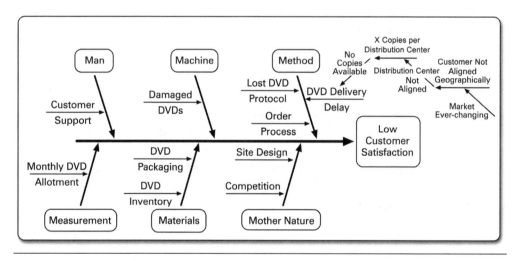

EXHIBIT 56.2 Cause & Effect Diagram.

You can have the same input under more than one category, but be careful not to list slightly reworded duplicate inputs under the same category.

4. Ask Why

Now, for each input (potential cause), drill down by asking, "Why would this input cause the effect in question?" Repeat this process until an underlying reason cannot be articulated. For example, asking why DVD delivery may be delayed, we might determine the following:

- *Why?* There are no copies of the DVD available.
- *Why?* We only have *X* number of this DVD in the nearest distribution center.
- *Why?* The distribution centers are not aligned with our customer base.
- *Why?* Because our customer base grew disproportionate to geographic populations.
- *Why?* Because the target market for our service is ever changing as the service matures and more people take advantage of DVDs by mail.

5. Discover Root Causes

Continue to drill down on each possible cause, asking, "Why?" When you finish, you will have narrowed down the potential causes to the main root causes. These can be further investigated using a Cause & Effect Matrix (Technique 57) to determine which inputs have the greatest impact on customer-centric outputs, and thus, need to be addressed to maintain customer expectations.

Cause & Effect Matrix

Identify the key input-output relationships in need of attention.

A cause & effect (C&E) matrix helps you determine which critical process inputs have the most impact on process outputs. For example, you might have a new product that stores an exabyte of data on a very small device. However, the process used to create the device might have an extremely poor yield. You could use a C&E matrix to identify which factors you should focus on to improve the yield.

In essence, a C&E matrix allows you to qualitatively determine the importance of cause-and-effect relationships between process inputs and outputs. This can be especially beneficial when you don't have enough quantitative data to define cause and effect, as may be the case with a new product, service, or process. The only caveat is that participants must be familiar with the process, its inputs, and its customer-driven outputs.

You can use a cause & effect matrix at any stage of your innovation process when you need to understand the relationship between inputs and outputs, or figure out which factor has critical influence.

Steps

Scenario: In the DVD-by-mail example from the Cause & Effect Diagram (Technique 56), we looked for the root causes (inputs) contributing to customer dissatisfaction. We can also use a cause & effect matrix to discover which process inputs affect customer satisfaction *the most* and, therefore, need attention and improvement.

1. Identify and Rank Process Outputs

List the customer outcome expectations, or outputs, across the top of the C&E matrix (Exhibit 57.1). Underneath each output, rank it on a scale of 1 (less important to the customer) to 10 (more important). If it takes too long to get consensus, use 1, 5, and 9 for the rankings to give the outputs more relative separation.

If the team disagrees as to which outputs are important to the customer, make sure the customer is well-defined: Is it the end user, an intermediary, or a fixer? For more on customer types, see Functional Requirements (Technique 33).

---

2. Identify Process Steps and Inputs

In the far left column of the C&E matrix, enter the process steps that contribute to the outputs listed on top. Also, list the inputs for each process step.

			Outputs							
			Helpful Support	Quick Delivery	User-Friendly Website	DVD Selection	Affordability	①		
		Customer Priority	3	9	7	9	5			
	Process Step ② Process Input		(3x0) + (9x9) + (7x0) + (9x9) + (5x3) = 177							Total
1	Select DVD	Web interface	9	0	9	3	0			117
2		Inventory system	1	5	5	3	0			110
3	Check available inventory	Distribution center locale	0	9	0	9	3	③		177
4		Inventory system	1	5	1	9	0		④	136
5	Check customer allotment	Customer database	1	3	1	0	9			82
6	Pick/ship DVD	Customer database	1	9	0	0	0			84
7		Shipping	0	9	0	0	5			106

EXHIBIT 57.1 Cause & Effect Matrix (Downloadable).

You can gather this information from your Process Map or Value Stream Map (Technique 51), or even a Cause & Effect Diagram (Technique 56).

To save time, the facilitator can complete steps 1 and 2 beforehand, allowing the group to focus on evaluation (steps 3 and 4).

---

3. Rank Process Inputs

As a group, rank the potential contribution, or effect, of each input on each output. Use 0, 1, 3, 5, or 9, with 0 as no impact on the output, and 9 as maximum impact. It's important that all team members share the definitions associated with the ratings. Enter the results in the body of the matrix. For example, the DVD-by-mail team believes the *distribution center locale* input has a significant impact on both the *quick delivery* and the *DVD selection* outputs, so they rated each of these effects a 9.

If you have a complicated process, you can do a *macro* C&E matrix using just the process steps (omitting the process inputs). This will tell you which steps have the most impact on the outputs. Then, you can do a more detailed C&E matrix using the inputs for only the critical process steps.

---

4. Calculate Cumulative Effect

For each process input row, multiply the impact value against the output priority for that column (Exhibit 57.1). Do this for each input/output combination, then add the results and put the total in the far right column. The highest totals represent the critical inputs to the process, and the ones you need to focus on to solve the problem.

A cause & effect matrix enables the numerical representation of process inputs and outputs, and the relationships between them. This quantifies the knowledge of each process expert.

Control Plan

Ensure that your new solution becomes commercialized as planned.

A control plan is critical to ensuring that your innovation will be produced or delivered according to your careful design, regardless of location, personnel, environment, or other variables that you won't be able to control. The plan helps you mitigate risk when moving from a controlled environment (such as a lab) into an operational environment (like the factory floor).

Customers have been conditioned to expect consistency thanks to businesses like Starbucks, McDonald's, and countless others that strive to deliver the same product regardless of location. Control plans enable any organization to replicate the customer experience by clearly documenting how to keep the process in control, what to do if it goes out of control and who is responsible for putting it back in control—all of which results in a reproducible process that delights customers and maximizes profits.

It takes many hours, even days, to complete a thorough control plan. This time can be minimized if you have already applied several techniques including Process Map/Value Stream Map (Technique 51), Design Failure Mode and Effects Analysis (Technique 44), and Measurement Systems Analysis (Technique 52).

Steps

Scenario: Imagine a drive-through fast-food chain that recognizes customers using facial recognition software, and predicts their orders based on their most recent and most frequent preferences. A control plan, if adhered to, will ensure that customers receive the same high-quality service no matter which drive-through location they visit.

1. Process Step

Refer to your process map or value stream map. Each key process step should have a row on the control plan. In our example, the process of taking a customer's order at the drive-through would entail many process steps—facial recognition, order processing, payment, and so on. We'll fill out our sample control plan (Exhibit 58.1) using the process step *facial recognition*.

We've included a recommended control plan form (Exhibit 58.1). But remember, the information collected in the plan can vary. Don't make it too complicated. For instance, if process capability is overkill for you, leave it off the plan.

---

2. Output

The output is the desired result of the process step. It could be an outcome or event, or it might be the next step in the process. You may have more than one output for a given process step. However, if all your process steps have several outputs, your process steps are probably too high-level. For our drive-through example, if the process step is *facial recognition,* the outputs are *cycle time* and *accurate identification.*

3. Input

The input is different from the process step. Inputs are determined by asking, "What are the key inputs that make the *output* possible?" It's normal to have several inputs for any given output; however, only list the inputs that directly affect the output. You don't have to list inputs that are assumed, such as the presence of the customer.

Process Step	Output	Input	Spec Limit	Process Capability	Measurement System	Current Control Method	Who	When/ Where	Reaction Plan	Transition Plan
Facial Recognition	Cycle Time	Camera	1.5–3.5 Seconds	1.33 Cpk	Time	Camera System	Manager on Duty	1 per Month/ Sample of Stores	1–Restart 2–Tech Support	Drive-up Plan. Doc
	Accurate Identification	Image	80%–90% Accuracy	4 σ (sigma)	Report	Software Algorithm	Tech Support	1 per Month/ Sample of Stores	Contact Vendor	Drive-up Plan. Doc
		Database Record	Yes/No	6 σ (sigma)	Report	Manual	Employee Taking Orders	1 per Month/ Sample of Stores	Add Customer to Database	Drive-up Plan. Doc

EXHIBIT 58.1 Control Plan (Downloadable). This example shows the control plan for just one step (facial recognition) from our sample fast-food, drive-through process.

Include inputs that you can't necessarily control, such as weather conditions that cause poor visibility. You don't have to go crazy with scenarios, but if it's likely to happen and if it will cause the process to go out of control, document it and try to plan for it.

4. Specification Limit

Now that you've identified the key inputs, the rest of the plan will concentrate on how to keep the process in control. Specification (spec) limits are proven standards or measurements that set the boundaries for each input or output. When the output is operating within these boundaries (*in spec*), the process remains in control. When the output operates outside spec limits, the process goes out of control. Spec limits can be a variable range (such as the 1.5 to 3.5 second range for our drive-through camera to snap a picture), or an attribute (we use *yes/no* for our database input because the driver's image is either in the database or it's not).

5. Process Capability

Process capability is the ability of the process to meet or exceed the specification limits you've defined. Capability is based on the number of times the process output failed (defect rate) or succeeded (yield). For more details, see Process Capability (Technique 41).

6. Measurement System

What type of measurement system will you use to gauge whether the process output is within spec limits? Measurement systems can be as simple as a stopwatch or as complex as an electronic data-capture process. Keep in mind that the simplest solution is usually the best; the goal is to provide an exemplary product or service, not to create elaborate measurements that delay delivery.

Measurement Systems Analysis (Technique 52) will make sure your measurement system is accurate and doesn't introduce variation into the process.

7. Current Control Method

How will you know when the process goes out of control? The control method typically results from a process failure mode and effects analysis (FMEA), where you have determined what could go wrong (how the process could go out of control), and what will be done to correct it if it does. For instance, if our drive-through camera cycle time is too slow, the system automatically alerts management.

8. Who

When you identify clear roles and accountability prior to delivering a new product or service, you can better predict and control the customer experience. This field simply documents who (or what) is responsible for keeping the process step in control. It could be an employee, a supervisor, a supplier, or even a machine setting or software program.

9. When and Where

This area documents two important elements: when (how often) will you measure the process to determine if it's in control, and where will the measurement data be recorded? Depending on what you're measuring, the *when* may be a designated frequency (daily, weekly, etc.). Or, it could be based on the number of transactions (e.g., products manufactured or customers served).

Either way, measurement data needs to be recorded consistently and accurately to help you compare data points over time. If your process is complicated, you'll want to employ Process Behavior Charts (Technique 55) to quickly and visually track when the process goes out of control.

10. Reaction Plan

We already have who, where, and when, so this section documents the *how*—how you will get the process back in control if it goes outside the spec limits. In our example, when the camera process goes out of control, the manager restarts the camera. If that doesn't work, she contacts technical support.

The *how* is often the hidden delighter in the customer experience. Customers will be infinitely more forgiving when something goes wrong if the response is appropriate and is delivered in a predictable manner.

11. Transition Plan

A *transition plan* includes any additional information, above and beyond the control plan, needed to move from a pilot or small-scale production to full-scale production and delivery. Typically, this documentation is detailed and so is merely referenced in the control plan. In our example, the transition plan might include tech support and vendor contact information, and suggested scripts for taking orders or soliciting customers to add to the facial-recognition database.

ACKNOWLEDGMENTS

Since we like to practice what we preach at BMGI, we viewed this book as an opportunity to involve the entire company in what was, in itself, an innovative approach to writing a book. From our master consultants, many of whom contributed their expertise, to our global staff, everyone was invited to share their knowledge. As a result, we have a long list of people that we'd like to acknowledge and thank for their time, counsel, and contributions.

First and foremost is Debra Jennings, who wrote and edited large portions of the manuscript, transforming a formidable variety of inputs into their final form. We can't say enough about Debra's incredible talent, tenacity, and wisdom. There is no question that without her, this book would not exist. You have our deepest thanks, Deb, for your incredible and impeccable work!

Next, we'd like to offer our sincere appreciation to several people who not only authored or contributed to one or more techniques in this book, but who also stepped forward to help with examples and research. These individuals are (in alphabetical order) Riaan Brits, Randy Herrera, Liz McArdle, David McGee, Rishab Rao, Steven Ungvari, Don Wilson, and Don Wood.

Of course, countless thanks go to the many other contributors who compiled and drafted techniques in this book, in addition to their normal teaching, consulting, and mentoring. These contributors are (in alphabetical order) Lee Adanti, Cynthia Bloyd, Jorge Garcia, John Gaul, Perry Giles, B.J. Goclowski, David Hermens, Tom Jones, Leslie Karnauskas, Kevin Kelleher, Russ Kiehl, Larry Kosta, Paul Massey, Scott McAllister, Jill Mead, Michael Ohler, Cary Paulin, Ed Pirino, Michele Quinn, Luis Ramirez, David Rasmusson, David Rasolt, George Rommal, Vince Ruscello, Joanne Sauvey, Christina Schlachter, Naresh Shahani, Renee Snell, Chris Taylor, Luc Vander Beken, Wes Waldo, and Brian Watson.

381

A special thank-you goes to graphic artist Scott Stoddard, who built off of the former work of Colin Moore to perfect the more than 150 exhibits and illustrations in this second edition. And not enough can be said about Joanna Barth, who worked closely with Scott to produce, check, vet, and check the artwork again to ensure its accuracy and quality.

Still others contributed in other capacities. Wendy St. Clair helped formulate the book's early outline. BMGI's general counsel, Marc Pappalardo, advised the team about copyright law. Jeannine Hall, BMGI's marketing leader, freely gave her unparalleled energy and insight while formulating and executing book promotion plans. A special thanks to Jessica Harper, who jumped in to tirelessly and meticulously copyedit on short notice, leaving no stone unturned. Kimberley Carrington and Melissa Madtson put their skills to work in helping format and check the manuscript for accuracy.

We'd be remiss to forget the staff at John Wiley & Sons, especially those with whom we worked closely. Our editor, Richard Narramore, was an incisive guide for us, keeping us on track at just the right times in the most gentlemanly way possible. As well, editorial assistant Lydia Dimitriadis served us with efficiency, professionalism, and sunshine on a weekly and, sometimes, daily basis. Finally, production editor Linda Indig was nothing less than a perfect, pleasant professional—just as she was the first time around when we published the first edition of this book. We have been fortunate and delighted to have such a great publishing partner in John Wiley & Sons.

Of course, our families were right there for us as they always are—not only accepting the long, extra hours working but giving us tangible support along the way. We love you and thank you for this!

As is said, last but far from least, we'd like to acknowledge the many organizations that have helped shape our understanding of innovation and our approach to making it more predictable, repeatable, and sustainable. Your trials and successes have inspired us, and we hope you continue to make innovation common and eventful in your organizations.